MAGICIANS OF THE SOUL

Books by Ted L. Orcutt, Ph.D.

NO BEGGARS JUST BALLOONS
— *A Practical Approach to
Self-Transformation*

**INTEGRATIVE PARADIGMS
OF PSYCHOTHERAPY**
(with Jan R. Prell)

MAGICIANS OF THE SOUL
—*Exploring the World of
Paranormal and
Mystical Experience*

MAGICIANS OF THE SOUL

Exploring the World
of
Paranormal
and
Mystical Experience

Ted L. Orcutt, Ph.D.

Global Village Publishing
San Diego, California

GLOBAL VILLAGE PUBLISHING AND THE AUTHOR will donate a portion of the proceeds of this edition to the Rainforest Action Network for the manufacture of this book.

Grateful acknowledgement is made to **Oxford University Press** for permission to reprint copyrighted passages from *The Tibetan Book of the Dead* by W. Evans-Wentz, (Ed.), 1960, New York, NY.

MAGICIANS OF THE SOUL: *Exploring the World of Paranormal and Mystical Experience*. Copyright © 1995 by Ted L. Orcutt, Ph.D. All rights reserved. Printed in the United States of America. No part of this book may be used or reproduced in any manner whatsoever without written permission except in the case of brief quotations embodied in critical articles and reviews. For information address Global Village Publishing, 10601-A Tierrasanta Boulevard, San Diego, CA 92124.

FIRST EDITION

Publisher's Cataloging in Publication Data

Orcutt, Ted. L.
    Magicians of the soul : *exploring the world of paranormal and mystical experience*. / Ted L. Orcutt. - 1st ed.
    p. cm.
    Includes bibliographical references.
    1. Mysticism-Philosophy. 2. Parapsychology.
    3. Transpersonal Psychotherapy. 4. Orcutt, T. I. Title.

ISBN 0-9623434-4-7
Library of Congress Catalog Card Number: 95-94237

---

95 96 97 98 99 10 9 8 7 6 5 4 3 2 1

This edition is printed on acid-free paper.

ACKNOWLEDGMENTS

In addition to the mystics, masters, paranormally adept, and otherwise auspicious people identified within the narratives of this book, I wish to express my gratitude to the following persons for their invaluable assistance in the conceptual clarification and editorial guidance of this project: Reverend Cassandra Cholaki, Venerable Tenzin Dhonden, Reverend Craig Dorval, David Hatherill Ph.D., Reverend Chris Meredith, Mira Nakashima, Jan Robert Prell, Ph.D., Mark Rubin, M.D., Walt Rutherford, Ph.D., Dale E. Schroeder, Arthur Stirling, Ph.D. and Geshe Lobsang Tsephel. Also, I extend appreciation to my wife, Melissa, and my son, Greg, for their spiritual optimism and devoted support of this project during the four years of its preparation. Finally, I am grateful to all of those unnamed persons who have been part of my mystical journey and therefore part of these stories.

CONTENTS

Acknowledgements		v
Prologue:	*The Soul's Immortal Quest*	1
Chapter 1:	*Mystical Awakenings*	15
Chapter 2:	*Paranormal Stepping Stones*	41
Chapter 3:	*Harvesting the Tao*	67
Chapter 4:	*Masters Just Practice*	95
Chapter 5:	*Zen Currents*	121
Chapter 6:	*Mindful Intentions*	147
Chapter 7:	*Discarnate Spirits*	171
Chapter 8:	*Reincarnated Lamas*	201
End Notes		233
About the Author		253

PROLOGUE

THE SOUL'S IMMORTAL QUEST

Now, I lay me down to sleep
I pray the Lord my soul to keep.
If I should die before I wake
I pray the Lord my soul to take.

For thousands of years on this planet, the common denominator of the human experience has been emotional and physical suffering. Different from treasured animals and plants lower on the food chain, human beings are more self reflective.[1] As such, the emotional and thoughtful experience of suffering is primarily a human affair. The usual and oppressive interpretation of this global experience is that life is a struggle.

The harsh presupposition of this existential belief is that human beings are thrust into an alien and hostile environment without choice nor adequate defenses. Struggle commonly represents the expected nature of being human. Even with optimal genetic and environmental circumstances, most people expect life to be extremely difficult. Emerging from this belief, undesired events define the context of conventional experience.

Conventional experience also bears the burden that disagreeable events provide a needed comparison to experience pleasure and fulfillment. When people interpret dissatisfaction and fulfillment as opposed, struggle becomes the primary reference by which they experience celebration. The absence of stress and sickness defines health. The fulfillment of desires and success occur through expected failure and mistakes. Envy and pride invite competition. The belief in original sin demands the need for redemption and salvation. A lack of evil implies morality. A scarcity of war and violence defines peace.

As struggle becomes the means for identification, communication, and affiliation, empowerment reveals a shallow cup. When fulfillment is defined by an absence of dissatisfaction, the opportunity of embodied life erodes to a balancing act of toleration and compromise. Even the news media cannot promote empowering stories of fulfillment when most people live by complaint. My favorite adage that exemplifies this pessimistic interpretation of common experience is: "Lord, lead me not into temptation. I can find it myself."

If all reality was defined by this limited belief and discouraging interpretation of experience, I would agree with a comment that Ronald Reagan made at a political demonstration before his presidency. Governor Reagan was in a bus that paused among hundreds of demonstrators who were protesting every known structure of modern civilization. One painted sign raised high above the crowd read, "We are the future generation of America!" Ronald Reagan scribbled on the back of a piece of cardboard and pressed it against the window in response. It read, "I am cashing in my bonds."

Fortunately, there is a profound alternative. It is not mythological. It is not a story defending struggle or a promise of celestial joy. Neither is it an abstract philosophy, institutional religion, nor New Age nonsense. The alternative is a mystical realization collectively shared by magicians of the soul in every traditional tribe and civilized culture throughout the world. Magicians of the soul are people who use traditional magic as transformational powers for the benefit of themselves and others.

The Roots of Traditional Magic

Illusory magic references the mechanistic illusions of stage or film where magicians perform their art for entertainment. An illusion means that the event perceived is not an accurate representation of reality. Rather, performed illusions are perceptual tricks created by muscular flexibility, mechanical devices, intentional deception, smoke, mirrors, hypnosis, and hologramic representations.

Aside from illusory magic, the traditional roots of magic symbolize the *tree of life*.[2] The earthly roots reach toward self empowerment. The trunk and heavenly branches extend toward self transcendence. The word *magi* is the plural of *magus*, meaning sorcerer in old Persian. The word *magic* stems from this word and the root *mag* means extraordinary states of being.

In diverse ways, traditional magic is practiced by: Catholic,[3] Taoist, and Shinto priests, Hasidic zaddiks, Tantric and Tibetan Buddhist lamas, Zen and Sufi masters, Native American medicine and holy people, witch doctors, shamanic healers of tradition, yogis, masters of martial arts, alchemists, homeopathic and faith healers, mediums, Spiritualists, paranormal magicians, and mystics. Even the three kings in the nativity story of Jeshua of Nazareth's birth were actually traditional magicians, priests of the Zoroastrian religion of Persia.

Historically, traditional magicians have always emerged to teach and heal. In far greater numbers today, cautiously they offer their wisdom with procedural maps for sincere travelers. These maps offer clear directions to transform conventional experience in this life now. Inevitably, they offer empowering lessons to evolve the soul for either reincarnation or eternal life. It is because traditional magic recognizes the limitations of conventional experience that it focuses on self empowerment, healing, and self transcendence.

Undesired events always occur. Magicians of the soul have discovered methods to shift the ways they respond to undesired events. People cannot always control events nor their emotional responses to them. However, they can learn to interpret their responses differently. With practice, magicians of the soul can even change the way they emotionally respond to events. With advanced skill, they can alter events directly.

Traditional magic divides into two domains by awareness and purpose. Low magic (Occidental tradition) or mundane magic (Oriental tradition) represents *paranormal experience*. Paranormal experience exercises empowerment of the self. With empowerment, people can redefine struggle as an optimistic challenge for paranormal intervention. However, different from ordinary or scientific opinion, the paranormal experience requires enough practice and evidence to substantiate an expanded dimension of reality.

In the Vajrayana or Tantric Buddhist tradition that originated in the eighth to twelfth centuries, mundane magical attainment was represented by the Eight Great Siddhas (powers), the six extrasensory powers, and the four transformative modes of action. A convenient translation for this categorization are the six extrasensory powers, mental powers that are similar to the great siddhas. Phrased in modern paranormal language with the original definitions of the Tibetan Siddhas, these abilities include: centering (dissipation of emotional reactivity); telepathy; clairvoyance (especially those 'visions' of human suffering); clairaudience (understanding of all languages including those of animals and birds); psychokinesis (originally known as the performance of miracles, they included the manipulation of elements, walking through walls, levitation, flight, walking on water, and healing the sick); and retrocognition (recalling the memory of past lives).[4]

High magic (Occidental tradition) or supreme magic (Oriental tradition) represents enlightenment or *mystical realization*. Mystical realization orients toward self transcendence. Mystical realization, however, demands mind control and satisfaction of self identity before focus beyond the self. Simply, there needs to be sufficient self identity before self transcendence can be realized. From the perspective of traditional magic as inevitably governed by high magic, this is what the human experience is all about.

The Advantages of Paranormal Ability

Paranormal ability is the intentional use of various psychic powers. These powers include telepathic, clairvoyant, precognitive, psychokinetic, and psychosomatic healing experiences. These phenomena are discussed in reference to experiences in later chapters.

I have used the following metaphor many times to discuss the advantages of paranormal ability, "To what advantage is walking on hot coals?" There are four sequential advantages. In order of empowerment, they are: (1) entertainment, (2) practical convenience, (3) diverting self or others from immediate danger or illness, and (4) using paranormal evidence as incremental stepping stones for mystical realization.

Similar to illusory magic, the first advantage of paranormal ability is entertainment. However, different from illusory magic, the paranormal magician does not have a mechanistic explanation of how the result actually occurs. The illusory magician knows exactly how an illusion must unfold to deceive the observer. The paranormal initiate knows the incantations for the experience, but even with mastery cannot mechanistically explain the result. While mystical explanations may be given, the mechanics of replicated events remain a mystery.

Like most novel experiences, paranormal ability is initially entertaining. However, once skill is achieved, entertainment looses its fascination. Continuation of practice eventually becomes boring. It is like watching the same movie several times and knowing the conclusion before the same repetitious results unfold. In summary, entertainment has a useful though limited function.

The second advantage of paranormal ability is practical convenience. Implementing these skills makes life adventurous. Also, it offers an opportunity to refine, enhance, and confirm paranormal skill. Within conventional reality, these paranormal results enhance self esteem, confidence, and responsibility. Convenient practical skills include: locating old friends, missing persons, lost objects, archaeological sites, hidden natural resources, and parking spaces. Other convenient skills include: gaining material objects of need or desire, fortuitous business decisions, forecasting future events, intuiting dangerous mechanical defects, and applying the contents of dreams.[5]

The third advantage of paranormal ability is diverting immediate danger and promoting healing. These practical advantages are more crucial than those of convenience. As a result, incremental skill in diverting harm and the act of healing enhances increased levels of self empowerment and evolved states of consciousness. Such experiences erase the fear of death and confirm the soul's immortal quest.

The forth advantage of paranormal ability is to use such experience as incremental stepping stones toward mystical realization. Indeed, the focus of traditional magic has always been toward self transcendence. Self transcendence means that the focus of concern is primarily oriented toward the welfare of others. Mystics serve as spiritual mediators to those in need. Attainment at this level often leads to a primary function as teacher or healer.

The Caveat of Desire

Once upon a time there was a tribe dominated by soldiers who desired to conquer the known world. Traveling far across arid lands, they reached a protected village. The population of the village was ten times larger than their tribe. They camped on the far side of a ravine and thought about a way to seize the village. After much consideration, they sought the wisdom of a powerful psychic. The tribe asked him, "What is the best way to conquer this village with the least loss to our tribe?" Consulting the astral plane, the psychic shacked a rattle. He tossed bones into the sand and cast secret herbs into a flaming fire.

Eventually, in the morning, he told the chief what to do. Following his advice, the tribe conquered the village with great success. After killing the men in the village, they raped the women and subjugated them and the children into slavery. Soon, afterward, they rewarded the psychic with many riches of desire.

The tribe continued their travels and seized more land and wealth. Eventually, they moved into an unfamiliar forest region and discovered a fortified city. This city was the largest they had ever seen. It had high stone walls and cannons protruding from tall turrets. The tribe summoned their noble scout to seek another psychic. After seven days, the scout returned. He told the chief that no psychic in this kingdom was to be found. However, he had located a mystic, an old, holy, crazy man who lived in a cave high in a sacred mountain. Perhaps he could help.

Desperate, the chief led a delegation of uniformed soldiers to the mystic. The tribe asked him the same question, "What is the best way to conquer this city with the least loss to our tribe?" The mystic told the delegation to give him three days to consult the Great Spirit. As the tribe's food and water supplies were sparse, the chief was annoyed. This adventure was taking three times longer than their previous experience with the psychic. They argued with the mystic to no avail.

The mystic fasted, danced, prayed, and meditated.[6] On the morning of the third day he summoned for the delegation camping in the woods beyond. The mystic spoke, "If you would get rid of the hatred, anger, and greed in your hearts, you would not need to continue to kill your brothers and sisters. As soldiers of fortune, you are mercenaries who rule by desire and covet your neighbors possessions. While successful, you dominate by greed and control. Were you warriors of spirit, you would know that the greatest energy is within yourself. You would know that the greatest reality is to conquer oneself and all desire. I have spoken." After listening to this message, the soldiers tortured and then killed the mystic.[7]

Greed impedes higher forms of consciousness. For higher forms of consciousness represent compassion rather than consumption. Ordinary people can use paranormal experience independently of pursuing mystical realization. Harmful results may evolve if such implementation is initiated by self concern and remains the exclusive focus of attention.[8] Extraordinary perceptions and the control of events, objects, or people by manipulating the laws of nature has limitations and consequences. Intentionally using paranormal processes and emotionally attaching to the power of control is frequently a regression of mystical realization. Indeed, Zen, as representative of one theme of mysticism, strongly discourages any attention to paranormal experiences occurring as a result of meditation.

Nonetheless, paranormal experience can be a useful stepping stone. It is particularly useful within Western civilization and Occidental thought. That is, the purpose of paranormal experience is not only to confirm personal power, but to offer evidence for mystical realization. The practical aspects of paranormal experience withstanding, they provide an evidential bridge to enlightenment and do not always represent mystical realization.

The Advantages of Mystical Realization

Mystics function within a more inclusive order of phenomena than those who exclusively implement paranormal experience for entertainment and practical purposes. Mystics do not use paranormal skill for entertainment. They rarely use paranormal skills for convenience. If required, they use paranormal skills for avoiding harm and for healing. Even then, they act only with spiritual reverence and consideration of the ultimate effects to self, others, and the universe.

There is an old Tibetan hermit who lives in a cave high in the Himalayas. Isolated, he has been meditating for sixteen hours a day for more than twenty years. In a recent interview, he was asked why he was spending his life this way. Calmly, he lifted his serene face and answered, "I am making the world work."

An interesting quality of conventional experience is that people continue life-limiting habits in spite of negative results. Mystical awareness breaks these chains of bondage. The advantages of mystical realization are the dissipation of emotional reactivity, non-attachment to the ordinary experience of identity, inner peace, and evolution of the soul. These qualities of elevated consciousness collectively contribute to resolving the global problems of world hunger, disease, overpopulation, pollution, and violence.

A conventional priest, rabbi, or minister receives authority from ordination by a senior elder of an institutional religion. All major organized religions are theistic. Theists believe in a duality of the (human) soul and the (Divine) spirit. This belief means that the spirit of God is separate and outside the spatial and temporal realm of the human soul. Prayer is necessary to establish rapport and contact between the human soul and Divine spirit. The religious aspiration is to seek an intimate relationship with the God "beyond" for emotional comfort or spiritual salvation.

In contrast, mystics receive their authority from direct personal experiences that exemplify a unity of soul and spirit. Mystics are ordinary people who believe in the unity of soul and spirit. Through meditation and altered states of consciousness, they experience the inseparable unity of all existence. Prayers, chants, and dances are offered to the Great Spirit, God, cosmos, or Divine power as mystics honor the universal or encompassing aspect of the immanent spirit or God within all forms of life.

Mystics view individual souls as particular expressions of the universal force or supreme consciousness. They believe and identify that the unity of the universal has been directly experienced. Also, mystical realization includes altered states of consciousness, paranormal phenomena, or shamanic powers associated with these experiences.

Confirming Traditional Magic

The reality of traditional magic requires an alignment to a new dimension of experience. This new dimension of experience must be both understandable and confirmed. This is particularly applicable in Western civilization. Confirming experience based on personal belief is *subjective experience*. While often more sensitive and imaginative, individual interpretation is prone to error and critical judgement the further it deviates from ordinary reality. Obvious examples that deviate from ordinary experience include dementia, schizophrenia, and delusions.

Confirming experience by common sense and agreement is defined as *consensual experience*. Consensual experience is supported by the most frequent, dominant, and political beliefs of a culture. As common sense represents consensual reality, it is prone to the hypnotically induced beliefs of consensus. Consensual experience is limited by the availability of accurate information as governed by politics, military power, and wealth. Dramatic examples of limitations include the Holocaust, religious cults that enslave individual freedom, and the influence of the media in judicial commentary and advertising.

Confirming experience based on the principles of conventional science is defined as *objective experience*. Objective experience has the obvious edge of being neutral and unbiased. Paranormal experience often uses similar principles. Rigorous paranormal research is conducted in scientific laboratories. Personal paranormal practice uses the principles of establishing a hypothesis and then reliably replicating the results.

The caution of objective experience, as represented by Newtonian science, is that it is limited by the intentions and circumstances of inquiry. Also, it is limited by a mechanistic description of the results as they apply within the scope of its own system. This is also true of paranormal experience when the manipulation of natural laws is viewed as simply a result of mechanistic cause and effect.

Confirming experience based on the collective authority of paranormal experience and mystical realization is known as *mystical experience*. Magicians of the soul who represent divergent nations, tribes, languages, and themes understand one another. As required occasion demands, divergent magicians communicate and share similar observations and prophecies. That is, regardless of cultural tradition and metaphor, both the maps and observations of the territory are remarkably similar.

All views of reality represent different metaphors reflecting different hemispheric functions of the brain. They are merely different ways to experience, integrate, and communicate information. Anyway, the issue is not whether magicians of the soul actually perform extraordinary abilities or display evolved states of consciousness. Of course, they do! Rather, the immediate issue is how traditional magic empowers people to transcend ordinary limitations, and live an increasingly integrated, satisfied, productive, and wondrous life.

While I value conventional science based on Newtonian physics, I often find this theoretical framework neither inclusive nor expansive enough to provide an adequate understanding of traditional magic. Exclusively relying on conventional science has obvious limitations that I find cumbersome, misleading, and inaccurate. Even within the practicality of everyday life, this mechanistic and dual world view does not match nor encompass paranormal and mystical experience.

I have always had some difficulty understanding what I considered as an arbitrary separation of various phenomena. One common example is the separation of mind and body. Another dualism is soul and spirit. Many other dichotomies exist within conventionally held views of linear time, quantified space, morality, and the beliefs surrounding will, luck, fate, and destiny. Once dissected and compartmentalized, conventional science attempts to understand and explain. More accurately, it attempts to describe a conceived and causal nature between the contrived separateness of two or more entities or events. When applied beyond its empirical scope of understanding to traditional magic, it often confirms an inaccurate and homogenized metaphor or mythology.

Simply, the scientific method cannot test the scientific method. Neither can faith test faith. Ultimately, then, conventional science and faith are beliefs in "themselves," in different methods of validation. The premise or presumption of both systems of checking evidence and discovering truth is that each model is accurate within its own limitations. Testing either model can only be accomplished by the biased positions of the evaluating model, or by a third system. And, this is where we are! Inclusive third systems are emerging with hologram, biochemical, and quantum theory. Cautiously, parallel information is now being revealed by magicians of the soul throughout the world. And, what is being discovered across the spectrum of these orientations are new integrative paradigms that are starting to map increasingly inclusive perspectives of reality and knowing.[9]

The Approach to this Book

This book is about the optimal possibilities of human experience as historically recorded and shown by thousands of people who have become healers, shamans, psychics, and mystics. The magicians of soul represented in this book exemplify models of attainment. The lessons offered are for anyone who is willing to practice and accept the necessary risks and responsibility.

The personal narratives beginning each chapter are true stories based on my experiences of real people and actual events. In most instances I used documented names. However, where I thought such accuracy might invade privacy, I used a few pseudonyms, preferring to respect confidentiality.

Each chapter features magicians of the soul as represented by a different theme of traditional magic. While each theme represents a unique metaphor, the similarities represent a shift of consciousness when collectively compared to conventional experience. Since this book chronicles a personal quest of soul, I have presented the themes in the order that magicians of the soul presented themselves to me as a result of my own quest of soul with informed intent.

Traditional magic provides opportunities to restructure and assimilate prior beliefs. An openness to inclusion of less familiar experiences increases the frequency and power of unfamiliar occurrences. Indeed, this is the reason myself and others with similar awareness and intent experience far more than the usual unfamiliar paranormal and mystical phenomena. In addition to experiencing more than the usual number of magical experiences, we experience them to be not only believable, but accurate representations of an expansive and superimposed reality.

Following the narratives are educated critiques and informed observations. These elaborations and explanations are an integration of objective research, professional, paranormal, and mystical experience. These observations may be particularly helpful to those desiring further clarification of essential principles.

An Omen For Exploring the World of Paranormal and Mystical Experience

An omen for exploring the world of traditional magic requires an open mind. Following the pathways suggested by magicians of the soul requires risk, adventure, and discipline. I expect those readers acquainted with traditional magic, mystical, and paranormal experience will stroll through this journey with ease. For you, I trust the reading provides emotional support, magical confirmation, mental clarification, and an occasional rocking of the soul.

For the many people less familiar with paranormal experience and mysticism, some experiences you are about to read may seem unrealistic, fearful, or even offensive. If this shows true with your experience, remember that within your current beliefs, the possibility of traditional magic represents alternative realities beyond your current experience and referential beliefs. Remember, that while this may be the case, paranormal experience and mystical awareness are well within your ability to experience and confirm. Indeed, this is one reason magicians of the soul are on this earth, to teach and to heal. It is also the reason I wrote this book.

Collectively, as an international world community, we are awakening to a spectrum of consciousness that defies the current beliefs of conventional experience as relied upon by the influence of Western civilization. Beliefs, also known as temporary conclusions, are a matter of personal responsibility and personal evolution. These changing forms of interpretative experience change every minute as the tides ever change the patterns of sand.

CHAPTER ONE

MYSTICAL AWAKENINGS

I grew up in a Christian family in Los Angeles, a city named by Spanish missionaries in honor of the Queen of the Angels of Porciuncula. My mother was a liberal Methodist from Missouri who valued the socialized respect and moral conduct that institutional religion champions. More than eighty years young, my father is a fundamental Baptist from Ohio who believes the kingdom of heaven favors entry to those who work hard and minimize sensual pleasures.

During my early years, my parents faithfully attended only the yearly ritual of Easter observance. Nonetheless, they colluded in demanding my regular attendance to either salvage their devotional neglect, or God forbid, store *karma*. Along the way, I didn't know whether God blessed those who believed in naive faith or religious protocol.

At the age of twenty-six I graduated with a doctor of philosophy degree in human behavior. My first position was as an Assistant Professor of Psychology at Dominican College in Wisconsin. Within the first few months, I learned that funds were available for a guest speaker. Following several requests through the academic hierarchy, the Monsignor invited me to select a person of academic distinction and notoriety. This guest speaker was to represent the concerns of the combined departments of psychology, religious studies, and philosophy.

My attention had expanded to focus on the mystical aspects of world religions. As a result, I became curiously interested in Alan Watts.[1] Raised in England, Alan was ordained an Anglican priest, the Episcopal Church of England. He earned a master's degree from Seabury-Western Theological Seminary and a doctor of divinity degree from the University of Vermont. However, similar to my rebellious spirit, he had difficulty conforming to exclusive interpretations, politics, and precepts of institutional religions. As a result he had become a wayward priest and now identified himself with mysticism.

As a prolific writer, Alan brought the spiritual importance of Eastern religions and philosophies to the West. With unabashed humor, he was quick to show that truth is not the monopoly of any one school of religious or philosophic thought. Advocating the expanded-consciousness movement, his teachings were a blend of Christian mysticism, Taoism, Zen, Yoga, Vedanta, Vajrayana Buddhism, Sufism, Theosophy and psychoanalysis. I viewed Alan as the perfect selection with which to satisfy personal and diverse academic interests.

I suggested the idea to a few colleagues. With a consensus of enthusiasm and curiosity, I submitted a proposal in the Fall of 1972. The dean immediately accepted it without difficulty. Confirmation was subject to the condition that the college publicly advertise an evening lecture for the entire community.

The next morning I anxiously telephoned Alan at his home in Sausalito, California. A forbidding and hoarse voice in British dialect answered. After offering him my name, rank, and collegiate affiliation, I ardently proposed a weekend of casual and intimate seminars. Most of them were to be private for selected faculty and students. We also wanted a public lecture and dialogue in the auditorium for the community. The college would advertise this event at a modest cost to help defray Alan's consultant fee.

Alan became extremely cordial, flattered, and enthusiastic. We negotiated a contract and scheduled a meeting during the Winter break the following January. He was to arrive Friday in the late afternoon and leave after the public lecture late Sunday evening. Little did any of us know how timely we were spending our money. Alan Watts died the following November of the same year.

I met Alan at General Mitchell Field in Milwaukee. He was smoking a black cheroot cigar. His dark hair was shoulder length, touching the collar of his black silk jacket. Fancying a well trimmed and pointed beard, his face appeared drawn. A tall lanky person with chestnut hair well below his shoulders accompanied him. I was soon to discover this quiet young person was his son. As it was late in the evening, we decided to forgo dinner.

I chauffeured Alan and his son back to the college campus through softly falling snow. Arriving at campus, I helped them with their luggage into two stark rooms of the nuns' old rectory. The faded drapes that hung from the high ceiling covered the waist high window. Alan walked over, spread the drapes, and gazed out the window. I knelt down and turned on a radiator that sputtered and hissed.

Walking over to Alan, I parroted his behavior of looking out the window. The room was about a hundred yards from a weather sculptured beach that overlooked Lake Michigan to the east. A half moon shone brightly on the frozen lake spiked with white caps paralyzed several feet in the air.

Wondering whether the spartan ambiance of his accommodations were satisfactory, I inquired, "Well, what do you think?"

Still fixed in a gaze out the window, Alan immediately responded, "I think I'm tired, and the moon is laughing."

Captured in a gaze of not-thinking, I played along. "Yes, but it's only a crescent."

Never looking in my direction, Alan immediately resounded, "That just means it is laughing twice as loud."

Saturday mornings, most college campuses look like a ghost town. This is especially true at Winter break in inclement weather. As I drove onto the campus, it was the first time I found a parking space directly in front of the Administration Building. The Academic Dean and invited professors met with Alan for a modest continental breakfast in the faculty lounge. Aside from meeting Alan, the morning agenda was to confirm a schedule for the weekend. Including Alan, his son, and myself, there were eleven of us.

The lead of the remaining eight was Monsignor Conrad who was the Academic Dean at the age of thirty-two. Before, he was President of Carthage College. Conrad was brilliant, witty, cunning, and courageous. He was one of ten who attended a weekend workshop in sensitivity training that I offered to the entire faculty.

Sister Theresa Lentfoehr was the venerable beacon of our flock.[2] Before coming to teach at the college, she was a poetry editor for the New York Times. She was also a dear friend and confidant of Father Thomas Merton until his death in India in 1968. Father Merton was a renowned author and Trappist Christian monk of the Gethsemani monastery who spent his later years committed to synthesizing Asian wisdom with Christian thought. Gentle, charitable, and mysterious, Sister Theresa was the resident poet of the college. In addition to a couple of priests, there were a few students who swore they had seen Sister Theresa actually float through the college hallways about a foot off the ground.[3] While these experiences reportedly occurred when the campus was nearly vacant, they rarely occur in crowds.

Sister Regina Williams held a Ph.D. in English literature and was the head of the University Without Walls Program on Campus. Regina was also a poet and perhaps the most sacrificial and inspiring of the group.

Dr. Luke was a cheerful priest who was researching biological ethics. A tasteful array of primitive masks and weaponry artifacts from Africa decorated his office. This displayed collection was a result of his previous travels as an employee of the National Geographic Society.

Dr. Veronica was the head of the psychology department and held a Ph.D. in physiological psychology. Veronica donned wire-rim glasses and draped her willowy body in tie-dyed skirts and cheese-cloth blouses. On campus, she was strictly academic and identified herself with early feminism. In the confines of her private social life, she was a warm and respected confidant to many students and faculty.

Arthur, Mario, and Bruno were members of the religious studies and philosophy department. Arthur Stirling was the Chairperson and was to become a friend for life.[4] Mario was pure Italian, married to an Italian wife with pure blood Italian children. He was one of the two philosophical skeptics of eastern mysticism and therefore questioned the credibility of Alan. The other was Bruno who held a graduate degree from the University of Chicago. Harboring a full beard and cynical attitude, he decorated his office with an altar of candles and a bronze incense burner.

Andre was a french romantic priest in the charismatic image of Dudley Moore. Nearly bald at thirty-four, he was the only drama instructor. Typically, he wore ragged, baggy jeans and tee shirts far before they were fashionable. Full of inspiration, he expressed an infectious laughter that could inspire the dead. Andre's office was sparsely formal and elegant with crystal glasses on a polished silver tray.

Breakfast concluded with a reasonable consensus that Alan start by meeting with the forty students in the University Without Walls Program for a four hour seminar in the afternoon. Students gathered and sat on the floor and stools in a large room in the basement of the dormitory. Alan brought a brocade, silk pillow on which he sat Japanese style on his heels in front of the audience. After three hours of lecturing on oriental thought, he invited questions from the audience.

Alan had written *The Joyous Cosmology*, a popular, however frequently misinterpreted treatise on the consciousness expanding use of hallucinogenic drugs. Knowing this, the first student queried.

"You say that you have benefitted from using drugs in your mystical quest. I want to know the dosages that were helpful to you and how many times you think people should use them?"

Alan gazed sternly at the young person.

"You understand, I presume, that first, I am neither talking about generic nor chemically synthesized drugs. I am talking about hallucinogenic herbs that have been used by mystics and shamans for thousands of years. Second, I trust you understand that I am not talking about using these substances for escape or entertainment. I am talking about using them as an enhancement for a life-style directed toward mystical awareness and only then expressively to ease breaking the chains of rational consciousness. Now, with these considerations, allow me to answer your specific question. I have always felt than an adequate gage of dosage and frequency is that when you get the message, hang up the phone."

A serious and bright young person sat on a stool above the others. After several other questions, he directed his attentive anger to Alan in a loud voice.

"I've been sitting here all this time and listening to you carefully. I am disappointed and angry that you don't take religion, mysticism, and spirituality more seriously. I don't believe you. I believe you are a fake and abuse the sacred with profitable mockery."

The outrage froze the crowd into complete silence. Alan rocked back and forth on his silk pillow and laughed from the depths of his belly. Even his feet jiggled with laughter from bellows that resonated off the walls. After his laughter subsided, he addressed the young man.

"Sir, I have never advertised myself as anything, but a philosophical entertainer. I am enjoying myself and I am truly sorry if you are displeased. For another matter, how indelicately you propose to castrate me with your self-gratifying expectations. As a matter of preference, my expectations exist to satisfy myself and I do not impose them on others. Serious you may remain. However, I prefer the validation of sincerity over the rigidity and stiffness of those who consider insipid intellectualism to be sanctimonious and indicative of either wisdom or spiritual revelation."

Shortly thereafter, the seminar ended. I invited Alan back to my office for a cup of tea. I walked ahead, allowing Alan to answer additional questions, mingle with the students, and attend to faculty. Half an hour later, Alan walked into my office. He closed the door and flopped in an overstuffed chair.

I served him Darjeeling tea, British style, with milk and sugar. After sipping, he nodded in appreciation. We sat quietly. Snow gently drifted outside my tall office window. Alan looked weary. After ten minutes, I broke the silence with a statement that he looked tired. He said that he was on route back to Sausalito from the east coast where he had bailed his son out of jail from a drug charge. Shifting from his public image of witty sage, he candidly shared with me that he was emotionally upset about his son. He thought, perhaps, he had not been enough of a father. We talked about this matter for a while and he appreciated my words of support.

After an hour, I told Alan that I did not experience him saying anything significantly different from Jiddu Krishnamurti, the Indian mystic and philosopher. The Theosophists acclaimed Krishnamurti to be the incarnation of Maitreya, the returned Buddha. Believing in personal *witnessing* through *choiceless awareness*, Krishnamurti was adamantly against any following. He publicly denied his bestowed title and disassembled the organization that created itself to spread his message. Alan woke up and responded enthusiastically.

"I have read and followed everything that Krishnamurti has realized. Frankly, I have borrowed many of his ideas and made them my own. I cannot think of a conflict that I have with his messages, except of course, that he is a boring soul.[5]" A broad grin daunted his weathered face.

Nine of us met outside the administration building on campus around seven in the evening for a coordinated caravan to dinner. The Wagon Wheel boasted the only prime beef north of Chicago. It embraced a meat-and-potatoes Western ambiance complete with captain's chairs. Wagon wheels hung high from a rustic ceiling. A hostess seated us at a heavy planked table surrounded by an assortment of families. Many represented the local dairy and agricultural industries. Silverware clamored amongst a background of Polka music. A waitress in a red-checkered skirt arrived and took our orders.

Initially, the conversation was cautiously academic with erudite questions directed to Alan. What little communication occurred was awkwardly vain and competitive. Scholars, often obsessional and compulsive, either remain silent or make an issue of a specific point from self-interest. Those more histrionic, dramatically play attention to whoever responds, regardless of the point. The game of social ambiance drifts between the scientists and the artists. Scientists usually invest in the content of their message. Artists dedicate to the expressive process and cast meaning later.

I wanted Andre to enter the conversation and save us from this clumsy contest of wits performed to impress Alan. After all, it was dinner, time to enjoy and just be with the person. Aware of the stale air, Andre shifted the conversation.

"Oh, c-o-m-e o-n! There is wine on the table, fresh maidens serving the feast, and this conversation is absolutely boring me to death."

Alan laughed loudly. The group relaxed and silenced as the red-checkered *Alice in Wonderland* served a meal in mid-western splendor.

As the evening closed, we all went our separate ways home. Each of us held our own views of Alan, both the person and the philosophical entertainer. Nonetheless, he was making an impact, sometimes as a deer on newly packed snow and at others as a cougar stalking its prey.

On the final evening, Alan opened with a public lecture in the college auditorium with about two hundred people in attendance. He sat on his brocade, silk pillow center stage with those of us who dined the night before.

Alan began. "The government sense of the individual is what prevails in the civilized world. This reflection of individuality is what I call the **skin encapsulated ego**. It means that I am a particular center of conscious attention. I have volitional control over a musculature that is unique, alone, and separate from the rest of the natural order. Incidentally, from this perspective, the natural order of the world outside human skins is a manifestation of completely blind and stupid entities. These unaware or foolish entities, somehow or another, occasionally fall into wonderful patterns that we see in crystals, or in the cross markings on window pains. We see them in the shaping of flowers as a result of purely mechanical combinations. In the same way, you can get interesting designs by putting sand on a drum, tapping the drum, and seeing how the sand behaves. So, this nonsensical and stupid world occasionally creates interesting designs."

"We cannot help feeling alone in this view of self. The feeling of impotence we all have, in the face of any crisis, is as if nature were saying to us, 'Wake up! Wake up! Wake up! Don't you understand that what you call YOU is a hallucination? Of course, YOU can't do anything. Your YOU is not real.'"

"The kind of individual that you think you are, this skin encapsulated ego, is a social institution. It has the same order of reality as the line of longitude. It is what other people have told you that you are. It is your assumed and conventional idea of yourself. This is what you think of as yourself."

"Your idea of yourself is a symbol that has no effective reality, as a dollar bill is inedible. A dollar bill has power only when everybody agrees it has value. If the United States should loose confidence in its currency, people could paper the walls with dollar bills. As long as we continue to play the game and agree this idea is valuable, the economy works. That's all it depends on. It doesn't depend on anything else whatsoever. An economy does not need to have gold, silver, or any other substantial value behind it. It works simply because people agree that it works."

"In the same way, people are encapsulated egos because they agree on the symbol. People pride themselves on their identity and assumed accomplishments. However, the idea of the ego has the same relationship to our living organism that a dollar bill has to just over one pound of mushrooms. They are eighty-nine cents a pound right now. Which would you rather have, a dollar bill or a pound of mushrooms? I would go for the pound of mushrooms. I can eat that and cook them very nicely."

"So, we have all been dissuaded into the idea of our own identities. People place a tremendous investment into the idea of unique separateness. They believe they have to protect it. They believe it is something that is one's self."

"You have a soul. You have to save yourself either by doing what the religions tell you to do, or on the other hand, by becoming a real person, like getting integrated, by making something of yourself in life."

"Suddenly, people get into a situation like we are all in now. People discover their assumed, real person cuts no ice. However, during history, there have been people who did cut some ice. There have been individuals who really moved the world such as Jesus, Buddha, Lao Tzu, Saint Francis of Assisi, Martin Luther, and John Wesley. These people really got something going. So, did Einstein and Oppenheimer. Each person looks into his or her soul at sometime and says 'Why can't I have that sort of effect?' The reason is very simple. People who have an effect on the world are inspired."

"When an inspired person talks, they become a channel. Something terrific moves through them. Socrates always said, 'It is not me that speaks, it is my *daemon*.' This word has degenerated and because of time has become our *demon*. A *daemon*, in Greek, meant my inspiring spirit, my contact with the Divine. So, people feel frustrated because they cannot have any effect on the world. It is because they do not have a *daemon*, spirit, or contact with the

Divine. People are not open to the Divine because they are under the hallucination they are a particular ego, separate from the rest of this universe."

"In a merciful way, nature leads us into this intense state of frustration where we feel there is absolutely nothing we can do about anything. The message of being in this state is the YOU that you think you are does not exist. So, my gamble is that if I get you thoroughly frustrated, you will find this out for yourself."

"With such knowledge, people sometimes get raving mad and even violent. Such people will learn nothing. However, they will work off a lot of steam. They may put someone in their righteous place. They may temporarily feel better. This game is great as far as it goes, which is not very far. Transitory happiness makes people no wiser. This activity further isolates one as it provokes other people to become angry and increasingly protective. This kind of sounds like the possessive and paranoid state of affairs the world is in, doesn't it?"

"On the other hand, the gamble is that people may, through this feeling of frustration and complete impotence, suddenly discover their reason for feeling impotent. They discover that the ego identity they thought they were, does not exist. This is the reason people cannot do anything. They discover that the sense of self they believed in, is fiction."

"This is a great awareness to discover. Some people discover this in the moment of imminent death. They are lying in a hospital bed. Physicians enter the room with the kind of face that anybody can tell what it means. It's grit to you. When you get that real loud and clear, right on the end of the line, you can go three ways. You can say, 'Put me out of my misery. I want to be unconscious for the whole event.' Or, you can say, 'Why, why, why, is this happening to me?' You can get angry. You can get the screaming me-me's."

"Or, the other possibility is that you can see there is absolutely nothing to do about it. You're finished. You have no further power or responsibility. There is nothing you can do about your starving children or whatever. It's all beyond your control. And, you give up. You just give up. People to whom that happens suddenly discover, although it's a little late in the day, they are full of delight, peace, and energy."

"I have attended too many death beds and seen this happen. It is wonderful that it happens because the person dies peacefully. However, look now! You are all as good as dead right now. All of you are going to die. I am going to die. There is absolutely nothing we can do about it. We are ephemeral fireworks. Beautiful! Look at you! You are so colorful and lovely! You can screech just a little while and then you disappear. You are not going to hang onto life, you know. And, if you could hang on to your life, you would strangle yourselves."

"So, why not let go now? Don't wait until the last minute in the hospital. The advantage of letting go earlier is that you become powerful. No one can bribe you. No one can frighten you. No one can put you down. When people do this, they face the world as if they were dead already. They realize they have no possessions. There is nothing to own. They realize they are a big act."

"I am not saying you should face this reality, like some kind of preacher. From my perspective, however, I don't know how people escape it. I am saying that if you face this reality and see what is going on, there is nothing else you can do. This isn't doing what you ought to do. It is doing what you must."

"So, you cannot congratulate yourself and say I've been virtuous for my awareness and deeds. This is merely an accurate awareness of the human condition. When people face the human condition, they are completely ephemeral. They notice they are disappearing rapidly into nothing or back into the pool of cosmic reality. When you accept this reality, you suddenly become alive and full of energy. You keep the credibility of simply being human. You can remain loving and yet non-attached to people. You can look people straight in the eye and know their difficulties result from not realizing they are God."

"Now, suppose you have a lot of money invested in a corporation that is involved in destroying the planet. In actuality, this corporation is raising millions of chickens. They have these chickens in cell blocks. The highly salaried research scientists of the corporation are working on ways to develop chickens that have no feathers. Getting rid of the feathers between the state of the egg and the cut-up-fryer is an inconvenient step."

"Now, this corporation has discovered how to raise them without feathers. The only problem really worrisome is that the chickens don't taste like chicken. They taste like papier-mache. The average stockholder in this corporation is investing in mutual funds and probably doesn't know what the corporation's money is going toward. He is bothered because the chicken he eats doesn't taste like chicken. He doesn't realize that he could control this if he would go to the stockholders meetings. He could say, 'Now listen, exactly what are you doing with my money about those chickens.' He doesn't do that because he is only interested in increased dividends. Meanwhile, the quality of his dinner decreases. This is a similar story to explain the pollution of streams, lakes, and the smog in the atmosphere. This person is not smart, you see."

"Do you think people are smart because they earn enough money to buy a wealthy house in an urban city and live in carbon fumes? Is that smart? Is that good business? You see, the trouble with this kind of thinking is confusing figures with facts. Once people understand this profound difference of values, they can meet a person who is in this situation and say, 'Look, you're not going to frighten me anymore with the amount of money you have or your impression of being a smart, clever business person. The truth is that you are a miserable person. You come on with this big revival that you are smart, rich, and a success in this world. More than likely, you are living on plastic. You are wired to the government's view of smart, rich, and successful. You are sucked into a diminished sense of reality."

"A revolution may arise. The centralized government may raise taxes so much that you won't have anything left. Sound familiar? You think you are an investor or a business man, and you don't even realize that taxation is obsolete in some counties, states, and foreign countries. You have put yourself down. Therefore, you have to make as much money as possible to protect your situation."

"You still think that underneath all of this, you are a poor little *me* living in a bag of skin. You don't know that every single person is the whole universe looking out through a pair of eyes. However, people can only find that out when they discover that the self they think they are, cannot do what they have been seduced into believing is possible."

Alan paused and then continued, "Okay, now I have spoken in monologue enough for the moment. It is your turn to take it on from here and ask me any questions you like."

A young well dressed person from the back of the audience stood and asked, "What can we as individual's do about the major economic, ecological, and political conflict in the world?"

"Now, here you see, this question arises repeatedly. This is good because I know when people ask this question, that we are getting right down to the heart of what you and I can do as individuals about these matters. First, you have to get a new experience of your personal and professional business in life. I am sorry. This is the fastest way through. You know, many people say the world will never change until each person changes his or her self. And, people know they can't change their self because the self they are supposed to reform is the same self that is supposed to do the reforming."

"All I am pointing out is that YOU, as you think of yourself, are not real. You are not that ego. And, it's a very simple matter to find out that you are not. This is not a royal challenge. This is not going to require terrific effort of will. It is simple! Only, you have to be willing to admit that it is simple. Many people don't want to admit that anything is simple. They say their efforts don't really amount to anything unless it took them thirty years and maybe at several hundred dollars a consultation. Then, they feel they have really paid their dues and suffered their time. Something better should happen. Of course, it doesn't."

"Realization is not a matter of time at all, either short-time or long-time. Realization is fundamentally an awareness, right now, that your supposed self cannot do anything at all. You are already completely washed out. You have no debt and no responsibilities whatsoever. You are as good as dead. Nobody has any use for you. There is nothing you can do to improve anything, not only in the world, but much less yourself."

"Let's get into this frame of mind, all of us. There is just nothing at all we can do about anything whatsoever. Isn't that a relief? Now, if you have that sense of relief, you have a lot of energy available. You have been using your energy to try and lift yourself off the ground by pulling your own bootstraps."

"I find people seriously saying today, 'You've got to lift yourself up by your own bootstraps.' Well, you can't do it! No amount of pulling is going to get the whole of you off the ground. It won't work."

"That's what we're all doing. We're spending hours upon hours a week trying to do this very activity. And, we're doing it by going to religious meetings and psychotherapists. 'Doctor, please help me with this task of getting myself up by my bootstraps.' You cannot do it. You cannot do anything. Once you realize that, you suddenly feel relieved, energetic, and free."

"Now, what are we going to do with the extra energy? Are we really going to improve the world? Are we going to improve it like all of our escapades in Vietnam, Venezuela, Panama, and Guatemala? Quite sincerely, these invasions were conducted with the best of intentions to bring the clean American way of life to all those poor nations. And the road to hell is paved with good intentions. Has it worked? Of course not! England did not help Japan or India. Columbus failed with the indigenous Indians of the islands off Florida. Spain and England failed with the American

Indians. France and the United States failed with Vietnam. This record has proved itself hundreds of times across history."

If people stopped wasting their energy with these resented improvements, their extra energy could in fact, do a lot of cooperative good. I know this may sound strange to you. That is precisely the problem. If we had a world in which everybody surrendered to improving their particular view of how the world should be, people would say, 'Isn't it strange how life has improved.'"

"The basis of my proposition is for you to realize that you cannot do anything. I am saying that you must go through the crises of experiencing that you cannot do anything to have the power to do something. That's the only position from which powerful energy arises. Then, when you realize that YOU, as you, can do nothing, you can link in with the real energy. Real energy is the energy of the universe. Indeed, as you use this energy to become a metaphoric channel through which Krishna plays his flute, you become the flute."

A young, accusatory college student stood and with a French accent exclaimed, "The other night I was looking at the stars. I looked out into the sky at the Big Dipper. I realized that what we call the Big Dipper is actually our interpretation. So, the stars are there and we organize our own reality. When you talk about energy, it seems to me that you are doing the same thing. I don't really know where you are getting this. It seems that you are just putting one set of values on top of another. If that makes you feel more powerful, then fine. However, it doesn't mean that your way of viewing the world or universe is an accurate perception. Do you understand me?"

"Yes! I understand you to be saying that I am talking about two systems of values. I am. If I understand you correctly, I am also saying there is no accidental system of values. That is, the Big Dipper is only important because of its usefulness in identification as an intellectual abstraction."

"However, if you are understanding me as saying that the way I am telling you will be the successful way, you don't understand me. I am saying to you there is no successful way. That's what you've got to understand first. Your religion does not matter. It does not matter whether you believe there is a God or there is no God. It does not matter whether you believe in a personal God or an impersonal God. It doesn't make the slightest difference what you believe. You have no faith.[6] You are wishing. Let's get rid of all plans that we can figure, all programs of success whatsoever. This is what I am saying."

"Let's recognize ourselves now as completely washed out without resources. Then, and only then, an energy will develop. A faith will develop, not in something that is an intellectual object, idol, or sacred cow. However, you first have to get down to nothing before anything will happen, because oddly enough, nothing implies something. There wouldn't be something without nothing, just as there wouldn't be nothing without something."

A person in his early thirties, clad in a grey suit and conventional tie stood and asked, "I am looking for the practical effectiveness of your wisdom. Could you give us an example of how this might work in our daily lives?"

Alan responded, "So, which of your daily lives would you like me to give you a practical example?"

The person clarified his question, "Well, not in your daily life because you have the advantage of all of this energy and experience. You might well live differently. I want to know how this might, for example, be helpful in dealing with my children and what the results might be."

"Well, I wonder why you are asking the question that way. You are saying to me, 'I'd like to be sure that what you are saying will be safe if we try it. What I am saying to you is that I cannot guarantee that. I just won't guarantee it because a way of life lived on the supposition that it will be safe, that it will work, will always get you into trouble. If you never take a risk, you will not achieve anything creative at all."

"The reason so many of our children today are so difficult is they have been over-protected. They have never been allowed to do dangerous activities because everybody got anxious. A law was passed against it. The insurance premium was refused. Somebody was embarrassed. So, the poor kids are not allowed to be dangerous in a way that all children should be allowed to be. When I was a child, I could do the most fantastically dangerous activities. We could ride our bicycles at tremendous speeds over the most disastrous trips. We thoroughly enjoyed ourselves and nobody noticed. I have watched children in Japan doing activities that would horrify the PTA in this country. I am afraid that some of them get killed. Some of ours get killed too. You have to take risks. So, I am saying, I cannot guarantee that what I am saying would have so-called practical results for family life. While you must have practical results in family life, if you depend upon them, your family life is going to be a mess."

Another person in the audience spoke, "I want to know how this applies to increased responsibility in marriage and relationships. I know of no culture where people are not social beings and effectively survive."

"I am not talking about dropping responsibility in the ordinary way. A person who is of the ordinary way sacrifices responsibility and does so because they are frightened of it. It's too much work. I'm not talking about it from that point of view at all. I am talking about it from the point of view that you realize, the responsibilities you have assumed, you cannot fulfill, whether or not you want to fulfill them. You, as ego, cannot do what you have committed yourself to do."

"For example, suppose you as ego get on your knees in front of the altar. You swear that you will love this person until 'death do you part.' You have no right to make such a statement. You are kidding yourself. You are being emotionally dishonest. You may feel like that at the time, but you've got hot pants. More importantly, if eventually you stop feeling that way, you suddenly feel guilty because you have made this rash and terrible vow. Then, you start pretending that you love. You put on another big act."

"Although your lover won't admit it, they know it is not true. You are then involved in terrific emotional dishonesty. Nonetheless, you say, we have a lot of children or responsibilities. We have to stick together to deal with these responsibilities and love the whole situation. Everybody knows you don't and they resent it. They hate you and they hate themselves for accepting it. And, they hate you for pretending it."

"Now, you have to be honest and say, I just discovered that I cannot command my feelings with my ego. My ego has no influence over my feelings. My feelings do not listen to my ego because my ego isn't really there. Face it! That's the way it is!"

"Now, what I am saying, is that if you face this reality, the energy you have wasted by trying to do impossible things will become available to you to do impossible things. That is, you will be able to fulfill responsibilities and do things that really must be done for people without saying that you do them because you love them so much, when YOU don't."

One middle-aged person raised her hand and asked, "I don't understand how to make time for all this mystical stuff. I've got three screaming kids, a heap of laundry, and a load of dishes that fills the kitchen everyday. How do I make time to let go without making meditation another time-consuming activity?"

Alan paused and then answered, "The next time you are washing dishes I want you to remember one internal message, and that is, that in these circumstances, we have only one dish to wash, this one!"

Another younger person in the audience raised her hand and was called upon.

"There are many gurus running around today. How do you tell the difference between a true mystic and a phony?"

Alan pondered for a moment and then gazed in the direction of the high-pitched voice in the dimly lit auditorium.

In his resounding English dialect he bellowed out, "Well, madam, I guess you have to be one to know one,"[7] and then robustly laughed in only a way that he could serve when honoring the angels.

Mystics Often Live Unconventional Lifestyles

Standards of convention include beliefs, perceptions, and ethical conduct. These standards are usually associated with technologically advanced cultures. Statistically, mystics are clearly in the minority. As such, their standards are outside conventional experience. Most mystics do not have notoriety. Many are wayward priests or tribal shamans. Some have a significant following that is strange and often threatening to conventional experience.

Alan Watts was a mystical sage who advertised himself as merely a "philosophical entertainer." By conventional standards, he was eccentric and mysterious. After years of serving as an Anglican priest, Alan lived his later years on a fairy boat in Sausalito, California. He did not live by values of fidelity nor a conventionally healthful diet. He built a private meditation center in the middle of a forest on the northeast side of San Francisco and walked through the nearby mountains in Asian clothing.

Alan was fond of living the whimsical lifestyle of a bohemian led by permissive desires of the present moment. Incorporating mysticism meant living the joy of excess sensuality. He spontaneously appreciated life to its fullest hedonistic extent and without conflict between spirituality and sensuality. Savoring caviar and Coquille Saint-Jacques with an aged bottle of delicate sauvignon blanc was as gloriously spiritual to Alan as sitting in *zazen* was miraculously sensual. It was for this reason that some people discounted Alan as a mystic.

At Alan's funeral service, entitled a "Crossing Over Ceremony," the Abbot of the San Francisco Zen Center bestowed on him the rare title *Dai Yu Jo Mon*, which means "Great Founder, Opener of the Great Zen Samadhi Gate." His ashes were interred in a *stupa* on a hillside behind the Zen Center's Green Gulch Farm.

Unconventional lifestyles also occur in the documented histories of mystical leaders such as: Zoroaster, Socrates, Lao Tzu, Moses, Jeshua of Nazareth, Gautama Siddartha Buddha, Mohammed, Dante Alighieri, Francis Bacon, Al-Hillaj Mansoor, and George Fox as founder of the Quakers originating in the middle of the seventeenth century in England.

In the seventeenth through early twentieth century, unconventional lifestyles were represented by: William Blake, Walt Whitman, Henry David Thoreau, Madame Helena Blavatsky as co-founder of the Theosophical Society, Joseph Smith as founder of Mormonism, and Mary Baker Eddy as founder of the Christian Science religion.

In the twentieth century, personal idiosyncracies that represent unconventional standards are exemplified by: Da Love-Ananda, Meher Baba, Sun Bear, Carlos Castenada, Padre Pio Forgione of Pietrelcina, Mahatma Ghandi, George Gurdjieff, Jiddu Krishnamurti, Swami Maharishi Mahesh Yogi, Father Thomas Merton, Swami Prabhupada as founder of the Hare Krishna movement, Osho Rajneesh, Swami Satya Sai Baba, Mother Teresa, Rolling Thunder, and Swami Paramahansa Yogananda as founder of the Self Realization Fellowship. Additionally, there are thousands of unknown mystics alive today spiritually serving the needs of cultural tribes, nations, and human welfare.

Conventional and Mystical Experiences are Qualitatively Different

Lisa is the name of a person. Buff is the name of a large domestic calico cat. Lisa eats more food than Buff. Buff climbs trees faster than Lisa. These examples describe quantitative differences between Lisa and Buff. Quantitative differences are measurable by amount or degree.

Qualitative differences define the peculiar or essential character of an object or event. They represent the distinguishing feature that identifies the object or event as unique. In comparison to Buff the qualitative difference of Lisa is that she can combine symbols of language for rational communication. No cat can perform this function. In comparison to Lisa, Buff and his friends have been known to find their way home from thousands of miles away without a known map.

Conventional experience represents ordinary sensation and perception through the five senses. Conventional experience of God or the universal force is perceived as separate and external to the embodied self. As such, it acts within linear and measurable time. Also, conventional experience usually assumes that evil is an active force within the universe.

Mystical experience is qualitatively different from conventional experience. In addition to the five known senses, mystical experience encompasses intuitive, psychic, and mystical perception. Mystical experience reflects union with God, the universal, or cosmic force. This experience is unitive and inclusive of universal forces. Linear and measurable time become an abstract illusion. Evil is an interpretative value based on the intent and use of conventional and magical power.[8]

The abstractness of mystical experience is notably more difficult for non-subscribers to agree upon. However, this is true only from the perspective of conventional experience. Since mystical experience has a different reference for confirmation, similar to subscribers of conventional experience, mystical subscribers agree amongst themselves. For example, when Native American holy people meet with Zen masters from Japan, Taoists from China, and Tibetan Masters, there is common agreement about beliefs and perceptions. Agreement includes visions, prophecies, dream interpretation, political and ecological issues, and medicinal and spiritual healing. This transpersonal agreement also distinguishes mystical realization as essential for the ease of human suffering and the successful evolution of the species.

Mystical Experience Accepts Personal Idiosyncracies

The Western conventional delusion is that since mystics are ostensibly perfect of spirit, their personal behavior should exemplify the stellar expectations of personal development. Human imperfections are mistakenly used as evidence against spiritual attainment. There is the widespread notion that to be a holy person or to engage in powers of the spirit, one lives a pious or pure life. Such characteristics include associations with celibacy, abstinence of materialistic and sensual pleasures, and subscription to conventionally healthful standards. These associations represent institutional religions that promote saints. However, they are not always applicable to mystical experience.

The saintly belief of spiritual experience is completely burdensome as a criteria by to which to gage mystical realization. Such a lofty image, for that person who may desire to pursue mystical awareness, is yet another interference and excuse for remaining embedded within an attached sense of self.

People often speak of apparent incongruence within the contexts of the sacred and the profane, the spiritual and the sensual. While it is human for people to search, it is not as acceptable to find. Skepticism arises toward those who claim they have had a mystical experience or are walking a spiritual path. When people separate heaven from earth, heaven is perfect, and earth represents heaven's fallacy or folly.

Mystical paths include personal idiosyncracies. Disapproval of the frailties is a conventional abstraction that affirms imagined limitations rather than a mystical relationship with the universe. While sometimes related, personal development and the evolution of the soul are separate human functions. The development of the personality depends on self identity. Spiritual evolution depends on identity with universal forces. Personal imperfections cannot discredit mystical realization. The most frequent judgements by those operating from conventional experience are an excuse for maintaining familiarity. Such excuses reinforce earthbound and finite awareness.

From the perspective of mystical experience, accepting developmental flaws is accomplished by reinterpreting specific behaviors and events. Developmental flaws of personality serve as signposts from which to learn. Life limiting behavior is part of being human. All human error is another opportunity to align with the universe. Human imperfections are reminders for people to pay attention. They are tests to keep people on track.

There are no dichotomies within the spiritual field. Dichotomies and apparent conflicts exist only within conventional experience or ordinary consciousness. These apparent opposites are necessary and useful for conventional rationality. The mystical dimension makes room for human idiosyncracies. It allows the personal weird to spice the cosmos.

Each dimension reflects the other as a mountain reflects its majesty in a still lake. It is not that the lake adds a little flavor. Rather, the lake serves as the manifestation of a different experience of the mountain. The mountain is the brush and the lake is the rice paper.

Mystical and Pathological Experiences are Dissimilar

People sometimes confuse mystical experience with conventional psychopathology. It is erroneous to equate mystical experience to psychopathologic beliefs and sense-perceptions. Such psychopathology includes hallucinations and psychotic delusions. Hallucinations and delusions are diverse because they deviate from the norm. This is because hallucinations are perceptions of objects when no such objects are present. Specifically, hallucinations are sensual perceptions that have no verifiable external stimuli. Delusions are either separate or accompanying false beliefs. Their "falseness" or degree of error is determined by comparing them to conventional experience.

This is not the situation with mystical experience. There are, of course, schizophrenics who have mystical experiences as there are mystics who have schizophrenic experiences. However, to equate mystical experiences with madness is, itself, a grandiose delusion. As Ken Wilber[9] has humorously pointed out, "Zen Master Hakuin left behind him 83 fully transmitted students who together revitalized and organized Japanese Zen. Eighty three hallucinating schizophrenics couldn't organize a trip to the toilet, let alone Japanese Zen."

Hallucinations and delusions restrict organismic freedom, emotional stability, meaningful perception, cognitive intention, and behavioral options. They generate from a fragmented sense of self. Such experiences do not serve or benefit the life enhancing options of either the person nor communal well being.

In contrast, a well developed and healthy identity generates mystical experience. Personal development is sufficient enough that elected focus of attention extends beyond the self. Mystical experiences are expansive. They characterize elected control, mindful intention, normal and paranormally enhanced sensitivity, and agreed upon perception. Mystical experience increases life enhancing options that serve both the organism and communal well being.

CHAPTER TWO
PARANORMAL STEPPING STONES

Stepping Stone One

When I was fourteen, the neighbors across the street installed a concrete swimming pool. The rectangular pool was twenty feet wide by forty feet long and landscaped with tropical palms, exotic boulders, and lava rock. Several of the adolescents in the neighborhood exchanged chores for desired swimming privileges. One hot summer day, three of us invited ourselves to this suburban paradise. The owners welcomed us to stay, but cautioned us about safety as they needed to leave for the remainder of the afternoon.

After an hour of smimming, my friends fell asleep drying themselves in the sun on the patio above the sidewalk deck surrounding the pool. I approached the diving board. Suddenly, I believed I could run the length of the board and vertically soar without touching the water until I reached the far end of the pool. In the moment, I did not consider the irrationality of my thought processes.

I ran, leaped, and focused only on the shallow end of the pool. All awareness of myself as a material body faded. I became a sailing point of awareness of wind, sun, reflective water, and the surrounding landscape. My gaze remained fixed on the far side of the pool as I freely glided about ten miles an hour. My body drifted evenly in a vertical position about a foot above the surface of the water.

I remember seeing the end of the pool coming near and became frightened I would hit the other side. With this awareness, immediately I dropped through the surface of the water five feet from the shallow end. I turned around and glared back at the diving board. I had accomplished an act beyond any satisfactory conventional explanation. Yet, without any doubt, the reality of my experience was unquestionable. My two friends were asleep and had not seen me. A new fear emerged. I knew that no one would believe me and that my experience would have to remain a secret.

Sixteen years later, I joined the United States Navy with a direct commission as a Navy Lieutenant. My goal was training in a clinical psychology internship at the Naval Hospital in Bethesda, Maryland. Several months into the internship, a fellow intern stopped by my office to show me some Navaho poetry. Jim was stout, a little bald, wore glasses, and had an infectious sense of humor. As an amateur mountain climber he had visited Nepal. While there, he made some serious climbs and became enchanted with Tibetan Buddhism. As a result, he now devoted an entire room of his country estate to meditation.

The Navaho poetry reminded me of my flight above the swimming pool at fourteen. I closed the door to my office. For the first time I shared my adolescent experience of levitation. During my story, Jim listened intensely without any change of expression. After several minutes, I finished my story.

With a broad grin on his face, Jim said, "I believe you."

Cautiously, I asked, "Yes, but aside from you believing that I am telling the truth, do you believe the actuality of the event itself?"

He laughed and said, "I'm not sure there is a difference. What are you really asking me?"

"I want to know whether you think that my experience actually happened or whether I made it up because I wanted to believe it."

"Did you?" he asked.

"Did I what?"

"Did you make it up or did it actually happen?"

"No," I said with a smile. "I didn't make it up. I have gone over it a hundred times in my mind and that's what I experienced! I know it happened though it is contrary to conventional and scientific experience."

Jim paused and said, "Let me tell you a story that I have never shared with anyone. Then we can both be crazy together. I was about sixteen when I practiced mountain climbing in the Blue Ridge mountains. One early morning I stood at the top of a thousand foot cliff. It had rained the night before. Moss heavily covered this range of slopes. That morning the slopes were extremely slippery."

"I reached a precipice and looked down into the valley below. A canopy of dense fog clung to the lower slope. I looked down the rugged mountain. Intuitively, I knew I could jump without ropes and make it through a veil of fog safely to the base. I didn't think about it. With a full backpack, I impulsively jumped. Like a character in a cartoon, I casually bounced from one moss covered boulder to the next without stopping until I arrived safely at the bottom."

"From below, a clearing opened through the fog. I looked up at the precipice with binoculars. I had accomplished what no professional climber could do in dry conditions with three times the amount of time. Also, the distance between two of the boulders prevented a single swing jump even with ropes."

We looked at each other in silence. After several minutes, Jim excused himself, stating he had a patient waiting. In the remainder of the year we knew one another, we never discussed these experiences again.

Stepping Stone Two

At twenty-one I was about to graduate with a bachelor of arts degree in psychology. I knew I wouldn't have any further complimentary medical services from the Student Health Center. Later, I would have to pay for the surgical removal of several warts on my left hand. I made an appointment for three weeks before graduation. However, I didn't like the idea of having these eruptions fried with the same kind of tool I used in a wood-burning set as a child. I experimented with a change in diet in the belief that it might get rid of the warts.

In spite of a major in psychology, I didn't know about clinical hypnosis at the time. My primary motivation was to avoid the pain of surgical removal. My only advantage was a belief that a change of diet might make a difference.

I followed an exclusively vegetarian diet. I devoured salads for breakfast, lunch, and dinner for three weeks. Two days before the appointment for minor surgery I stood in the shower and noticed my hand was completely normal. I had been so busy studying for final exams that I had not noticed if there were any incremental improvements. All of the warts, some of them large on several knuckles, had now vanished. I called the Student Health Center and canceled my appointment.

Stepping Stone Three

After graduation I became a close friend with the older brother of a classmate I had grown up with since the sixth grade. We developed a new bond enhanced by both of our wives being pregnant. Barry was a fire fighter with the Los Angeles Fire Department. He competed in playing pool as a member of a team sponsored by a local pub.

We frequented a variety of striper bars once a week, but only those with pool tables, the non-regulatory ones that feed on quarters. Barry could usually run several consecutive tables.

After six months of observing naked breasts, the finer points of pool artistry, and monetary reacquisition, I was bored watching Barry play pool all evening. To entertain myself, I conducted an experiment. I wanted to see if I could psychically control the movement of pool balls on the table. While I maintained a positive belief in the likelihood, I didn't expect to be as successful as the results confirmed.

Barry's skillful performance was undaunted. He was a consistent and reliable player and one with whom, I would not expect to have paranormal advantage. Secretly, I decided to focus my attention on his athletic skill for my experiment. I stood outside the respectable range of playing. I checked Barry's intended shot between the targeted ball and pocket. Mentally, I pictured a line from the targeted ball to an imagined spot on the cushion. This spot was near the targeted pocket, yet where it would honorably miss. In the beginning, I chose his most difficult shots and focused on them missing by half an inch. Somewhat to my surprise, I was successful on several non-sequential trials. However, since I was distracted and just amusing myself, I did not credit his errors to my success.

On following evenings, I decided to take myself more seriously. I increased my risk of failure by choosing his easier shots and reduced the distance by which I expected the targeted ball to hit the pocket. While Barry still played well, his performance had become inconsistent enough that I actually began to feel guilty. He missed simple and short shots that even I could make reliably. Also, I noticed that I was practicing my paranormal skill as much as he was practicing his gamesmanship.

On one particular evening, Barry ran two tables. In the middle of the third game, the cue ball was a foot away from a three foot straight shot. I had never seen him miss such a shot. I focused on my imaginary line of deviation. Barry missed the shot and lost the game to his competitor who ran the remainder of the table.

Of course, easily his errors could be dismissed as either random mistakes or the result of drinking a few beers. I chose to believe otherwise since his margin of errors over the past few months increased particularly at the times of my intervention. I remember feeling that I was influencing disruption without mutual consent and then primarily for amusement. I had become successful enough for my own purposes and abandoned the experiment.

Stepping Stone Four

I was attending graduate school in the evening and taking care of my three-year old daughter, Karen, during the day. One afternoon, I was working on my dissertation. I received a long distance call from my older cousin expecting wise counsel. I had not heard from her in many years. She called to say that she didn't know how to console her eight-year old son. He had climbed a wire fence and severed half the first finger of his right hand while trying to climb down. I remember saying a few shallow words of consolation. The phone conversation ended and I returned to my writing.

Karen walked toward me as I began to type. She had awakened early from her usual afternoon nap and climbed out of the low crib fence. I turned around to greet her. Looking at her right hand, she casually said, "I have all my fingers Daddy!" I asked, "What did you say?" She repeated herself for my conventional disbelief.

After questioning her further, I knew that Karen did not have any conscious reason for her statement. She was in bed during the phone conversation. Her bedroom was forty feet away through a corridor with the door closed. Also, she was very emotionally bonded to me. She simply and psychically interpreted my unusual interruption as an understandable concern to her.

Stepping Stone Five

Several years later, I taught a graduate class in Cross Cultural Personality and Mental Health in Los Angeles. Most of the fourteen people in the class were already various professionals taking courses for advanced degrees in psychology. The focus of the course was to explore the psychotherapeutic healing systems of diverse cultures and understand how these methods influence personality and increase mental health.

Jennifer was an American high school teacher in her fifties who had lived in Japan for two years and trained in *ikebana*, the art of Japanese flower arrangement. She suggested that the class arrange a visit to the local branch of the Church of World Messianity. Her request reminded me of my fourth grade field trips to Helms Bakery and China Town in the same city. Also, I was suspicious of the "savior" undertones of the name of the church.

Jennifer assured me the church was respectable. It was headquartered in Atami, Japan with a membership of one million members, another 200,000 in Brazil, and 2,500 in the United States. It was neither Christian, Shinto, Buddhist, nor Spiritualist based. Rather, it focused on a system of energy-healing called *Johrei*.[1] Other branches of its ministry focused on flower arranging, ceramics, and natural farming. Quenching a thirst for the paranormal, the class and I unanimously agreed to visit.

I telephoned Reverend Thelma Dowd. After disguising our curiosity as academic observation and research, she graciously offered an invitation. She would allow our entire class to attend an evening meeting if we met with her an hour in advance for an introduction.

The class met in Reverend Thelma Dowd's office of the church on an early evening during the week. She gave an hour lecture on the benefits of energy transformation[2] and the Johrei Fellowship. Also, she cautioned us. The ceremony we would first witness downstairs was one performed for the safe travel of the soul of a church member who recently died.[3]

Following our briefing, we attended the end of the service already in progress. Quietly, we entered and sat on folding chairs. There were about forty people in the sanctuary. No one gave noticeable attention to our entrance. Most of the people were of Japanese descent. I did not understand their concluding remarks as they spoke in Japanese and I did not. Shortly after our admission, the formal service concluded. Reverend Dowd asked volunteers from the congregation to remain for a demonstration of Johrei. Members individually approached and paired with each of us.

A Japanese middle-aged person approached and asked me whether I was willing to work with him. I was delighted. We sat for about twenty minutes and talked. George told me that a few months ago he admitted himself to the University of California at Los Angeles Medical Center for evaluation of a pain in his lower back. Following tests, his physician informed him that he needed a kidney stone operation. Since he preferred to avoid invasive surgical procedures and believed in the power of Johrei, he demanded all staff to leave him completely alone for three days. He asked for a private room and required that he not be disturbed in any way. Visitors were not to be permitted. Food was to be left inside the door entrance without comment. His physician reluctantly agreed. After three days, further tests concluded the absence of kidney stones. George's physician released him from the hospital. I asked George what the physician said. George replied, "He said it was a miracle."

After our conversation, George instructed me to relax in the chair. I looked around the room. Now, other pairs of people were performing the same exercise. Members of the church were sitting behind each of us. They moved the palm of one hand about a foot away from our backs in circular form. George positioned himself directly behind me and told me to close my eyes. After a few moments, I felt heat enter my back and move around in circular form. My entire body was relaxing as a result of this heat sensation. This sensation continued for twenty minutes.

Following this demonstration, George and I talked again. He explained to me the physical effects of purification and the transmission of Johrei. George explained that Johrei was a method of transmitting *divine light* to a human body through the palm of its administrator. He defined *divine light* as a purificatory energy flowing from the realm of spirit that cleanses clouds in the spiritual body system. As these spiritual clouds in a specific region are dispelled, the physical toxins existing in the same area of the physical body expel. The harmful bacteria or viruses located in the diseased part of the body are deprived of their life force and rendered harmless. Eventually, these are also discharged.

I thanked George for his gracious offering. As the last member of our class finished, I offered my appreciation to Reverend Dowd. In our next class, ten of the fourteen students reported various physical sensations from Johrei. Three students reported relief of various pains that had occurred for more than a year.

Stepping Stone Six

Dr. Arthur Stirling was the Chairperson of the Department of Religious Studies and Philosophy that helped sponsor Alan Watts. Arthur graduated from the University of Edinburgh with his doctorate degree in theological ethics. Following, he took a ministerial position with a small rural parish in the countryside of Scotland. Arthur made a traditional yuletide Christmas pudding that weighed seven pounds from a 19th-century Scottish recipe. It included pork lard that he bought from a local country farmer, whole eggs, plump currants, and crisp English walnuts. All ingredients soak in two fifths of Puerto Rican and Jamaican rum for four weeks, four Sundays in Advent, until the "pudd" is aged.

Arthur lived in a double story brick home across from a park in the downtown older area of Racine, Wisconsin. His family included four daughters with his wife, Margo, who was half the size of his physical presence. Margo was the homemaker. She grew and picked her own herbs, was a gourmet cook, and practiced yoga daily.

This was the time at which Jose Silva was starting his seminars, not surprisingly called, the *Silva Mind Control*[4] method. Jose Silva made various practical claims. They included developing abilities to use psychokinesis, see auras, determine points of physical illness, self-healing, and locating lost objects. Arthur,

Margo, and their oldest daughter, Elizabeth enrolled in the week workshop. Elizabeth was in sixth grade at the time.

Several months after the workshop, Elizabeth's sixth grade teacher raffled several gifts to her class for the celebration of Thanksgiving Day. Students wrote their names on pieces of paper and placed them in a ceramic jar. The teacher drew a piece of paper from the jar each day of the week and gave a surprise gift to the winner. Elizabeth wanted to win. On the first day, she concentrated on the teacher drawing the piece of paper with her name on it.

Elizabeth came home and told Arthur how she had won. Arthur was a little upset. He scolded Elizabeth and told her that she should not be playing with powers of the mind in this manner. Elizabeth listened, but the temptation of winning another prize was too much. On the second day, the teacher placed all the children's names back into the jar. Again, Elizabeth concentrated on the teacher drawing her name. Once again, the teacher drew her name. The same result occurred on the third day. Frustrated, the teacher stopped the raffle.

Stepping Stone Seven

Arthur and I decided to test a clairvoyant technique he learned in the Silva Mind Control workshop. We conducted these experiments with an attitude of sincerity blended with the playfulness of parlor amusement. I would hide something in his house. Arthur would concentrate and usually find it within fifteen minutes. We traded turns and successfully did this on more than thirty occasions.

Years later, I lost a star sapphire gold ring my father had made and given to me for a birthday present. I was living in Virginia at the time. My morning routine was to rise at five thirty in the morning, and for an hour go outside and practice *t'ai chi chuan*.[5] One winter morning, I practiced in a clearing among pine trees. It snowed the night before and more than a foot of snow covered the ground.

After looking for the ring in vain, I employed a different method. I remembered the technique of locating lost objects. I closed my eyes and went into a light trance. I pictured the ring in the foreground and focused my attention on the background. After a few minutes, I saw the ring laying on top of a brown background. The brown color didn't make any sense to me. I looked inside and outside the house trying to locate something brown. Finally, I gave up.

The following morning at dawn, I went outside as usual to practice. Soft snow had now melted leaving scattered patches of brown earth. Gazing down at one of the patches, I discovered my ring on a background of wet dirt. The ring was exactly as I had viewed it the evening before during my attempt to locate it. Obviously, I had flung it off my hand the morning before during practice. It had fallen through the soft snow and become buried below.

I learned in these exercises not to confuse the symbol with the object. "Brown" was the symbol for the object "dirt." An object cannot both look *like* an object and *be* that object. If you are trying to find your watch and it looks *like* your watch, you can bet it is not your watch. If on the other hand, you either picture the watch directly, or have a vision that resembles a clock, bingo, you locate your watch.

Stepping Stone Eight

Arthur and I wanted to prove to ourselves that clairvoyant skills worked at greater distances. Like children fascinated with a new toy, we played a game of first locating and then creating parking spaces. Finding a parking space was easy, but we had to specify a site or location.

I focused on a familiar site, viewing it from above in advance of arrival. I looked for the nearest and most convenient parking space to my destination. Sometimes it was not there. Sometimes I needed to focus again a few minutes past my original try. When I focused on finding a convenient parking space and located it, I continued to focus on the empty space. The process was similar to an anti-ballistic missile moving toward its designated target. Inevitably, I drove directly to the available space and parked conveniently.

Sometimes, Arthur and I would collaborate our visions. We tried to coordinate our efforts, such that in our novice view, it would double the likelihood of the result. Later, I discovered that when increased numbers of people focus on the same target, it may or may not increase the desired effect. Other variables include contamination of focus and distraction. This is known as *psi* interference or *mental noise*.[6] These distractive thoughts and images arise from memory elements or imagination. Such interference often results from excessive comparative analysis of target elements.

With increasing skill, I began to trust myself. In a few instances I was surprised to find that the focused upon parking space was already occupied. I learned to wait a few seconds. Timing was not always precise, but quite near. Several times I waited for no more than three minutes. More often than not, in less than a minute, someone approached his or her vehicle and left the exact focused space to me.

As I became more practiced, rather than find a space and then continue to focus on it, I created a parking space. Creating parking spaces is more difficult for the believer, but not always the act, because of an expansion of belief. However, I became as adept with this skill as well. As I continued to practice creating spaces, I began to feel that I was using cosmic credits to satisfy unnecessary needs of a temporal nature. The results were not only a product of selfish concern. They were unnecessary for my well being, like killing animals for sport rather than for food or required provisions.

Locating parking spaces and then taking advantage of the opportunity is in harmony with the natural order of events. This is the way events are mostly going to be anyway. Continually creating parking spaces, while successful, invites interference. The process of creating events requests universal forces to yield for selfish concern. In this sense, I became conscious of mystical abuse. Mystical abuse is simply using inclusive power for exclusive and needless purposes.

While I did not fear cosmic retribution, I had mastered the skill by replication and could fulfill my desires by the less disruptive process of locating. I now knew I was tapping into a universal consciousness and energy beyond myself. Respectfully, I did not want to take advantage. Also, I didn't know the entire consequences of psychic influence and didn't want to find out too late. Besides, my craving for something more than empirical reality was now satisfying my hunger. Later, I was to learn how these paranormal experiences connected to the mystical realization that was still missing in my life.

Stepping Stone Nine

In July 1977 I attended the Sixth International Congress of Group Psychotherapy in Philadelphia, Pennsylvania. I went to one workshop the first morning and took the remainder of the day to vacation with my wife north along the Delaware River. On the second day I noticed a hand written advertisement for a four hour workshop entitled "Energy Transformation" offered by Tilak Fernando. People interested in attending had to pre-register. Admission was limited to twenty participants and then only to those on time. The workshop was scheduled for three hours. These were extremely unusual requirements for a professional conference. The requirements, workshop title, and the name of the leader captured my interest. After briefly discussing the opportunity, my wife and I decided to attend.

We arrived on time at eleven in the morning. People seated themselves in metal folding chairs in a traditional audience seating arrangement in a large room. A few minutes past the hour, an assistant closed and locked the double doors. The secretive ambiance set a mysterious mood.

Tilak was trim, slight in stature, and of East Indian origin. Professionally, he introduced himself without credentials as merely a psychologist from Sri Lanka, Ceylon. None of the printed brochures of the conference mentioned his name. No one with whom I talked knew of him. No one understood how he managed to gain approval for this unrelated topic at a scientific conference on group psychotherapy.

For more than an hour, Tilak delivered a vague and tiresome lecture. He sprinkled his message with occasional Sanskrit terms, the meanings of which I did not know. I do not know whether others found it to be explanatory or entertaining. I only know I was beginning to wish I was under an umbrella at the restaurant overlooking the canal in New Hope where we had lunch the day before.

Tilak finished his lecture and ask that we fold the chairs and remove them to the sides of the room. He asked for volunteers for three demonstrations and chose nine people including my wife. He directed three people to stand at shoulders length from one another and face the same direction. He asked them to close their eyes. He directed three other people to stand two feet behind the first three people, facing the same direction.

Without warning, he walked about two feet in front of the people in the front row and moved the palm of his right hand toward them, as if forcing air into their chest cavities. His open palm stopped nearly a foot in front of their chests. Suddenly, each of the three people fell in a vertical radius into the arms of the person behind them. It was as if they were struck by a moving force the length of their bodies. That is, they did not just fall. First, they moved with a force that could not have been initiated by physical effort even if physical contact had been made. Second, all three people fell completely stiff from their heals backward. Third, Tilak's only preinduction suggestions were asking for volunteers and asking for three other people to stand behind the three primary targets of the demonstration. Also, the time between these people initially closing their eyes and then propelling to the ground was less than ten seconds.

Each of the three was then gently leveled to the floor by the three people who caught them. The three people on the floor were in deep trance. I use the word *trance* because the people on the floor looked asleep. With these people *resting* on the carpeted floor, Tilak asked another person to stand about twelve feet from them and hold a rolled newspaper in her left hand. Within five seconds of her grabbing the newspaper, Tilak snapped his fingers in front of her eyes and lit the newspaper on fire with matches. Her eyes open, she merely gazed at the flames surrounding her hand, wrist, and lower arm. She continued until she held nothing except small fragments of paper and ashes. Later, she reported no pain. Group observation confirmed there were no burned areas or even singed hairs of her skin.

Tilak then asked for two chairs to be placed about five feet apart facing one another. My wife volunteered for this demonstration. He asked her to place the back crown of her head on the edge of one chair and the tip of her heals on the other. He directed me to support her weight underneath the middle of her lower body. He then told her to relax and close her eyes. Without further instructions, he asked me to raise the weight of her body. As she became completely stiff and horizontal, he directed me to let go and remove myself from the area.

The person, whose hand had held the burning newspaper, was still staring at her upright hand in front of her face. The three people on the floor were still in trance, except that one of them was beginning to writhe in involuntary convulsions. In a moments notice, Tilak immediately went over and knelt by the person. Without speaking he stiffened his right hand. Starting at the person's throat, he pressed into his body cavity and ran his hand the length of the person's chest into his diaphragm and then pressed deeply. The person on the floor sighed a deep breath and his convulsions subsided. Tilak returned to my wife still in her rigid horizontal position.

He turned to the participants and said, "Anyone can do this with two chairs. I will try to show you that it can be done with one."

Tilak tried to move the chair from underneath her heals. It was far more than half tilted and almost removed when she started abdominal convulsions. Her breathing became extremely deep and erratic. While her eyes remained closed, her eyelids fluttered and her head jerked. Tilak gently replaced the chair and she regained a relaxed composure in a horizontal position. He looked at me and said, "Perhaps there is too much distraction. She is not ready today."

He then asked me to position myself to regain her weight and without any countdown, awoke her from trance by snapping his fingers. Immediately following, he did the same with the three people on the floor and the person holding ashes. After a few closing remarks, none of which offered any rational explanation, an assistant opened the locked doors and the crowd quietly dispersed.

Varieties of Paranormal Experience

Paranormal experiences include telepathy, clairvoyance, precognition, and psychokinesis. Of these, telepathy is the most common. Telepathy is receiving information directly from another person's thought processes without the intervention of the ordinary five sense organs. It is knowing something in the present that is not perceived through the five senses or could have been known from other available information.

Clairvoyance is the acquisition of information about an event, object, or place without the intervention of the ordinary five sense organs. Clairvoyance refers to gaining information through a vision.[7] Clairvoyance is similar to telepathy except the information is supposedly not known to any other physically living person, except clairvoyants. Interestingly, clairvoyance cannot be distinguished from telepathy in laboratory experiments. Regardless of experimental design, clairvoyance cannot be excluded as a possible explanation because even a telepathic target must be communicated to an experimental subject for confirming or denying accuracy.[8] This is the reason parapsychologists simply refer to telepathy and clairvoyance as general extrasensory perception (GESP).

More than half of psychic experiences occur precognitively. Precognition is the ability to know something in the future when there is no known available information now from which such awareness can be known. While half of paranormal experiences reported are pre-cognitive, they are less specific and practical because they usually arise within dreams that occur during sleep.

Psychokinesis (PK)[9] refers to the ability of people to influence events, objects, or people at a distance without physical intervention. Usually, psychokinesis refers to the intentional and conscious influence of physical or material systems outside the initiator's embodied self. Psychokinesis can occur near the targeted object or across the world. Distance is not a factor.

At the turn of the century, there was much interest in psychokinesis because of the extraordinary events reported at Spiritualist meetings or seances. Objects moved through the air. Rapping noises were heard coming from furniture. There were reports of tables floating in the air completely suspended from the floor. Most of these cases involved fraud and serious investigators were reluctant to verify psychokinesis.

Levitation is a subcategory of psychokinesis. Levitation usually refers to people physically rising without physical support in the air. However, this general definition does little to distinguish the observable varieties of levitation from thousands of reported incidents throughout the world. Reported incidents vary in: (1) the length of time of suspension of the physical organism [from a few seconds to hours], (2) the planetary position of the physical organism [vertically, horizontally, upside down, irregular tumbling, or within a seated lotus position], (3) control in the directional movement of the physical organism [from random to planned], and (4) the distance covered by the physical organism [from none to hundreds of miles]. Examples of levitation include bouncing, suspension, hovering, floating, and trance-walking.

One popular example is the claim made by advanced devotees of transcendental meditation™, those followers of Swami Maharishi Mahesh Yogi. This practice is an initial stage of yogic flying.[10] However, many of the observable reports of this meditative activity claim people "hop" for several seconds at a time within the air without apparent muscular activity rather than suspend within the air for three or more minutes. This example of levitation demonstrates: (1) levitation that occurs for several seconds, (2) within a seated lotus position, (3) with planned control, and (4) a few inches of vertical distance above the ground with no horizontal distance.

As a bizarre example, Douchan Gersi reported a personal observation at a Voodoo ceremony in a Haitian village. A person, in a completely vertical position, arose from the ground above the crowd. As he continued to dance in slow motion, he slowly began to turn upside down. With his head six feet from the ground, he swiftly traveled through the air and landed several feet from the ground against a tree on the other side of the plaza. Still head down, he climbed the trunk and sat upright on a lower branch. With cheers from the crowd, he climbed down and behaved as if nothing happened.[11] This example of levitation demonstrates: (1) levitation that occurs for nearly a minute, (2) within an upside down position, (3) initially planned and then without control of posture or location, and (4) six feet of vertical distance above the ground with fifteen to thirty feet of horizontal distance.

Yet, another classic example of levitation is trance-walking The Tibetans refer to this practice as *lung-gom*.[12] The actual meaning of *lung-gom* is that with meditative practice of uniting the subject-object relationship and then mindful concentration, mind is conjunct with matter. This is a more accurate description than the conventional one of mind over matter or mind conquering materiality.

Trance-walking does not represent either a lofty rising of the physical body from the ground, a physical suspension, or hovering within the air. It is the ability of people to move their organism across distances above the ground or water with only intermittent physical support. The intermittent physical support far exceeds even the Olympic physical ability to run and jump fantastic distances.

Trance-walking demonstrates: (1) levitation that occurs from a few seconds to hours, (2) within a vertical position and forward movement of legs intermittently touching ground or water beyond any ordinary physical possibility (3) controlled and directional movement of posture and location, and (4) vertical distance slightly elevated several inches above the ground and from a few feet to hundreds of miles of horizontal distance.

I prefer to include psychosomatic healing as another subcategory of psychokinesis. The difference, here, is that the occurrence is self-initiated and focused within the physical body. Psychosomatic healing is mental and spiritual healing initiated by self and separate from the effects of diet, herbs, vitamins, or any physical manipulation or intrusion by another person. It includes miraculous healing, spontaneous remission, psychokinetic, and spiritual healing when initiated by self. When initiated by others through prayer or energy transformation, it is external psychokinesis.

The primary difference of general extrasensory perception (GESP) and precognition as opposed to psychokinesis (PK) is that psychokinesis rarely occurs without intention. An exception to this general principle is poltergeist phenomena, those reported incidents in which objects randomly move about without declared intention by any observer. While not always, poltergeist phenomena are associated with young people experiencing psychological stress who "unconsciously dissipate" energy through unintentional psychokinesis. The evidence for this reasoning is that such phenomena cease to occur on physical removal of the focused person of suspected poltergeist activity.

With reference to the stepping stone vignettes earlier, general extrasensory perception (GESP) includes my daughter's telepathic experience and the clairvoyant experiences of locating lost objects and parking spaces. Psychokinesis includes Jim's and my experience of trance-walking[13], influencing the direction of pool balls, Elizabeth's influence of the raffle, creating parking spaces, and Johrei healing. Psychosomatic healing includes the example of my removal of warts. Tilak's performance was a combination of highly skillful hypnosis and psychokinetic abilities.

I did not present any examples of precognition because I find these experiences to be impractical, unreliable, and potentially hazardous to one's well being. First, precognitive experience does not as easily emerge by intention. Second, the information from precognitive experience is usually vague in the form of "hunches." As a result, these experiences are open to considerable interpretation. Third, when information is received about a future event, it is often tragic.

Personally, I don't like to clutter my mind with avoiding tragic events. In attempting to "avoid negatives" people empower the likelihood of their occurrence. Some evidence supporting this arises from parapsychological research. However, there is corroborating evidence within clinical hypnosis and cognitive psychotherapy. People often empower that which they fight against, as in a self-fulfilling or rather self-defeating prophecy. The mind cannot directly remove negatives. It can only successfully neutralize them by a replacement of desirable targets.

Paranormal Skill Begins with Trust

Conventional science begins by doubt. Scientific hypotheses are stated in the negative and are called "null hypotheses." Null hypotheses are assumed to be false until proven otherwise. Thus, desired expectations are false until refuted and positively confirmed at a respectable level of statistical reliability. By this belief, trust requires empirical evidence. I consider this to be an essential process of eventual confirmation of paranormal skill, but not in the initial stages of paranormal empowerment.

Similarly, common sense requires reasonable explanations for occurrences that fall outside ordinary understanding. Here, trust needs to be explained. Common sense demands a rational justification. Even institutional religions presume original sin. Belief in salvation rests with the individual's response to the highest institutional authority and inevitably the grace of God. By this belief, the expected failings of trust require redemption and wishfully, salvation for failure.

Interestingly, the "law of the land," the secularly legal process of most all cultures, presumes innocence. The burden of proving guilt relies on the prosecution. Here, trust is assumed and quite ironically favors the individual's testimony of experience.

Within the paradigm of paranormal and mystical experience, beginning stages require trust in the actuality of experience. That is, it does not matter so much whether the event actually occurred according to conventional experience or conventional science. Initially, it is essential to believe the event of the experience occurred without reservation.

Jim's and my experience of trance-walking serve as excellent examples. Neither of us planned our experiences. Our experiences, however, did occur. Following, there was no way to prove our experiences since no one saw us and could therefore validate our experiences. Also, within our understanding of the "real world," the separate events as we experienced them at the time were not explainable, except as a conventional departure representing hallucinations or delusions. Our awarenesses of this context was evidenced by immediate decisions not to share the information for fear of being considered foolish or crazy.

For myself, there were only two choices after the experience. I could believe everything else I knew that supported conventional reality and disbelieve my experience. Or, I could believe my experience exactly the way I experienced it. Years later I questioned myself about understanding this experience and underwent regressive hypnosis only to confirm the results exactly as I have reported. Even years later I attempted to dismiss the "reality" of this experience within academically sophisticated paradigms of developmental fixations, mythological archetypes and even the narcissistic religious implications of "walking on water." However, while each these conventional explanations made some intellectual sense, they could not explain away the clarity of the experience. Indeed, up until recently, while I have doubted understanding this experience within conventional paradigms, it has never occurred to me to doubt its occurrence in any way. The occurrence and the experience remain as real as everyday life.

The essential point in the beginning of paranormal experience is that it does not matter whether the event occurred by empirical confirmation or not. Trust in the experience as experienced is what matters. This belief serves as an initial important stepping stone, paving the way to expansive experiences not known before. With sequential beliefs expanding the doors of perception, later paranormal experiences can be confirmed or discounted with incremental practice.

Paranormal Skill Increases with Incremental Practice

In the origination of martial arts in the Orient, all students were issued a white belt to hold together their *gi*, the uniform of practice. With years of practice, the cotton belt became worn and difficult to keep clean. Eventually, those with dirtier belts became known as more advanced. Confidence can most easily be built with incremental beliefs in self-mastery.

Paranormal stepping stones are incremental beliefs of empowerment. They result from paranormal experiences that are initially trusted and then practiced. Incremental practice and replication enhances skill. Initial steps are the curious tales and unexpected paranormal experiences of others. Intermediate steps are spontaneous occurrences to self by apparent coincidence. Advanced stepping stones must be initiated, directed, and verified by self.

Unfamiliar territory is more easily approached with incremental steps, even micro-steps. Stepping stones are small increments for getting accustomed to the unfamiliar. Paranormal stepping stones are non-ordinary accumulative experiences that are increasingly self-directed and eventually established as an ordinary function of everyday life.

Mastering Paranormal Skill Requires Confirmation

Similar to scientific investigation, in later stages, paranormal expectations must be confirmed by testing the results. Hypotheses need to be determined before conducting experimentation. Expectations need to be defined before implementation. Results are evaluated by whether the expectations are confirmed or not. Further evaluation is determined by replication and then determining whether the results match the experience of others. This occurs by trial, error, and observation. Practice continues until confirmation of the replicated results become "real." A separate sign that occurs when this happens is that self-importance initially becomes inflated and even narcissistic. Eventually, with continued practice, it fades into the background of experience when paranormal experience is used to confirm mystical realization.

Now, the difficulty with paranormal experimentation, when performed and tested outside a laboratory, is not only the obvious bias of the experimenter, but the lack of consistent regulation of control. According to empirical science, this is a reasonable criticism for doubting the result of one's experience. However, paranormal phenomena have been observed and recorded since recorded history. In this respect, consistent phenomena have been orally transmitted through the ages and in millions of instances recorded. That is, while regulated and confirmed by individual observation, the anecdotal results are remarkably similar in millions of reports.

Within paranormal field investigation, there is corroborative testimony as to both the rules of engagement and the expected results to be obtained. Results are confirmed by other paranormal magicians as well as realized mystics. The process of confirmation in the field can be as rigorous as scientific experimentation in the laboratory. Also, the rigor of investigation may carry greater life-threatening risk than the safety of a laboratory.

Paranormal Experience Is Natural

Within Western conventional experience, there is an arbitrary division between natural and supernatural. Natural is scientifically explainable. Supernatural is not. Supernatural phenomena are events and experiences that cannot be confirmed by either a current empirical or rational explanation. That is, supernatural is a label applied to any phenomena that cannot be adequately explained by conventional science.

In contrast with paranormal phenomena, conventional scientific explanations for supernatural phenomena appear unlikely. Since there is reasonable and emerging scientific evidence attempting to explain paranormal phenomena, supernatural and paranormal are separate phenomena. Within the paradigm of paranormal experience, natural and supernatural are the same. That is, both paranormal and mystical experiences are natural.[14]

Also, there is a difference between paranormal experience and mythological or religious explanation of such experience. There are many learned scholars such as Joseph Campbell and Carl Jung who, while extremely sympathetic to paranormal experience, consistently lean toward explaining away such experiences by reference to spiritual mythology. A classic example of this tendency is Sir James George Frazer's profound work, *The Golden Bough*.[15] Contributions of mythology and spiritual teachings make meaning of the world. Except for these contributions,, these systems of understanding the universe attempt to explain paranormal experience within the context of a resultant mythology and do not confirm the reality of paranormal activity and experience.

Paranormal Power is Neutral

The laws of the universe are neutral. The moralistic assignment of "good" and "evil" is entirely dependent on the way power is used. "Good" is an interpretation determined by inclusive and life-enhancing intentions or results. "Evil" is an interpretation determined by exclusive and life-limiting intentions or results.

From a conventional perspective, "good" and "evil" are interpretations determined by personal beliefs, societal, and cultural relevancy. From a paranormal and mystical perspective, "good" is applied to those evaluations in which the event includes and accommodates[16] discrepant values, and to which it promotes maximum life-enhancement. "Evil" is applied to those evaluations in which the event excludes or merely assimilates[17] discrepant values, and to which it represses or retards life-enhancement or encourages life-limiting options.

Magicians of the soul use their knowledge and powers with natural laws that govern cosmic and psychic forces for the benefit of all beings. Non-spiritually oriented magicians use their knowledge and power for personal and exploitative advantage. This essential characteristic distinguishes "white" from "black" magic. While traditional magic is based on singular principles, the results of its practice determines whether its character is beneficent or malevolent, or in religious terms Divine or diabolical. Simply, paranormal powers are neutral forces of nature. Interpreting such powers as either virtuous or evil is determined by the global life-enhancing or life-limiting results of usage.

CHAPTER THREE
HARVESTING THE TAO

Oasis was a personal development center located in Colorado that advertised a residential workshop entitled "Taoism, Meditation, and Psychotherapy." The workshop was scheduled for a full week in South Haven, Michigan. Participants would be told the specific location of the *Oasis* "farm" following registration.

Gia-fu Feng and his staff were the leaders. Gia-fu was the founder of the Stillpoint Foundation, a Taoist meditation center in Manitou Springs, Colorado. Taoism is a mystical Chinese philosophy with magical roots that extend back to the 6th century B.C.[1] Gia-fu was born in Shanghai in 1919.[2] Educated in China, he came to the United States in 1947 to study comparative religion. He held a bachelor of arts degree from Peking University and earned a master of arts degree from the University of Pennsylvania. Gia-fu wrote *Tai Chi—A Way of Centering & I-Ching*.[3] Also, he translated the *Tao Te Ching*[4] and *Chang Tzu*[5], the classic texts of Taoism.

Gia-fu was an early financial advisor of Esalen, the original mothership of personal growth centers. Located on a bluff overlooking the Pacific ocean in Big Sur, California, Esalen is still the largest personal development center in the world.[6] Gia-fu claimed he left Esalen as a result of a personal conflict with Frederick (Fritz) Perls. Fritz was a German psychiatrist and the founder of Gestalt therapy. Later, it was easy to understand why these two cantankerous titans might well clash.

Arthur Stirling and I registered for the workshop in the late Spring. A few weeks before the workshop, confirmation arrived in the mail with xeroxed instructions. They required we bring only sleeping bags and comfortable clothing. No liquor, tobacco, or food was permitted. There was a drawn map that showed directions and indicated that the "farm" was actually a school house.

Like children adventuring to camp, on the scheduled date we packed sleeping bags, camping gear, and a stash of cheese, crackers, nuts, and candy. North of Chicago, our travel route was to circle around the southern tip of Lake Michigan. Near our destination four hours later, we checked a map that looked like a child had drawn it. Like tracing the branches of a tree from the trunk, we followed increasingly narrow country roads. The experience reminded me of the scavenger hunts I embarked on in grade school with instructions like, "Turn north by the large tree on top of the hill."

Dandelions, wild daises, and tiger lilies flanked the roadside. Behind them were expansive pastures of tall grass yielding the sweet aroma that unfolds summer. Deciduous birch trees spawned new leaves and gently waved in soft currents of wind. On an adventure of soul and spirit somewhere between Tom Sawyer and Lao Tsu, our lack of expectations served to kindle our excitement.

We made our last turn on a dirt road for several thousand feet to an old defunct school house. The weathered white paint and rusty screens on the massive windows were badly in need of repair. The architecture indicated it was built near the turn of the century. No one was present. We were unsure whether we had followed the directions correctly. Believing we were merely early we stopped the car. Arthur turned off *Canon* by Johann Pachelbel and we opened all four doors of the Volvo station wagon. It was astoundingly quiet. Only the rustle of leaves and a few blue jays squawking in the distance broke the silence.

Dust still floated in the air from our arrival. I walked the well worn stairs of this traditional old school house and felt transported to the era of my grandfather. The screen door squeaked open. I knocked on the door. I waited for a while and knocked again. There was no response. Arthur grabbed his *Nikon* from the car and snapped a few pictures of the school and a field of buttercups and black-eyed Susans.

An authoritative oriental voice broke the stillness. "Welcome," he said. "You here for the workshop?"

Startled, Arthur and I turned around. A small person was standing to the left of the porch with a wide grin on his face. He fashioned a long, tapered beard and was almost bald. Nearly five feet tall and muscularly lean, he weighed maybe nine-five pounds. He wore a black loose tee shirt, sweat pants, and white sneakers without laces or socks.

We walked over to shake his hand and introduce ourselves. I hadn't seen any pictures of Gia-fu. However, since I didn't expect many old Chinese men to be wandering alone in the middle of a Michigan prairie, it was safe to assume this was the workshop leader.

He gently shook my hand.

"My name is Gia-fu," he said.

"You say it like *Jaw-foo*."

He quickly instructed us on how to pronounce his name properly to his satisfaction.

He continued, "It is good that you are on time, but no matter. Workshop starts when all the family arrives."

"What family?," I inquired.

Gia-fu curtly answered, "All members of the workshop!"

I ask him how he arrived since I didn't notice any other vehicle. I expected, perhaps, some mystical explanation. Gia-fu explained that the other people with whom, he had arrived earlier, went into town for supplies and would return soon. He told us it had taken three days to drive across country and they were tired from the road travel.

A rickety, foreign sedan pulled up the road. Four people got out of the car. They introduced themselves as Jane, Marla, Robert, and Rick. Jane, Marla, and Robert were on Gia-fu's staff at his Taoist retreat in Colorado.

Jane was thirty-one years old, twenty-three years younger than Gia-fu. She was also his wife. She was petite and sensuous with long sandy hair. Jane was a professional photographer. She received her doctorate from the University of Wisconsin for work in high-energy, particle physics. Recently, she had taught a course in Oriental thought and modern physics at Colorado College.

Marla was softly overweight. Comfortably, she wore a bulky saffron blouse outside a baggy pair of jeans. Later, we were to learn she was the dietician and chef.

Robert was tall and lanky with a receding black head of hair. He held graduate degrees in physics and had studied astrology for the past five years. Robert was the serious intellectual of the staff clan.

Rick, as we were to discover later, was a senior member of the sponsoring organization, *Oasis*. He was either sent to evaluate this new workshop or came as a result of his own curiosity and interest. I was never sure which motivation was accurate.

Arthur and I removed our gear from the car and moved into the school house. The inside was empty with worn oak floors. We threw our bags in a corner and walked outside into the afternoon sun. Slowly, other workshop members began to arrive. Curiously, and for better or worse, we would all now be compelled to be a family for an entire week.

I don't remember any of the other workshop members. It is not that they were so unnoticeable. Rather, I had many other considerations on my mind to which I was paying attention. Anyway, I was not here to learn from other workshop participants. I was here to learn from a maverick Chinese sage who, just maybe had an edge on the mystery of life.

The last of the registered participants arrived. I noticed there were only seven others besides myself and Arthur. Based on previous workshop experience, I expected nearly triple the number of participants. Of the fourteen of us, five represented the workshop staff. These were intense odds. After all, this wasn't an evening presentation. It was committing to living together with strangers for an entire week, a thought that kindled a fresh hesitancy.

Everybody scurried around the central room in the school house trying to find a private place for luggage and bags. No one was particularly territorial and the atmosphere was cordial. Gia-fu entered the room and clapped his hands loudly. Only half of us paid any attention. Again, he clapped his hands.

He yelled out, "Pay attention! Put your articles where you like for now, but keep them out of the center of the room. We will meet here at two o'clock for an introduction and have dinner at five." Abruptly, he walked out of the room, not waiting for acknowledgement.

As is usual in these circumstances, there are always a couple of people who turn around and say, "What did he say?" We whispered Gia-fu's message among us until everyone felt confident about following directions. We then became aware that our intimidated foolishness was like passing notes on torn pieces of paper in elementary grades. Indeed, we were all back in school.

Everyone promptly showed at two o'clock in the main room. Appropriately demonstrating our previous group training, we sat in a circle on the seasoned oak floor with huge stuffed pillows.

Gia-fu broke the conversational noise hanging in the air, "I am glad you are all here. I want you to know that from this point forward, we are all a family. All families need a father, or at least some authority figure. This is my workshop and I am going to provide that function. From this moment on, I am going to say what we do and when we do it." He then continued in a more casual manner and introduced each of his staff. The staff was adept in meditation, Taoism, oracle casting, nutrition, massage, physics, and astrology.

After brief introductions, he continued, "I have some rules that will help all of us work better as a family. First, you will eat what my staff and I eat and when we eat it. No one is allowed in the kitchen without Marla's permission. Marla will be in charge of what we take into our bodies at all times."

Gia-fu proudly extended his sinewy arm with his palm face up toward her and added, "At meal times, stand at the kitchen door and wait for Marla to serve your meal. Next, we will rise at five every morning and do whatever I decide. We will do all activities together as a family. I will schedule time for you to be alone. This is not extra time for self-indulgence or entertainment. It is time that I am scheduling for meditative integration. Right now, because I don't know how all will happen, I am unable to tell you when that will be."

"You see, this workshop is a living process that unfolds by the combined and unique elements of all its members. Since I don't know you and how you will evolve within yourselves and in relationship to each other, I cannot predict how this process will unfold. The interactions of our particular family will shape and influence the emergent patterns of our activities as they quite naturally appear."

"Marla will serve dinner at five this evening. After we finish our dinner, I want each of you to carefully select and introduce yourself more seriously to one other person that you do not know. I want you to find a private space. I want you to tell the person you select a secret about yourself. It should be something embarrassing or shameful you would not ordinarily share. However, you are to respect secrets. For, whatever someone tells you in confidence is never to be repeated. You are not to repeat it here at this workshop or ever again in your life. Are there any questions?"

No one spoke.

After a brief silence, he exclaimed, "Good! Then, after dinner and your secret sharing, we will meet again at seven. We will then talk so we can start to focus on the secrets of nature."

Gracefully, Gia-fu rose in posture and exited the room.

At precisely five o'clock people gathered in a line at the kitchen door. Those nearest the entry peaked in and tried to detect the dictated food for our palates. I harbored fears of tofu, soy beans, wheat germ, and beets, covered with a delicate topping of alfalfa and bean sprouts with a dollop of yogurt.

Conscientiously, Marla served the plates. I was pleasantly surprised. There was an appetizing mound of yellow squash, green peppers, leeks, celery, and ripe tomatoes served with wooden chop sticks. The vegetables were lightly simmered in olive oil, lemon, and dill. To the side was a filet of broiled chicken breast bathed in marinated chunks of garlic. Delightfully, there was also a ripped chunk of steamed wheat grain bread with real unsalted butter.

The people first in line to receive their plates immediately grabbed a spot on the floor and began to inhale their food. Gia-fu, recognizing this savagery and lack of consideration to family members, screamed for everyone to wait. As the last person received his food, Robert brought a large kettle of oolong tea and a variety of clay mugs.

Gia-fu then softly spoke, "You may now eat and preferably taste the food that nature has relinquished to serve you. The squash does not grow in the fields for you to butcher and ravage. We take it because we need it to nourish our bodies. The least you can do is appreciate it. Marla took care and time in preparing this food for us with the mindfulness that what we are about to eat also will eat us. Food influences our organism as well as our emotional well being."

His voice became sharply louder, "Also, and this is the last time I will tell you. We will begin eating together and we will finish eating together. Whether we starve or feast, we do everything together as a family!"

He stopped talking. Every one remained still until Gia-fu picked up his chop sticks.

After dinner, Marla gave us a brief lecture on her views about nutrition and diet. She handed out copies of a paper entitled "My Stomach and Me" and invited us to read it in our spare time. Marla asked for help in cleaning the kitchen. There were ample volunteers. By this time, everyone was elevating a social conscience.

At seven in the evening, the family met in the main room. Although Gia-fu's opening remarks said otherwise, I now felt the workshop was beginning.

He began, "I want you to know that our workshop began the moment each of you arrived. Since your arrival, I have been paying attention to each of you, what you do with your time and what you don't. I have been watching how you interact with one another and how you don't. I have been watching how you live in the moment and how at other times you either try to force events to happen or allow them to force you. This is what living Taoism is all about."

Gia-fu then introduced himself with a vocalized resume embellished with tones of pride and satisfaction. He told us of his childhood in China and rendered his version of relationships with the wise teachers and healers of Esalen. He spoke of his world travels and his contemplative life in Colorado.

He continued with a synopsis of what he would include in the workshop. "This workshop will be a blend of ancient Chinese ways and modern Western psychotherapy. Everything we do will be part of this workshop. Our relationships with nature and one another will show us ways for moving beyond ourselves."

After an hour of introduction, Gia-fu continued, "I want everybody to introduce themselves. I want you to share with our family why you came to this workshop and what you want from this experience. You will have plenty of time to tell us since this is all we have to do this evening. We will continue until midnight or early into the morning if introductions take that long."

One by one, the participants told their stories. As I took my turn, I started with my past education and recent achievements. That part of a personal tale is always easy and yet boring for me. It's usually like telling people what I want them to think of me. It also gives them categorical boxes and expectations within which to place me that I often regret later. Telling too much information is restrictive when people expect certain behaviors.

When it was time to explain my motivation for attending the workshop and what I wanted from the experience, I wasn't sure what to say. I'm not sure I knew. I remember saying something that was superficial, undoubtedly something I wouldn't accept from anyone else. Almost asleep, I offered an ambiguous statement about wanting to learn more about Taoism and meditation.

During these introductions, Gia-fu, his staff, and everyone else remained silent. The telling of tales was a monologue activity. No one had an opportunity to know how others were perceiving them. As people volunteered, their motivational statements sounded as superficial as mine. While this made me feel better, I noticed how all of us were treading softly on the rice paper.

We took several hours to finish our individual stories. Gia-fu was alert to the air of caution and asked everyone to express any current conflicts about themselves. One chic person in her mid-thirties shared the difficulties she was having in her marriage. A couple of people told how they were having difficulty feeling like failures in their careers. One or two people mentioned health problems.

At the risk of sounding like we were in denial, Arthur and I shared that our lives were going well. Indeed, they were.

Gia-fu assured everyone their difficulties were important and that we would work on each of them later. It was after eleven o'clock. Finally, he asked the group to share any concerns about what he had outlined earlier that evening. He was referring to the contents of the workshop or the process by which he would conduct it. A few members asked practical questions about sleeping arrangements and alarm clocks.

Gia-fu smiled and answered, "Jane and I will sleep in one of the other two rooms. Everyone else may sleep where ever you wish. As for alarm clocks, I'm it for now. I will wake you up in the morning, but I want you to start waking yourself up on time with your internal clock. It's very easy, you know. You already have exquisitely programmed your internal clock. It's time that you take advantage of all that work. Just tell yourself to wake up whenever you want before you go to sleep. You will be amazed by how well you do all by yourself."

The evening was winding down. Rick, the staff member representing the sponsoring center of *Oasis*, interrupted and directly addressed Gia-fu. "I have some concerns about the way you are running this workshop. I've been silent until now because I didn't want to interfere and make a judgement until I had more time to observe you in action. You know, I've been in the human potential movement for the last ten years and on the staff of *Oasis* for the last five. My experience with personal growth groups is that control is a collectively shared experience. Everyone equally participates in the decision making. All I've heard since I arrived here is that you are the authority. All I've heard is that this is your workshop and that you are going to run it anyway you want!"

Rick continued in a voice that became shaken, "The rest of us don't have any say in what you are calling a family. This is against all the principles of personal responsibility and interpersonal communication that I've struggled so hard to include into my life for the last ten years."

Gia-fu remained silent and still, softly gazing at Rick. Casually, but firmly he responded, "I am sorry that you are so upset. Did your father always tell you what to do, when to shit and when to shut up?"

Rick became aggravated. "This isn't about my past relationship with my father. I've worked that through. In fact, I think it's a cheap shot and an obvious therapeutic manipulation on your part to divert my feelings right now. I resent you for taking what I'm directly sharing with you and cleverly turning it into a one-upmanship game so you're still the authority. This is exactly what you've been doing since I got here. And it's not just with me, but with everyone."

The entire group remained silent.

Gia-fu remained firm and on his original track, "Your anger is not at me. Your anger is about your difficulty with authority and I represent that. In fact, in this workshop, I AM that. What is it that you want from your father that you never got?"

Ignoring his direct question, Rick angrily replied, "I want all of us to have an equal say in how this workshop is going to be conducted, in what we want and when we want it. And, I want you to stop playing therapeutic games with me right now. If I wanted psychotherapy, I would have gone to a psychotherapist. I came here to learn about Taoism and meditation."

Gia-fu responded, "You are so angry. I want to help you. I want for you to discharge all this anger that is eating you up in small pieces, a bit at a time. You are not letting me in. All you are doing is defending yourself, being righteous and trying to get the support of the group. I want to know what went on that was so bad between you and your father. Talk to me."

Their confrontation went back and forth for nearly an hour. Impulsively, Rick stood up. He started shouting in rage and pointed at Gia-fu.

Threatening him, he said, "You are still not listening to me. You continue to play your mind-tripping games. You intellectualize and play authority with me so you don't loose face in front of the group. If you continue, I am leaving the workshop and will report this entire affair to the director at *Oasis*. You will never be contracted to work with us again, or for that matter, with any of the other major growth centers."

I don't know how he did it, but remaining in a cross-legged position, Gia-fu rose all of his ninety-five pounds nearly off the ground. Only his feet appeared to remain on the floor for a few seconds.

His voice resonated like thunder from the depth of the earth. "How dare you challenge me! I have been all over China and studied with Taoist masters. I have devoted my life to transcribing ancient texts thousands of years old. I helped found Esalen, the mother of all the growth centers in this country. I have been in every single type of encounter, communication, and psychotherapy group you could possibly imagine and either before you were born or when you couldn't even wipe your ass. You are a very angry man. You have a rage inside of you that frightens me. I have tried to reach out to you and I am tired of your insults and threats. This is my workshop and I will run it the way I see fit. If you want to leave, go ahead and leave. Go ahead and burn buildings and murder people, but get out of my workshop if all you want to do is this competitive bullshit."

It was well past midnight. The room was still, except for the reverberation of emotion. Rick looked at Gia-fu. He quietly told him that he would let him know whether he would leave in the morning and walked out the door. Gia-fu calmly asked everyone to remain seated for a few minutes in silence.

After several minutes, Gia-fu broke the silence.

"I am sorry this had to happen. It upsets me very much. This is not a good way to start a workshop. However, issues must be addressed when they happen, to make room for new opportunities. As snow melts, allowing the earth to breathe, flowers can grow. We will go to sleep now, and I will see you at five in the morning."

Arthur and I unrolled our sleeping bags near each another and crawled in. Someone turned out the lights. For a few minutes before dozing to sleep, we wondered whether we had made a wise decision to attend this workshop. Quietly, we discussed Gia-fu's autocratic leadership. Independently, we dismissed considerations of narcissism in favor of traditional mystical protocol.[7] Also, for a change, we welcomed someone else taking full responsibility for directing personal development and the expansion of consciousness. While we disagreed with Rick, nonetheless, we wanted him to stay. After all, if he left, now it would be like loosing a family member.

My next awareness was hearing the sound of hands clapping together loudly. Gia-fu's voice yelled in the dark.

"Wake up! Wake up now! It's five and we have work to do. Hurry up! Hurry up! Get dressed and meet me outside in five minutes!"

The tone of his voice sounded urgent. I crept out of my sleeping bag and scrambled for a flash light. Two other beams of light flashed through the darkness by the time I found mine. I pulled on a pair of levis and a tee shirt, threw on a jacket and moccasins, and stumbled outside. One by one, people thumped down the rickety stairs in the dawn. A hazy yellow mist hovered the horizon.

Loudly, Gia-fu whispered, "Hurry! Hurry! Follow me!"

We walked for about twenty minutes on a dirt road. Gia-fu ordered us to stop, stand in single file, and not to talk.

He stood at the side of the single line of troops and said, "Watch what I do and follow in form."

He started a slow dance. Picking up one foot, he gracefully moved his arm, then the other foot, and then the other arm. Slowly, foot by foot, he moved forward. In a parade we imitated his directions. For the next hour, the promenade of people quietly crept like a snake through the early morning stillness.

From time to time, Gia-fu would approach people and correct their posture of movement in silence. He gave no explanation about our curious endeavor. The sun now fully above the horizon, he told us that it was time to return to the school house.

A couple of hours later we settled inside the school. Marla served a pot of spicy cinnamon tea.

Gia-fu explained, "You have just had your first lesson in meditation, through *t'ai chi*. *T'ai chi* is the Queen of Chinese martial arts. There is a difference between doing it right and doing it well. Doing it right means that you imitate the posture correctly. When one does it well, one's mind is with the Tao, the rhythm of the universe. This occurs through correct breathing and a clear mind."

He continued, "You all need to pay much more attention to timeliness and urgency itself. Urgency is living life fully. Next, it is vital to your life force to greet the sun, to participate in the celebration of dawn. Dawn has special mystical power. Twilight is the organ of this world inhaling with the movement of the universe. Like you this morning, the universe inhaled to greet the sun. Dawn and dusk are the times the universe shifts energies. And like your breath, sunrise and sunset are the earth's time of inhaling and exhaling. This is why it is important for you to pay attention to your breathing.

As most of us, I had been preoccupied waking up, following directions, and being captured by the mystery of the activity. I didn't notice that Rick was not among us.

Gia-fu spoke, "I heard Rick leave in the night. I am very sad. I feel bad. I am ashamed. I feel that I failed with this young man who is so angry. This morning, when we were out there on the dirt road, I meditated on this. I don't know what else I could have done. Rick would prefer to be right rather than well. I did not know this would happen though I should have suspected as much. Rick is a very sick man and I failed him. I am sorry we had to start our workshop like this. However, it happened. I shall speak no more of it."

We spent most of the day in group psychotherapy with those members who wanted to work on issues they mentioned the night before. All during the day, Gia-fu appeared sad. Around four in the afternoon, his mood shifted. He announced that since we were in school and had been here a full day, it was time to go on a field trip. Without further explanation, he laughed for the first time during the day. He told us to meet him in front of the school house in ten minutes. We clustered in three cars. Gia-fu, of course, occupied the flag ship and directed us to follow.

We drove north toward Saugatuck for nearly an hour. We stopped in a dense grove of birch. It was chilly. Robert told everyone to take a log from the trunk of his car. A couple of people grabbed blankets. Marla brought a kettle for tea. We walked through the towering birch shuffling on a carpet of dry leaves. We emerged from the forest onto an uninhabited sandy shore on the east side of Lake Michigan. A cool wind stirred white caps on the lake and scattered the reflection of the sun from the west.

Robert arranged the logs compulsively in a tripod and fanned the fire with a paper plate. Gia-fu walked toward the beach. He yelled for the rest of us to take off our shoes and follow him to a distant edge of the lake. We reached a cove in the sand where the waves had smoothly sculpted the shore. Gia-fu asked for silence.

He waved his arm in an expansive gesture across the horizon and said, "Dusk is when the universe exhales. It's when the organ of the earth surrenders to the dark forces. This is the spirit of rejuvenation. We have had a lot of talking today. Now, it is time for silence. It is time to let the water wash your thoughts away. Most of you have learned to crawl and be lazy in your thoughts and actions. Many of you have learned to run very fast with your body and especially in your mind. Few of you have learned to be quiet inside your head. It is time that you learned to walk."

"You all think you already know how to walk, but I have listened to you. I have watched your bodies reflect your minds. And, I am telling you, you don't know how to walk any more than you knew how to breathe this morning. I am going to teach you an ancient Taoist meditation technique, the way the old masters learned to walk. This walking will silence your mind. Spread out. Get far away from one another. Stay quiet and watch me."

Gia-fu stood still with his feet together and gazed south along the shore. Slowly, yet with conviction, he picked up one foot and then the other. He placed them directly ahead of him, gently planting them in the sand. At first, his demonstration appeared no different from normal walking, except slower. With further attention, I noticed that the ball of each foot touched the ground before his heel. I also noticed that his entire body was in perfect balance. He was gazing straight ahead.

After a few minutes, he stopped, turned around and said, "Now you practice."

For more than an hour we walked silently in the sand. Occasionally, Gia-fu approached each person and gave specific comments and directions. Initially, I found this exercise extremely awkward, reversing all logic of early imprints. After half an hour, just when I thought I was learning the basics, Gia-fu approached me. Without a word, he gently pushed my shoulder. I stumbled in the sand and he laughed.

"You're working too hard," he said.

"Your mind is too filled with doing something and with doing it perfectly. Remember this morning. I don't want you to do it right. I want you to do it well. Let your feet take you and stop giving them so much attention. You're missing the sunset."

He walked away. He was right. I was trying so hard to walk correctly that I had been unaware that the sun was nearing the horizon. I now noticed our silhouetted shadows reflecting on the upper bank. As hues of sapphire and crimson gold floated on the horizon, Gia-fu called for us to gather at the fire. Marla served German potato salad with cooked cabbage and grilled sausage flavored in the smoke of the fire. This time, at the expense of the meal getting cold, we waited until Marla served everyone before we began to eat. I looked at Gia-fu. He looked pleased.

After eating, he asked us to share what we had learned about walking. For the first time since we arrived, our family was expressive, open, and alive. Some people shared their difficulties with the mechanics of the exercise. Others talked about how focusing on a simple task cleared their minds of the gibberish inside their heads.

Gia-fu spoke, "This exercise was originally practiced on rice paper, the task being to walk a length without wrinkling or imprinting it or making any sound. However, your physical aptitude is merely a reflection of paying attention to your surroundings. Learning to walk is not about the relationship between your feet and the earth, or between your mind and what you ordinarily perceive as the external environment. Learning to walk is merging the two so they become one. With practice we become one with our environment."

It was immediately clear that Gia-fu's timely selection of this field trip and exercise had brought the family closer together and cleansed its crisis.

The following afternoon Gia-fu told us to gather outside. Robert and Jane raked an area in the field next to the school house and erected a volleyball net. All of us met outside. Gia-fu told us to separate into two teams. On reviewing all the activities until now, it was peculiar to me that we were going to play volleyball. After negotiating back and forth, we arrived at what we considered fair teams.

Gia-fu was holding the ball in his hands. He looked over the net at me and inquired, "Where is Arthur?"

I responded, "Oh, he's not coming. He said he's got a headache."

Gia-fu snapped back in a voice loud enough for everyone to hear, "Arthur is constipated. He needs to take a shit."

Everyone laughed.

Without warning, Gia-fu served the ball. He abruptly stopped us after several games and directed us back into the main room. I learned to expect that everything in this workshop had a purpose. Every moment and event, whether we were forewarned, paying attention or not, had a meaning. My curiosity was alert.

Inside the main room, Gia-fu began the group, "You have just played volleyball. We are now going to engage in volleyball therapy. Until now, we have been learning how to be in a state of presence with our environment, from the food we eat to experiencing the earth, wind, fire, and sunsets. Also, we have been building a functional family. We have been learning how to support one another for who they are and not who we want them to be. I wanted to see how you relate to one another when I put you in a competitive situation. You were playing volleyball. I was watching your decisive actions. Without you knowing, I watched how each of you related to your allies and your foes. I watched how you related to your teammates and your enemies. I watched how each of you helped and manipulated."

"Now, I want to discuss my observations with you. I want to see if you agree. I want you to be aware of your social nature. I want you to see how you include others in your life space and how you push them away from you."

One by one, Gia-fu addressed the group, including the staff. With sensitivity and humor he gave us his lucid observations that he compiled from earlier on the court. He had catalogued these individual observations in his mind. He had sorted them and then arranged them for presentation in a manner that was plain and easy for each of us to hear. His sensitivity softened our receiving the lack of praise.

He told me that I needed to increase my competitive nature and stop being so kind and caring to my foes.

"Stop being such a nice guy," he dictated.

When he came to Arthur, he told him that he was over-intellectualized and needed to learn how to share his feelings. He advised that he learn how to yield control and be spontaneous and then maybe he would not get headaches.

The next day, Gia-fu informed us that he was going to teach us to use the *I Ching*.[8] The *I Ching* is the ancient Chinese *Book of Changes*.[9] Reflecting Taoist and Confucian wisdom, it is used as a magical text of oracles for divination.

Gia-fu austerely spoke, "I will teach you with the use of the traditional yarrow stalks and not with the easier, faster, and modern version that uses Chinese coins with the square holes in the middle. I am sorry. We do not live in yarrow stalk country. However, anticipating our plight, I planned. I stopped at an oriental market along the way and bought bamboo skewers as a substitute. No matter! *I-Ching* not particular regarding instrument of casting. Most important, however, is the attitude of the person casting."

Querentes formed a *yes* or *no* question in their minds. From a bundle of fifty skewers, they removed one skewer and set it aside for precisely maneuvering the others after casting. Gia-fu directed querentes to write their question on a piece of paper and share it with the group. Prior to each of the eighteen castings for each question, the querente and group meditated on divergent aspects of the question.

For example, one question was, "Should I leave my lover of one year and move to Cincinnati for a career advantage?" Depending on our individual perceptions of the querente, with this question, each of the group members focused on individually projected opinions of career advantages, financial stability, emotional turmoil, fear of intimacy, or career success. Most importantly with each casting, the querente would focus on different ambivalent facets of the stated conflict. With each cast, the querente tossed the skewers in the air in an intuitive fashion that represented a specific facet of the conflict focused upon. The skewers always landed in a geometric pattern on the carpet.

Using the skewer previously set aside, Gia-fu then taught us how to divide the geometric design into two separate bundles. Complex instructions followed regarding the determination of numbers and placement of skewers in between the fingers of the left hand for the calculation of specific parts of each hexagram.[10] This entire procedure was then repeated seventeen more times such that the specific oracle was calculated with its answer to the question.

The entire process for each question took about an hour. Most of the time was spent by us in concentrated meditation on various aspects of each querente's question. After instructions, the remainder of the time was given to Gia-fu's interpretation of the oracle. After the workshop, I purchased my own bamboo skewers for a grand total of ninety-nine cents. I still use this same set today. The following morning Gia-fu made an announcement.

"So far in our journey, we have given a lot of attention to nature and the personal conflicts of many of you. Also, we have attended to the relational dynamics of our family. It is time that we draw on universal themes of celebration, wonder, conflict, and mystery."

He paused and continued, "We are now embarking on a new journey. For the remainder of our time together, we will orient our work around Tao therapy. Of course, Gia-fu thought that eating breakfast and even bowel movements were therapeutic.

He said we would base our work on the *Tao Te Ching*, the Taoist text that supports the underlying philosophy of the *I-Ching*. We would use these readings as a format within our family for the remainder of the workshop.

The *Tao Te Ching* was written by Lao Tsu, an older contemporary of Confucius in the sixth century B.C. The essence of Taoism is contained in the eighty-one poetic chapters of this text. This text provides one of the major underlying influences in Chinese thought, culture, proverbs, and folklore. While Confucius was concerned with ethics and everyday rules of conduct, Lao Tsu focused on mystical realization.

The following lessons over the next few days had a profound influence on my life. In every group session, we cast the *I-Ching* and allowed the oracle to select different chapters for us. Each chapter represented a different theme for our group work. Interestingly, while we allowed the *I-Ching* to *select* our themes for several days, no chapter or theme was ever repeated. Each time we cast the *I-Ching*, it clearly gave advice by a different chapter and theme. Various themes included issues such as: guilt, material acquisition, productivity, possessiveness, aggression, patience, satisfaction, and inner conflict.

During each group session, we worked with one to three of these themes. Each of us would share the good, the bad, and the ugly about our experience of the selected theme in our life. Now, everyone was enthusiastic to participate without emotional reservation or protective and embarrassing concerns.

The afternoon before the end of the workshop, Robert gave a presentation on astrology. This lesson was to compliment our training in oracle casting and experience of the *Tao Te Ching*. He had collected our places and dates of birth on the first day of the workshop. He said that later he would spend time with each of us and review our horoscopes. However, the focus of his presentation was something I had never heard before. Robert, you will remember, had a background in physics. Robert's theory on astrology was that it was misrepresented by astrologers and foolishly dismissed by scientists.

"Astrologers," he said, "persuade people into believing that the merit of astrology is a result of a cause and effect chain with the movement patterns of planets and the solar system. The notion that planets and their evolutionary movements determine either human personality or events is ridiculous, silly, and absurd. There is no evidence in physics or astronomy to even suggest the possibility of such causal relationship or interference. The difficulty with professional astrologers is they don't know how it works and try to legitimize it by using the principle of science that assumes causal relationships."

"On the other hand," he said, "just because there is no direct causal relationship between the planets and human personality or events, does not mean that astrology is not scientific. Science prides itself on replication. Whatever experiment is conducted in one laboratory, with prescriptive notes, can be replicated in another laboratory with the same results. In this sense, astrology is a superstar of scientific success. It is the most replicated and sophisticated science of human personality ever devised. It makes psychoanalysis, the most comprehensive personality theory, look like it belongs in kindergarten."

Robert concluded with a seductively clever rationale, "In science or the *I-Ching*, when you base billions of natural observations on a constant fixed event, then that system becomes both diagnostic and predictive according to the volume of observations given over time. It is not that the stars are causal influences. It is that they are a reliable point of reference on which to base human observations."

"After a few thousand years of applying observations to a reliable reference, the system itself becomes an accurate indicator of events. The system itself becomes a functional reality. The planets and stars don't make anything happen. They are a reliable grid or map on which we have superimposed our interpretations of how and why events occur. Since several billion people have done this for several thousand years in several thousand cultures, astrology, as a diagnostic and predictive system is mysteriously awesome."

Robert looked at Gia-fu, smiled for the first time, and quickly added, "And so, is the *I-Ching*."

The group dismantled. Gia-fu called for a "school recess" and laughed. He dictated we reconvene in fifteen minutes for massage training. One at a time, those of us who wanted, could meet with Robert individually outside to schedule our personal horoscope.

People met back in the main room. Gia-fu said he was too tired to talk about the details of Chinese acupressure or Swedish massage. He laughed and said he would prefer to get one right now. He told us to break into pairs, with one person lying on the floor. We would focus on the upper torso. I was in a daze when everyone chose partners and ended up without one. Only Gia-fu, Jane, and I remained.

Gia-fu crawled over to me and said, "Looks like you're without a partner. You can share Jane with me," and started laughing again. Jane had remained fairly reserved the entire workshop. Petite, natural, and sensual, she simultaneously embodied earth mother and an erotic, spiritual power. In the entire week, I don't remember ever talking to her with more than cordial remarks. The three of us were sitting on a thrashed carpet. Suddenly, Jane removed her sweater showing her bare breasts.

She leaned over, kissed me on the cheek, and said, "I want you to massage me."

Surprisingly to myself, I was embarrassed. I didn't know what to say. Gia-fu was chuckling and in retrospect, probably enjoyed my embarrassment. Jane turned around and lay face down on the floor. Gia-fu told me to straddle her lower back and instructed me on message. He attended to my breathing and at times would instruct, "Now in, now out." The sexual over and under tones of the remark did not escape my attention.

Half an hour went by quickly. I removed my carcass from the straddle and Jane turned over. Boldly, she pulled me near her supple breasts and softly embraced me. After politely thanking me, she gently pushed me away and pulled her sweater back on.

"It's your turn," she said.

I started to roll over on the ground.

Gia-fu observed and instructed, "Take your shirt off."

After another half an hour, Gia-fu stopped Jane and said, "Okay, now it's my turn. I get double the amount of time from both of you because you have forced me into the despicable position of observing mutual sexual seduction. All I instructed was a physical reverence in the spirit of Tao. You have both taken carnal advantage."

His abrupt comment froze my posture and silenced my mind. I looked at Jane. As she was beginning to smile, Gia-fu laughed loudly and pounded his palms on the rug. Indeed, he was enjoying himself.

At five on the following morning we awoke by a mysterious whistle. I didn't know where it came from, but by now I assumed Gia-fu was having fun again. Anyway, the family was now accustomed to this wake-up routine and formed in obedient fashion at the kitchen door.

Marla served a modest and expedient breakfast, even by continental standards. I suspected the pantry was running out of food. No complaints surfaced.

Anticipating leaving, everyone was in a frenzy of readiness for breaking down camp. As no one was from Michigan, all of us had long distances to travel.

At seven in the morning, in the middle of apparent disarray, Gia-fu clapped his resounding hands. He appointed a clean-up crew to insure that we left the premises as found. Since we bid our farewells the night before, little was left to be said. By nine o'clock in the morning, everyone had left except Gia-fu, his staff, Arthur and I. In no particular rush, we waited to reap the last of the harvest. Arthur and I packed the remainder of our gear in the Volvo. Gia-fu emerged from the creaking stairs of the school house and walked toward the car.

"Nice car," he said, looking at Arthur, and added after a pause, "What is it?"

Arthur was reaching for his camera already carefully stowed in his suitcase.

"Volvo," he answered over his shoulder.

Gia-fu responded with further approval, "Nice car!"

Finally, Arthur found his camera and asked Gia-fu if he minded a few pictures. Gia-fu was delighted. Arthur snapped a few frames by the school house steps and walked back to the car. Gia-fu approached, put a hand on each of our shoulders and spoke one last message.

"You know my friends, Taoism isn't about having to make decisions all the time; it's just about having a good time."

The Tao is a Unity of Polarized Energy

Harvesting the Tao is simply yielding to the universe by arranging our beliefs and actions so they are in harmony with nature. Human beings, as an integral part of the universe, are subject to the natural functions of the universe that collectively are the Tao. Therefore, the Tao is translated as the way of the universe. Acknowledging this awareness with a sincere revelation, people can study the natural functions of nature and work in harmony rather than in opposition. The advantage of attending to this process is that fear and suffering simply disappear. After all, nature provides everything without requiring payment, gratitude, or even suffering.

Gia-fu was fascinated with the experiential dynamics of *yin* and *yang*, the representational polarities of manifested change.

He used these concepts as a way to mystically understand the universe. This included sunrises and sunsets, inhaling and exhaling, and walking in balance. Also, he employed the divining and paradoxical wisdom of the *I-Ching* as a way of making decisions in everyday life and determining future results.[11]

Nature represents itself through the polarized energies of day and night, summer and winter, water and rocks, willows and oaks. These interdependent manifestations of energy are in constant interplay and reflect the changes of life. The expression of these polar energies are inseparable from human life. The function of this explicit duality expresses the implicit unity of all materiality and processes. Rejecting this awareness, people further separate themselves from the universe. They then struggle against the inherent problems implicit in conventional experience, trying to control and conquer them as something external they must resolve.

The Tao Invites Effortless Action

Wu-wei is the principle of non-doing. It is impersonally initiated action. Action without striving is a state in which one merges with the *Tao*. It is effortless action that represents the element of water, which without resistance accepts lower levels, yet wears away the hardest substance.

Effortless action is swimming with the current or going with the grain. *Wu-wei* reflects a lifestyle of acceptance that enlists the least amount of expended energy. Trying to change *what is* only creates resistance. By taking the path of least resistance, people gain a sense of peaceful acceptance and a synchronized harmony with the universe.

In not following this principle, people aggravate their illusions of external control and are unable to trust themselves and others. While people may temporarily solve their problems, they do not resolve their limiting beliefs that make an experience a problem. That is, in focusing on a problem that we make by interpreting it as a problem, we do not resolve the beliefs that make it a problem in the first place.

Gia-fu instructed with concrete experiences such as awakening, eating, walking, talking, massaging, and playing volleyball. He used practical and obvious metaphors like the difference between doing things right and doing them well.

Gia-fu's requirement for total control of the workshop was a simple act of practicality, managing a school full of mystical children. This authoritative leadership characterized the respectfully traditional custom between mentor and apprentice. It is entirely consistent within Oriental and Occidental traditions of studying with masters of the martial, meditative, and healing arts. Indeed, his requirements were remarkably mild compared to the traditional expectations of many mystically oriented mentors. Simply, he led but did not dominate.

Gia-fu reminded us to accept immediate situations without wanting them to be different. Even with his comment as we left the workshop, he encouraged us to act from our intuitive mind in the moment. This method of effortless action demands that we know our direction and not always our method.

The Tao Expresses Unique Virtues

All people and creatures have their own special gifts. Lao Tzu, the acclaimed author of the *Tao Te Ching*, reminds us that fine horses can travel a hundred miles a day, but they cannot catch mice. The Chinese character *Te* represents unique reflections of the universe. While *Te* translates most easily to virtue, our virtue is also our curse. Each of us arrives in this world with our own advantages and disadvantages. We have unique lessons to learn and as a result, special contributions to make. *Te* represents the physical manifestation of our spiritual blueprint. It is the unique expression of our quest of soul.

One of Gia-fu's unique gifts was his ability to monitor the interactions of our entire family and each of our moment-to-moment experiences. Also, he expressed his awareness with an inviting urgency that demanded immediate attention. Everything we did was embraced with meaning within larger and larger contexts. No person or experience was ever out of place to him. Meditation and psychotherapy were not isolated events that we did at certain times and not others. Meditation and psychotherapy were an integral part of everyday experience.[12]

The Tao Embraces Non-Attachment

Gia-fu lived a rhythmic flow of physical, emotional, and mental movement relatively free from attached desire. He knew that change is the only permanence. The typical belief of permanence is an illusion. While he followed an agenda, he allowed the continuing changes of the workshop to influence the menu. This was shown from the first meal where he called our attention to not ravaging the food and being more considerate of others. In the negative, non-attachment is a lack of coveting. In the positive, people display it by appreciation of each present moment.

Gia-fu harvested the magic of Tao from the simple ordinary experiences of everyday life. He made the ordinary extraordinary for purpose and meaning. He experienced the universe as magical and chose to interpret it as complicated for fun. Regardless of his imposed rules for apprenticeship, Gia-fu was the most unassuming, non-judgmental, and gentle teacher I have known. His opinions were intentionally focused observations for either provocative effect or for fun. They held no after-weight, no intentional negativity with which he approached people at the next opportunity. Expressing a complete range of emotions from anger and sadness to joy and laughter, he was compassionate and shared of himself in every way that he demanded of his students.

CHAPTER FOUR
MASTERS JUST PRACTICE

A year after my experience with Gia-fu, I moved back to San Diego with my own family. I was unemployed. Thumbing through the local newspaper in an attempt to find the classified section, I noticed several large pictures of an old Chinese man wielding a cane. With interest I read the accompanying article.

His name was Liang Ting-Shuk. Sixty-two years old, he had studied martial arts in Peking since the age of twelve. He also held a bachelors degree in agricultural economics from Oxford University. Liang had just arrived from China and was teaching t'ai-chi chuan.

I interpreted my discovery as a fortunate omen. The opportunity to study t'ai-chi from another traditionally trained master was irresistible. After all, worse events could have occurred. I could have found a job and not had time to pursue paranormal and mystical experience.

I telephoned the Chung Hwa School at the Chinese Cultural Center. A soft spoken lady told me that Liang was starting a new class the following Saturday at seven in the morning. This synchronistic timing confirmed that my discovery was destined.

I arrived at the Chinese Cultural Center eagerly ahead of time. Several students of all ages were learning English in one of the stark class rooms. Not surprisingly, most of them were Chinese. About fifteen people were waiting to the side of an unpainted cement block building on a barren basketball court.

A mellow and round-faced Chinese man was standing near the edge of the court. He held an unpretentious posture with his hands folded behind him. About five feet and four inches, he was bald with a few swatches of gray hair above his ears. His sweat shirt covered a solid upper frame and fully extended belly. He wore black cotton pants with draw strings at the ankles and the traditional Chinese black canvas shoes that still cost only about four dollars. Responding to questions from several students, he was in no hurry to start the class. I waited for his attention. I formally introduced myself and asked him his name.

Without shaking hands, he said, "My name Liang Ting-Shuk. *Liang* is, how you say in English, my surname. It's my last name and that's what you call me."

"What does it mean?" I asked.

"Oh, in Chinese means Wooden Beam, Conqueror, and Schezchuan Province," he said in a revered tone.

Now, this is a serious legacy I thought. I always wanted to have an appointed name that represented a unique personality rather than the modern wishes of parents given before birth. In growing up, I remember many different minorities defending their cultural heritage. I remember being envious they, nonetheless had an automatic identity with which to defend. While bred from roots of German, Irish, English and Welsh, my genetic and cultural heritage was now an amorphous breed representing an All-American mutt. Among millions of others in search for some unified dignity, I identified with being a product of the sixties. Rebellious of everything that had stood the test of time through the Eisenhower era, it was only natural to rebel against it in search of an identity as a revolutionary. 'Counter-culture' we called it. That was a minus for everything that stood as a conventional plus.

I remember the political and ecology rallies on campus, the permissiveness of sexual exploration or was it exploitation justified by rebellion. I remember the music of Paul Horn playing in the Taj Maijal, Dillon, Beatles, Hendrix, and of course Ravi Shankar amongst the shelves of beads, bongs, and incense in head shops. I protested in Berkeley over People's Park with rebels pissing off the roofs of buildings, body painting in the parking lots, and smoking joints in the health food stores. The clothing, adopted from the poor, indigent, and the Eastern cultures was a symbol of rebellion against American bureaucracy. There was Big Sur, encounter groups, and human potential movements, where feelings reigned majesty and the intellect was subjugated for the first time in human history outside the excuse of ignorance and birth defects.

It was a time where the meaning of life and the plain dignity of being human was validated above materialistic mediocrity. Wind chimes, growing herbs, nude bathing in hot springs, and group sex were associative symbols. Maidens with flowers in their hair thumbed their way along the highways in paisley print dresses trying to find themselves. Bare-chest studs with pony tails, sweat bands, guitars, and sandals followed suit.

God, I would have died to have a name, an earned and given name like Wooden Beam-Conqueror-Schezchuan Province in those days. It is like the Native Americans who have names like Rolling Thunder, Sun Bear, and *Dances with Wolves*. Maybe I would have known who I was apart from the rebellion instead of becoming a part of it, instead of identifying with the only culture I knew.

Liang gazed calmly past my profile enough to attract my attention back to our conversation.

"How much are your lessons?" I asked.

"Group lessons are twenty dollars a month. Individual lessons are five dollars an hour. But, you don't pay this time. You might not like. Just follow with class and let me know later."

Liang walked over to one side of the concrete slab and faced away from the group. Obviously, most of this group had already taken lessons since they responded to his gesture as an immediate cue. The entire group stopped talking and faced forward. Similar to a traditional *dojo*, I took my place in the horizontal lines of people facing the *sensei*. As is traditional in the opening movements of t'ai-chi, Liang mindfully raised his arms up and out in front of him. Slowly, he started to move one leg and then suddenly stopped.

He turned around to everyone and said, "Now you practice."

I felt that I had barely completed one basic movement. For the next half hour, we all practiced this one simple gesture. Liang shuffled about the crowd, precisely correcting the posture of each student.

He approached me with a cane in one hand and silently watched me practice from a couple of feet away.

"Bend! Bend more," he said, referring to my knee.

I bent my knee more. He placed his cane at the side of my toes such that it extended vertically above my knee. While I had bent my knee more, it extended beyond the cane and my toes.

"No good for balance. Keep knee bent and not beyond toes," he instructed.

He continued to teach me the four main postures of the first movement. He explained the function of each posture in reference to balance, stability, and breathing. Probably out of embarrassment, I made a joke about my difficulty with one of the moves.

Liang was sharply critical.

"T'ai-chi not funny. T'ai-chi very serious business," he said, and walked away.

I felt chastised. I wondered where the humor was that I had learned to expect from my experience with Gia-fu. Obviously, this venture demanded that I adjust my preconceptions.

Liang looked at his plastic watch and stopped after an hour. Several people approached him and handed him money. I wanted to show the proper interest of a dedicated student. I felt that I should decide now whether I was going to take lessons rather than wait until later. The problem was that the group format did not offer me enough individually instructive attention. After the careful consideration that a full minute can grant, instinctively I approached Liang.

"I want to take individual lessons with you."

"Good," he said, and continued.

"I don't do individual lessons here. I do them in Balboa Park in front of the Federal Building, everyday but Friday. What time you want to come?"

I thought for a few moments and said, "How about Tuesday at ten?"

Liang walked over to a yellow, plastic bag with a smiley face on it and pulled out a tiny tattered black note book. Briskly, he thumbed through the pages.

He looked back in my direction and said, "No, ten no good. Have another student then. You come at eleven."

Obviously, he was not asking me a question. Rather, he was imploring me to fit into his schedule. I agreed.

On the day of our appointment, I arrived in the park early. Balboa Park emanates the earth first and then the spirit. Maybe this is why it has recently become a haven for the homeless. It was the site of the Panama Pacific International Exposition in 1915 and the California Pacific International Exposition in 1935. The park contains enough different buildings to resemble a small city. All the structures are ornate with Spanish colonial-baroque architecture. It is also known for the San Diego Zoo and more recently, its emerging Japanese Friendship Gardens.

Liang was easy to find. He was standing on a freshly mowed field underneath a giant yew tree providing ample shade. A wide concrete entry way divided the lawn in front of the Federal Building. It was an ideal setting. The Federal Building is of Mayan architecture. It was designed after the Palace of the Governor in Uxmal, on the Yucatan of Mexico. Now replaced, the second story glass figure originally displayed the colored version of a Mayan warrior and slave. The park appeared empty. Few people ever used this building, even as the alternate gymnasium, and then only occasionally for badmitten.

I parked my black TR-6 and walked across the park to Liang. I noticed that Liang was not teaching a student. I wondered whether he had actually scheduled an appointment before me. Perhaps he had wanted to change the time of my appointment just for the sake of establishing authority. Maybe this was his way of telling me that he was the mentor and I was the apprentice. I decided to question him about this indirectly.

I greeted him and asked, "Where is your other student?"

Liang casually looked at me and answered, "Oh, he no show up. We start now."

While I had received an answer, it did not resolve my question. Liang turned around with his back toward me and started the form as he had in the first group meeting.

He stopped at the same place and turned around toward me and said, "Now you do."

I tried to match his graceful movements and he continued to correct my posture. This went on for an hour, progressing no further in form than we had the previous week in the group session. He stopped, looked at his watch and said, "We stop for now. You pay me."

I thought his manner of requesting payment to be abrupt, but after all, it was practical. It got the job done. I told him that I didn't have any cash and asked him whether he accepted checks. Without a word, he nodded in approval. I didn't have a pen and had to get one from the glove compartment of the car. I came back and handed the check to Liang.

He was starring at my car and inquired, "What kind of car is that? Is it a General Motors' car?"

"No, it's a Triumph."

"Where's it from?"

"It's made in England."

"Does it have a radio?"

I tried not to laugh and answered, "Yeah, its got a radio."

I rescheduled with him for a couple of days later and walked to my car.

As I reached for the door handle, I noticed that Liang was right behind me. He had his hands politely folded behind his back and was looking directly at the dash board. I showed him where the radio was and he kept looking all over the entire compartment.

After a couple of minutes of silence, he looked at me and said, "Good car, see you Thursday."

I would have found our exchange to be unusual and awkward had I not experienced Gia-fu's appreciation of the Volvo. However, as I was to learn in the years ahead, Liang harbored a particular fascination for automobiles and their gadgets.

I arrived again in the park on an overcast Thursday morning. At dawn, cloud bursts had drenched the landscape. I was glad we had a concrete surface on which to practice. Liang was instructing a young Japanese female. Apparently, she was studying the same form that I was learning, except that she was much further along. This was my first opportunity to view the movements in this form that were ahead of me.

Silently, I stood on the wet grass and watched the power and grace of Liang. However, I found myself distracted by the delicate beauty and petite frame of the oriental girl. The girl's lesson finished. She paid Liang and walked away from us to a distant section of the park to practice.

Liang turned to me and abruptly said, "You like her?"

Caught off guard, I didn't know what to say.

He continued without giving me a chance to respond.

"Have you practiced?"

"Yes," I answered.

I was to learn that Liang would reliably ask me about my practice at the beginning of each of my sessions. It was, in fact, to become his usual greeting. After my session, I again paid Liang with a check.

He looked at the check and asked, "What kind of doctor are you?"

"Clinical psychologist," I answered.

He inquired further, "I don't understand why you want to work with crazy people. You need to be crazy to work with crazy people. Now you want to be healthy with t'ai-chi mind. Looks like problem to me."

I tried to explain to him that the two were compatible. I told him that I didn't need to be crazy to work with crazy people, at least not always. I did not impress Liang with my logic. He patiently stood there in silence, occasionally looking at me and then the ground. I finished my arduous explanation with considerable malaise. I might have thought Liang looked bored except that he rarely displayed any emotions.

He changed the subject and said, "What time you want to see me next?"

I scheduled two appointments for the following week and walked toward my car. On the way home, I wondered whether he was right. Until this time, I had not questioned why I was a psychotherapist. It was a choice I stumbled into from early interest. I pursued it because people encouraged me by saying they felt an ease in talking with me and that I made a difference in their life. Also, it was a skill with which I had become proficient. However, for the first time I wondered whether my career choice was wise and healthy for me. I wondered whether it was now a detriment to mystical ways.

I drove to my next session preoccupied and distressed. I had been harboring personal dissatisfactions with my wife for the past two years of an eleven year youthfully blossomed relationship. Within the last three weeks I had classically fallen madly and passionately in lust with an exotic and sensual goddess.

In retrospect, however, she was a sexy and seductive "daddy's girl" who was unhappily married to a career driven and successful physician. The classic triad emerged. I was both kissed and battered into the middle of it. The situation was also complicated by my two wonderful children whom, I loved. They were two and six years old. I felt an overwhelming pressure from all directions to make a responsible decision, though the inevitability of satisfying all concerned was an imaginary world of guilt-ridden omnipotence. One way or another, I knew I was doomed.

I met Liang as usual and we began our session. My mind distracted, my performance was a reflected travesty of concentration. Liang, however, said nothing. Surprisingly, he didn't even correct me once. I was glad when our session ended. Expecting conflict resolution, I decided to approach the wise one.

"I have a problem," I hesitatingly said.

I was waiting for an invitation. There was no response.

Bravely, I continued and told him my story of pain and conflict. He showed unusual interest by looking in my eyes. With watery eyes mirroring my story of pain, I explained my dilemma. I finished and looked at Liang. He had turned around to grab a ginger snap and lost interest.

"Have listened, but don't know problem," he said curtly and rather nonchalantly.

Emotionally engulfed in my desperate need for resolution, I repeated my tale. This time, however, I emphasized the alternatives of my impasse. I embellished the ending with a more charging invitation for advise. Liang looked at me like a French waiter who had just sipped a virgin-corked, two-hundred year old bottle of chardonney.

In complete repose, as if oven-warmed bread was in the left side of his cheek, he answered my initial question with profound brilliance.

"Why don't you live with both of them? What's the problem?"

I struggled a laugh.

"Liang," I said, "we don't do that here in America."

"We don't do it in China either."

"Then, why are you suggesting it as the solution to my problem?"

"Because I can't think of anything else. Besides, that's not your problem."

"Then what's my problem?"

"Your problem is that you worry too much. You look outside you and view situations as adversary. Then you view situations as something to conquer. Then you worry about how you are going to control these concerns. Then, when you don't succeed, you find yourself in problem situation. Funny thing! You were in problem situation in first place."

Emotionally, I was calm. However, my mental frustration was ballistic.

"So, how do I get out of the problem in the first place," I asked.

Liang more gently responded, "There is no problem in the first place. *You* are the first place. No you! No problem! Your way, no matter your solutions, you continue problem."

I was completely frustrated in the most peaceful of ways. I still didn't know what to do, but somehow I didn't care. Nevertheless, I knew that I still needed to decide. I inquired further.

"So, now that I'm in this mess and can't get back to the beginning, how do I solve it for now."

Liang looked back in my direction.

"Doesn't matter," he said.

"Live with both, live with one, live with none. Important point is to practice t'ai-chi. Now you pay me. Old man has talked too much and needs some rest."

After a few more weeks, I left my wife. I began dating and eventually married my new lover who after four years left me. Through the giving and taking of much emotional pain, I now know what Liang meant when he explained that it didn't make any difference which choice I made.

One day my lesson finished early. I asked Liang about the origin of t'ai-chi chuan and its mystical parts. Liang in his beach chair, I sat on the grass and he talked.

"One hundred fifty years ago, nobody in capital of China new of t'ai-chi.[1] T'ai-chi was in hands of lower classes and probably was fast. As it was brought to Peking about 1824, kings, emperors, and duchesses were ready to learn and pay for the art. These rich people always indulged, drinking, eating, women, opium, watching and playing with birds in cages. They became weak and could not fight. With t'ai-chi, they learned how to have strength without working fast. Breathing was incorporated for strength with slowness. In addition, it restored the health of these wealthy people. In the times of any country, not just China, the wealthy have always been responsible for making something popular."

Liang paused and gazed into the distance. I waited. After a few minutes he continued.

"As far as I know, but maybe I don't know enough, there is no philosophy to t'ai-chi, none of this yin-yang stuff or *I-Ching*. T'ai-chi is for fighting. Although t'ai-chi is for fighting, it does make health. Of all the people I've ever known, fifty percent got better. That is, some got a little better from sickness or disease. Some got completely well. The other fifty percent, no change, but never any harm or damage."

"There are many fighting systems of different countries, but of all, the Chinese is the most beautiful. And of the Chinese, t'ai-chi is the most graceful."

I asked him why so many people learned this art in China.

He continued, "There are many reasons people learned fighting in China. Villages always fight between one another. Each village needs its own fighting people. Each village needs fighting teachers to teach young, so fighting becomes a way of making a living. It is a way of supporting your family."

"Next, important people pay well for body guards. And, fighting is good, for how you say, Wells Fargo."

He paused with a rare and barely noticeable smile, clearly showing pleasure with his American metaphor.

He continued, "Learning fighting is good to guard and protect wagons of goods in travel. Also, people move from village to village. They set up tents and show fighting art for entertainment, then pass hat for coins. If performance no good or bad show, no money!"

I asked Liang why he had studied t'ai-chi chuan.

"When I was young my mother took t'ai-chi because she was very sick. She got well, healthy. She made me go and learn, but not for fighting. I took it for a while, but I did not like it. Too slow, not fast and hard like Shaolin. But, I went back after studying Shaolin. Someone told me that if someone tried to hit or strike a master of t'ai-chi that the aggressor would fall down. I didn't believe this. But, when I got older, I saw this with my own eyes, not once, but several times. But these people not masters, just good at t'ai-chi, just much practice. T'ai-chi learned by most for show, you know, like what you call circus, not very practical. But with practice, over years, most practical for fighting, particularly with Wu and cane."

After four months of studying with Liang, I learned the basics of the *Wu* form. This form is more subtle and practical than the *Yang*. Each of the lengthy versions that Liang taught took forty five minutes to complete. I was practicing two hours a day and was waiting to learn t'ai-chi *garn* or the cane. The cane's length is similar to the Japanese *jo*, but longer than Filipino *escrima* or *arnis* sticks. I had watched Liang practice. He wielded the cane as graceful as a swan and as deadly as an eagle in flight toward its prey.

I arrived one day to start learning the cane. Liang offered his usual greeting of asking me whether I had practiced. I affirmed my dedication and asked him about the origination of the cane as a weapon.

"Monks needed to travel from temples to monasteries and so forth. They needed to take food and money. The early monks only prayed and did rituals. They didn't know how to fight. So, renegade warriors and bandits would attack them. Many times, they were badly hurt and sometimes killed. The monks got tired of this so, they started training in both the hard and soft warrior arts.

But, many of them were very old. They couldn't move very fast and needed canes to walk. So, they figured out ways to use the cane as a weapon to gain advantage and neutralize many opponents. After while, monks not afraid anymore."

Liang stopped talking and sipped some tea. Unusually, he then spent the remainder of our session demonstrating the practical martial functions of stabs, thrusts, sweeps, overhead and side swings of the cane. He showed how to increase power of movement by twisting the body and springing the staff into movement. As with all weapons in all martial arts, he explained that the cane is only an instrumental extension of one's physical body. I was not to employ it as a weapon separate from my body.

He walked over and pushed his thumb into my clothing near my waist, at the side and top ridge of my pelvic bone and said, "Now you go find and make your cane this length from the ground and we start next week."

I tried to locate rattan in San Diego. I discovered there was a current embargo on shipping rattan with the peel on it into the United States. The only rattan I could find in San Diego had the peel removed for the making of furniture. This just wouldn't do. I drove to Los Angeles to a furniture supplier that had a few lengths remaining from his last shipment. I learned a long time ago that when I go out of my way for something important, it makes what I am doing more special, if not magical.

For the next year and a half I continued practicing *Wu* and cane. I learned the long form of *Yang*, the broad sword and double edge sword. The broad sword is the wide curved sword that looks like it belongs to a pirate or Sinbad the Sailor. The double edge sword is similar to King Arthur's in the legend of the Knights of the Round Table. In learning these weapons, I felt like I was living in far away storybook lands. This was a class that I had missed in childhood and needed to make up.

Also, in learning the use of the weapons, I experienced an aggressive sexual energy. There was no doubt in my mind that I was wielding phallic symbols and passing through my latent and earthly puberty rite. Of course, this developmental mythology is all part of the relationship between mentor and apprentice, and similarly between fathers and sons.

I had learned enough forms that I could practice for several hours without repeating any of them. In daily practice, sometimes I would question specific movements or their combat function. On one occasion, I wrote three questions on a piece of paper. I wanted to remember to ask Liang about them at my next lesson. On driving to the park for my next lesson, I remembered that I left the piece of paper at home. Nonetheless, I remembered the questions, perhaps just because I had written them down.

I arrived in the park and found Liang reading a substandard paperback novel.

Approaching him, he closed the book. Curiously, he inquired, "You ever go to female house?"

"What do you mean by 'female house?'"

In complete candor, he looked at me and said, "You know, where women take off their cloths."

I laughed and said, "Oh, do you mean a striptease bar or a whorehouse?"

Disregarding the two alternatives, he replied, "Yes, what's the name of it, down by the beach, on the corner?"

I still didn't know whether Liang was referring to a burlesque show or a brothel. Since I wasn't well versed in the local talent of the night, I could only make a couple of guesses about the name. We never did arrive at exactly the right one. Liang finally gave a motion to start my lesson.

After the lesson, I paid Liang and waited for his attention to ask questions. He bent over and put the cash in his plastic bag. He stood and turned around starring directly at me. Without my asking, he answered each question in my mind in exactly the order that I was thinking of asking them.

He then looked at me and said, "Was there anything else that you want to know?"

Stunned, I laughed and said, "No, thank you very much."

Liang didn't even grin. Liang never laughed and rarely smiled. He just sat down, poured tea, and ate a ginger snap.

In addition to t'ai-chi chuan, I knew that Liang taught forms of *Shaolin kung fu*. "*Kung fu*" is a frequently misused word. In Chinese, it translates to mean perfection in any art. In itself, kung fu is not a particular style of fighting. My old karate teacher had teased us one day by saying we were going to learn kung fu broom to clean the *dojo*. Shaolin kung fu was the style, ostensibly featured, in the television series *Kung Fu*. I was most curious to learn *dragon tiger fists*, a fast moving and lengthy form of over a hundred and thirty moves taking twenty minutes. I had now studied with Liang for three years and requested to learn Shaolin. He approved.

Liang usually waited until I perfected previous parts of a form to his satisfaction before he introduced additions. While all Chinese forms are circular in motion, Shaolin was very different from t'ai-chi chuan. It was fast, hard, and aggressive with low thrusts to the groin and multiple ways of damaging vital organs.

A paranoid thought occurred to me, that with this violent form, I might be encouraging confrontation since my lessons were in full public view of people meandering in the park. With forms such as this, I was familiar to working in a private *dojo* that did not permit public spectators. Additionally, self-conscious thoughts of performance and publicly wanting to look good crept into my mind during practice. I tried to dismiss these thoughts by telling myself this was part of the training and that anyone watching would be a stranger. This rational, however, was only marginally effective.

After a few months of practice, I completed *dragon tiger fists*. One day I arrived in the park, intending to focus my lesson on a review of my t'ai-chi forms. It was a warm Spring day and there were an unusual number of people in the park to view nature's display of trees and flowers in bloom. I was about to begin my session. Contrary to my agenda, Liang implored that I needed more practice in Shaolin. In more than three years of apprenticeship with him, he had never suggested the contents of my lessons. He always asked me to determine our agenda. I quickly dismissed the curious event and waited for Liang to walk ahead and turn around with his back toward me as usual.

Instead, he said, "I want you to go through all of *dragon tiger fists* for me."

His request for an entire form was also uncommon. However, following instructions, I began. I was about half way through the form. Liang corrected a movement and we continued together. For the first time in three years, a crowd gathered around us in a large circle. I followed Liang as usual. We moved through the form with speed and power. As the crowd grew to nearly two hundred people, I was conscious of performing and became distracted. While I was confident, I was not visualizing an opponent with every move as I was taught. We completed the form. The crowd whistled and clapped in praise. Liang motioned me back to the lawn. As he poured tea, the crowd dispersed. Within a few minutes, the entire area was vacant.

Liang exclaimed, "Good lesson!"

"Yeah, except there were too many people here today," I said.

"What people?" he firmly asked.

I replied the obvious, "All those people who were around us!"

Liang casually sipped tea and gazed across the field of grass. Several minutes passed. I took his silence to mean that I should not have given attention to the crowd. Nonetheless, I found his comment to be an unusual way for him to teach. I was already mildly dissatisfied with my distractions and was becoming increasing agitated at his response. However, after thinking about the situation for a few moments, my mind became completely blank of anything intelligent to say.

Finally, out of frustration I said, "I know what you are trying to tell me. You're trying to tell me that I should have given attention to my form and not worry about what those people might be thinking."

Liang gazed past me and casually inquired as if he didn't know what I was talking about.

"What people? Who are these people you keep talking about?"

His question was so puzzlingly sincere, that for a moment I questioned my senses. Liang was now looking in my direction as if waiting for an answer. I was about to repeat myself when Liang asked, "Does your radio still work?"

I was dazed with his question. I expected his question to be some philosophical metaphor like 'the radio inside my head.'

"What radio?" I asked.

"The radio inside your car," he emphatically stated.

"Yes, it works," I said.

"Good!"

Baffled, I looked at him in disbelief.

"Why do you ask?" I said.

Liang merely responded, "Important for radios to work inside cars!"

I was speechless. He had stated the obvious like a novel announcement of profound wisdom.

"You pay me now. I have another student to teach," he said.

It was ten minutes past the hour for another student to show. I looked around. There were no other students in sight. I paid him as requested and scheduled my next session. Walking to my car, I couldn't make sense of his strange comments after the lesson. I was filled with questions. I had no way of organizing any of Liang's bizarre requests or responses of the day. I got into my car and started to drive out of the park. I looked at Liang. He was sitting in his chair gazing in another direction. Still, there were no other students in sight.

For several minutes I reflected on the bizarre events of our session. Suddenly, I became aware the radio was not working. I had left the dial on when I turned the ignition off on arrival. I couldn't believe it. It had worked perfectly well on the way to my session. I turned the dial on and off again several times. It still didn't work. With a mixture of amusement, aggravation, and curiosity, I drove immediately to a mechanic. After playing with the radio for twenty minutes, he ferreted out the mischievous, mechanical demon. It was an incinerated fuse. With deft replacement and a generous five dollar charge, the radio worked perfectly well.

Driving home, again I tried to make sense of the unusual events of the morning. All the strange events became a harmonious and meaningful message. A central theme emerged. The evidence supported that Liang planned this session and its lesson in advance. At the beginning, he made a peculiar request for me to execute Shaolin and then a rare demand to proceed through the entire form.

After the lesson, he denied any obvious awareness of the crowd. Liang was telling the truth in relation to his experience. The people were not "there" for him. Quite simply and practically, the crowd did not exist because it was not a priority. The people were as much a part of the background for Liang as the grass, trees, and the flowers. His statements after the lesson were a clever ploy to teach me that awareness does not need to distract concentration. Awareness of the external environment does not need to interfere with an internal focus of consciousness.

Next, Liang asked an abrupt question about the function of the radio in my car. Then, as a metaphor for concentrated attention, he affirmed that it was important for the radio (concentrated attention) to work. A fuse is a circuit that breaks with an overload of energy. My concern with the crowd in the park had prevented me from the present-centered attention required in my session. My distractions represented a broken circuit of awareness.

Fuses eventually burn out sometime. However, given the sequential synchronism of events, I considered this mechanistic and merely coincidental explanation as obdurate and naive. Obviously, telepathy was out of the question because I was the one who expected the radio to work. The evidence supported that Liang knew ahead of time the radio or fuse would not work later (precognition), became aware of the malfunction during the session (clairvoyance), or directly influenced the malfunction sometime during our session (psychokinesis).

While possible, I dismissed psychokinetic influence because I did not believe Liang would go to this much trouble to teach. Rather, his method was to quite naturally take advantage of changing events as they occurred. Also, I rejected clairvoyance. Liang would have had to know that the fuse incinerated during the course of our session. And, while this was possible, fuses only incinerate with a new charge of energy. The evidence supported precognition in knowing that the fuse would incinerate on ignition of the car before I left the park. The session brought home the message that I needed to pay more attention to my awareness of the moment and less to environmental distractions.

A few weeks later, Liang's privileges were temporarily removed for operating outside the Federal Building. The park commission told him that he could temporarily use the defunct conference building. No one else was using it. This location was the best the park commission could offer until they resolved the details for the next summer. It was winter and Liang accepted the relocation without concern.

The following week, I arrived across the parking lot from where I regularly trained. The building was another two story massive structure of Mayan design. One of the double massive doors was ajar. I walked in. There was no sound or light. Spontaneously, the door opened again. Liang briskly walked inside and said, "Wait here."

Suddenly, a single hooded light, more than twenty feet in the air, cast a ten foot spot in the middle of the gymnasium, hardwood floor. The dark, open space was larger than the stage of the Metropolitan Opera in New York. At the level of the second story, an ornate walkway completely encircled the arena. I felt the emptiness as stark with only the sound of silence.

Liang walked toward me near the entry way. We stood in the dark, twenty feet away from the single spot on the empty gymnasium floor. He told me to follow him. We walked into the encircled lit spot on the floor together. As usual, he turned around with his back to me and instructed me to follow in form. Forty-five minutes later, he stopped and we walked back into the shadows near the entry way. After paying him, again I asked why he had stopped Shaolin to practice t'ai-chi. I mentioned that Shaolin was so crisp and powerful.

He looked directly in my eyes for a few moments and commanded, "Stay here!"

He walked in a perfectly straight line into the middle of the circularly lit spot on the floor again. In strict military fashion, he spun an about-face, such that he was directly facing me. After a few seconds, and from a standing position, he leaped into the air. Both of his feet were off the ground. His left leg moved straight out in front of him and up above his head. The tip of his right hand swept to the left and grazed the tip of his canvas shoe. His right leg was straight up and down, and nearly three feet off the ground. He landed on both legs and leaped into the air again. This time, his right leg thrust up above his head and directly in front of his face. He swept across the tip of his shoe with his left palm. He landed on both feet perfectly balanced and calm. He walked straight ahead and stopped in front of me.

Quietly, he said in an apologetic voice, "I'm very old man now. Cannot do Shaolin anymore and that's why I do t'ai-chi." His comment, of course, completely belied his performance. I knew that was the message he wanted to convey.

The following summer Liang was again permitted to conduct his lessons outside the Federal Building. One day when I arrived, three members of a gang clad in black leather jackets and dirty jeans hovered around Liang. Keys and ropes of chain drooped from their belt loops. Liang had just finished a lesson and was sitting in his low beach chair on the grass underneath his favorite yew tree. He was sipping his usual oolong tea from the stained red plastic top of a thermos bottle and munching on a couple of ginger snaps. It was the middle of the summer. These days he wore a frayed baseball cap.

Three people, in their early twenties, rudely tried to talk to Liang.

One of them said, "What is this you are doing here? It looks like some kind of dance."

Liang ignored them and gazed straight ahead. All clues missed, they continued invading with their conversation. The men spoke among themselves with intermittent laughter and with questions poked at Liang sometimes. This continued for about five minutes. Liang said not a word. He casually finished his tea and cookies, replaced the thermos in his black bag and gazed into the distance past their knees. Taking cue from my mentor, I remained silent as well.

By now, the men were talking about the obvious power of karate and how t'ai-chi just didn't look like a martial art. One of them directed his last question to Liang.

"So, what's it really for man?"

Liang slowly stood and for the first time looked directly at each of them and bellowed out in a voice I didn't now he had, "This is t'ai-chi. T'ai-chi for killing people."

He continued in an even louder voice again, "T'ai-chi for killing people."

Every casual stroller in the park for up to a block away turned around. The three men stood there stunned and immobilized.

Liang looked at me and said, "Time for lesson now and walked toward me."

The men walked away without a word. He conducted our lesson as usual. If he was upset in any way after the confrontation, he did not show it.

Several months after this event, a couple of other advanced students and I were in the park with Liang. One of the students asked Liang about t'ai-chi with multiple opponents. I remembered the day with the three men towering above Liang's small stature. I reminded him of that day and chimed in with a request for a demonstration with multiple opponents. Liang hesitated. No one to my knowledge had ever seen him use his art in actual combat.

Liang looked at us and said, "Okay, one time, maybe two, no more. One condition, no mess around. You all fully attack me any way you want. You actually try to hurt me bad."

We agreed and walked over to a more open area of grass. The three of us stood around him in a triad. Liang nodded showing that he was ready. Immediately, one student jumped and thrust a level side kick at Liang's chest. I saw Liang start to move toward him. I moved forward with a straight right punch to the head. The third student tried a round-house kick. My next awareness was that all three of us were on the ground, unhurt, and barely touched. Liang was standing calm. We got up and one of the students politely asked for our second try.

Liang said, "Okay, so you know no trick, but this time you get serious."

This time, the three of us planned a team strategy. Feeling more confident, we circled Liang and waited for our silently planned count. Simultaneously, we attacked with different kicks and strikes. The results were similar except that two of us were still standing and several yards further away from Liang. Liang walked back to his shaded territory underneath the tree and poured tea. We were not especially shocked that Liang had well defended himself, nor that we had never touched him. However, we were surprised that none of us were bruised. We had felt little more than softly being brushed by his clothing. In swelling pride of our master, we walked back to where Liang was seated.

We were about to thank him when he held up his palm for our silence and casually said, "No master, just much practice."

Martial Masters Appreciate Simplicity

I intermittently studied with Liang for more than seven years. During the first three years, I took private lessons two to three times a week. After stopping, I had asked him to give me a Chinese name. He said he would. Several months later he sent a letter. It read: "I received your letter long ago. This is an inexcusable delay, all because of my laziness. After thinking over your Chinese name for a long time I have decided on the following name of Iron Tree Branch. Maybe you will come across some Chinese in New York or East Coast who can give you better Chinese name. Yours, Liang."

Liang Ting Shuk lived a spartan existence. He lived in a sparsely furnished apartment in a low income district. He used public transportation. Rather than working in an office, he used public areas for practice. He always wore inexpensive cotton clothing. He read third-rate novels, frequented strip joints, and was thoroughly fascinated with the mechanics of Western civilization. His modest and healthful diet was vegetarian with an abundance of tea and ginger cookies. He did not live this way to increase an aesthetic meditative holiness. He said he was attempting to save money to enable his wife to join him in America.

Martial masters are warriors of spirit. They appreciate what would ordinarily be considered the irrelevant or meager details of everyday life. The bird that lands on the window sill, the leaves that fall from the trees, and the morning dew on the grass are all treats from the universe.

Martial Masters Commit to Practice

Liang's seminal lesson was that the belief in masters was merely an apprentice's illusion. Liang, himself, stated he had studied with many "masters" in China. However, Liang defined acclaimed masters as only people who had practiced more than others. Those who practiced were blessed with knowing how much more they needed to learn. Even after practicing martial arts for fifty years, he positively rejected the image of being a master. Genuinely believing that he had just practiced more than others, Liang clung to the portrayal of an advanced student of the art.

Everyone can learn to master various abilities that most people usually attribute to masters. Acquiring an extraordinary sensitivity to any art, whether it be martial, athletic, musical, carpentry, gardening, culinary, or psychic, requires practice. Masters of martial arts, herbal healing, meditation, flower arranging, tea ceremony, or yoga are regular folk who commit their life to a particular art and form of evolution.[2] All people have predispositions that allow them to be adept in some arts more than others. However, everyone can become more skillful by practicing a single art.

Martial Masters are Practical

Liang never discussed mystical beliefs. He viewed such endeavors as intellectual speculation and fantasy. Such abstract reflections were only detours hindering experiential realization. Nonetheless, he lived the mystical realization of being an integral function of pervasive energy. To Liang, t'ai-chi chuan was explicitly a practical fighting art. The effectiveness of t'ai-chi chuan demands merging with one's opponent to balance conflicted energy. Liang also considered t'ai-chi chuan as a preventive and reparative health exercise. Implicitly, it was a method of maintaining complete attention and harmony with one's self and the universe.

Liang represented a mystical earth father. I learned from him simplicity of routine and efficiency of action. He simplified life in a concrete and innocent way. Liang rejected the belief of studying t'ai-chi chuan as a method to achieve enlightenment. He never mentioned the word meditation, yet was one of the most contemplative people I have ever met in my life. He never discussed t'ai-chi chuan in relation to attaining higher states of realization, transformation or transcendence. Liang was the quintessence of practical mysticism and viewed philosophical and mystical interpretations as a disruptive amusement that only impeded progress.

Masters and mystics with whom I have studied exemplify similar teachings through different skills, methods, techniques, and metaphors. No master or mystic has a monopoly on the secrets of enlightenment. People follow teachers or teachings they find helpful because of a particular personality or consciousness in life at different times. Any master or mystic who claims to have a monopoly of methods to extend beyond self-gratification is: [A] playing and having fun, [B] intentionally projecting this message for apprentice motivation, [C] competing in the conventional world for glorification and enthronement, [D] delusional, or [E] any combination of the above.

Martial Masters Discourage the Importance of Paranormal Experience

Liang showed unquestionable proficiency in telepathy, precognition, psychokinesis, and a debatable ability in clairvoyance. Abundant other mystics demonstrate a variety of paranormal phenomena. There are also many notable mystics who do not show these abilities. Paranormal skills are not a requirement to define mystical identification. Neither do paranormal skills evidence mystical affiliation. Paranormal abilities and mystical realization describe distinct phenomena. While these phenomena frequently occur together, they are not dependent upon one another.

Liang never discussed his paranormal abilities nor ascribed them any special value. He simply viewed his expanded sensitivities as part of his everyday, usual perception for gaining information and teaching. Martial masters value these abilities for self-awareness, self-healing, control, and instruction. Nevertheless, they typically discourage or forbid students from pursuing these skills directly.

Paranormal experiences can easily distract and mislead beginning students from the basic lessons of martial masters. That is, paranormal experiences can initially enhance self-glorification rather than contribute to extending awareness beyond the locus of self. As a result of their initial dramatic nature, while paranormal experiences are recognized by mentors, mentors dismiss the importance of them. It is common that when people begin practicing various forms of meditation, they have particular paranormal experiences. Enthusiastically, they run to tell their mentor, believing this event to be a sign of spiritual attainment. Usually, the mentor agrees these experiences are to be expected and to pay no attention to them. They will go away.

As stated before, my position on this matter is more respectful of paranormal experience. While I completely agree that paranormal experiences can hinder mystical realization, I am convinced they can be a special gateway and significant enhancement toward mystical realization for the Occidental mind.

Martial Masters Discourage Personal Adoration

Years after I studied with Liang, I visited him again. He was still in the park in front of the Federal Building. He gave me a warm greeting. It was, perhaps, one of the few times I saw him smile. I wanted to polish the few forms I still remembered which were *Wu* and cane. As we began a series of twenty sessions this summer, I noticed that Liang had changed the details of specific forms. He would continuously correct my postures that I had so carefully imprinted with practice over nine years. As his corrections became more conspicuous, I asked him if he had changed his forms. He unequivocally denied that he had changed anything, inferring that I was incorrect. Knowing that I had practiced exactly as I had been originally taught, I interpreted the experience simply to mean that both of us had changed.

Some mystics demand apprentices to follow their precise advice for reprogramming and proficiency. Even with novices, some mentors intentionally give vague directions or require their students to discover their own unique answers. Regardless of teaching methods, all mystics demand complete attentiveness to their teachings from apprentices. As students evolve, mentors eventually discourage apprentices to follow their particular interpretations of mysticism or metaphoric styles. This is so, precisely because all mystics understand that personal metaphor is essential for understanding. Regardless of national, cultural, or racial persuasion, all mystics understand that the universal manifests itself through the easiest and most agreeable symbols for the initiate.

CHAPTER FIVE
ZEN CURRENTS

Four years later, many personal circumstances had changed. The college at which Arthur and I employed claimed bankruptcy. Arthur moved to eastern Pennsylvania and took a position as a Unitarian minister. I divorced and remarried two years later. During that same time, I elected a commission as a Lieutenant in the U.S. Navy in a clinical psychology internship at the Naval Hospital in Bethesda, Maryland. Graduating after a year, I transferred to a staff billet at the Naval Hospital serving the largest fleet on the East coast in Portsmouth, Virginia.

For three years, Karen and I drove from Washington D.C. and Virginia to Pennsylvania about once a month to visit Arthur and Margo. Their home was always a haven from the military and hospital environment in which I was now involved. During one visit, the poet and activist Daniel Berrigan visited Arthur to share his recent joys and tribulations. Daniel and his brother Philip Berrigan, a Catholic priest, were known for their prominence in the late sixties as Vietnam protesters. Daniel was later convicted for breaking into the Pentagon and burning draft records.

With a passionate desire to make a difference in what appeared to be a crumbling world, the four us decided to purchase a farm. Our idea was to use it for family living and to create a residential center for personal and spiritual development. We looked at more than forty properties for nearly two years.

We became passionately attracted to a twelve acre farm three miles north of Quakertown, Pennsylvania. An hour north of

Philadelphia and two hours west of New York City, the location was ideal to draw people from these large urban populations.

None of the dwellings were visible from the road. The gravel entry circled the length of a field of grass to the double story main house. The four thousand square foot house was built in 1850. Much of the interior woodwork was restored in 1911 in Victorian style. It fashioned twenty-two inch stone walls, a full basement, and a planked floor attic. The attic had full head-room which we thought might be useful after negotiating with the resident bats. There were four stone walk-in fire places. The outside walls were stuccoed and painted white. With its black slate roof, it looked as if it belonged in New England. Four tall pine trees shielded a covered front porch and granted it the name of Whispering Pines.

To the northeast of the main house stood a stone smoke house, once used for smoking meats, fish, and cheese. To the south and across the road was a spring fed acre lake encircled by a mowed lawn path lined with wild flowers. We were told the pond was over seventy feet deep and included water snakes and large turtles. A dilapidated dock butted up against one end of the pond. A small wood row boat leaned on the lower bank.

Further to the south was a stream winding along the length of the property for half a mile. On the other side was a dense forest of birch that shielded the property from the road and protected it from the north winds.

Down on the slope from the main house was a stone spring house with a walk-in fire place. An old wooden door with an iron latch faced the north. We were told that a grounds keeper once lived in the attic of the spring house. The attic's only entrance was from the outside by a ladder through a small opening above the door. The basement of the spring house served as the primary well for the property. Deep underneath flowed a stream and fresh water pumped to the main house all year long.

To the north was a double story barn. A round Pennsylvania Dutch hex decorated the upper front story, ostensibly protecting it from demonic spirits. However, I noticed that the hex was added after the tornado flattened the roof. Someone hastily reconstructed the roof ten feet shy of its original peak.

In an extended family meeting, we decided that Arthur, Margo and their four children would live in the main house. To the main house, we would add an upstairs bathroom. Karen and I would live in the spring house. We wanted to increase its living space while preserving its historical authenticity. We would convert the barn into residential housing and restore the original stalls as rustic rooms for workshop participants.

Arthur had a friend who was an architect. Sebastien Hagenau was a pupil of Mies van der Rohe of the Bauhaus in Dessau, Germany. He was on the faculty at the Illinois Institute of Technology. Fifty-two years old, he was second generation Czechoslovakian and a confirmed bachelor.

The four of us cast the *I-Ching*. As a result of its oracle, we called Sebastien and ask whether he would examine the property. We wanted him to design the architecture for the spring house and the restoration of the barn. Sebastien expressed interest with the qualification that we pay for his travel expenses and a modest fee for the plans after reviewing the property.

Three months later, following a severe January storm, we met Sebastien at the Allentown-Bethlehem-Easton airport. I had seen him a few times before in Pennsylvania. He embraced a rotund frame beneath a bulky sweater outside comfortable trousers. His remaining swatch of silver hair now fully distinguished his unpredictable personality. I knew he owned and lived in a house in downtown Kenosha, Wisconsin. I respected him for his metaphysical perception of nature. Nonetheless, I had forgotten his droll manner and provocative wit. In near silence, we returned to Arthur's row house in Bethlehem.

Arthur and Margo prepared their usual feast on the redwood picnic table in the dinning room. A carbon knife stuck in the table along side a brazed loaf of freshly baked herb bread. To its side was a crock of white butter. Blocks of Jarlsberg and Norwegian goat cheese flanked rolls of Thuringer and summer sausage. An enormous ceramic bowl of romaine lettuce with pine nuts, almonds, tarragon, dill, and olive oil crowned the center of the table.

Arthur and Margo's four daughters joined in the nightly celebration by sneaking a few bites and then seating themselves on the benches. Arthur offered a prayer as the nine of us joined hands around the table. From the living room stereo, sounds of Scottish folk ballads whispered in the background.

Dinner aside, three of the children ran to various rooms of the house to play. The monthly scheduled child started "kitchen privileges." Everyone helped return the food to the refrigerator and stack the dirty dishes atop the tiled counters. The adults adjourned themselves to the living room and sat on a large Oriental rug.

Margo brought in a pot of steeping English tea with an assortment of mugs, a tin canister of sugar, and a pitcher of milk. Superstitiously grabbing our symbolic pieces of identification, each of us carefully scrutinized and selected a representative mug of mood. Undoubtedly, this ritual always made tea taste better than it would, had we not taken such interest.

The recording changed. Classical guitar now melodically strummed to complete the after-dinner ambiance. The conversation spun around stories since last together. Our attention shifted to a knock at the door. Arthur rose from his half lotus position to answer. A gust of frosty wind blew past the heated radiators and slithered along the floor as Arthur opened the door. We noticed that it was snowing heavily outside. I turned and saw a distraught woman dressed in a drab, grey coat with a hood covering her head. Her hands clutched a scarf tightly around her neck and face.

Arthur appeared to know her.

"I really need to talk to you," she said.

Arthur was hesitant. "This is probably not a good time. We have guests from out of town and have just settled from finishing dinner. I would be pleased to meet with you tomorrow at the church."

"I am awfully sorry to trouble you at home, but you don't understand. I am falling apart and I need to see you now. I promise, I won't take too much of your time."

By now, the chilled wind had completely displaced what little heat already warmed the lofty room.

"For God's sake, Arthur, invite the poor girl in before we all freeze to death," Sebastien interrupted and yelled out.

"Please, come in and I will see you for a few minutes," Arthur responded.

The woman entered, looked around, and apologized for interrupting. "Oh, I didn't know you had such a full house. I am sorry to interrupt like this. I appreciate you seeing me. I promise I won't take much of your time," the woman reiterated as she removed her wool scarf.

Margo approached the woman, said hello, and helped her remove her cloak.

"Would you like a cup of hot tea?"

"Oh, I would love a cup of tea. Thank you."

As Margo poured tea, Arthur introduced Tanya as a member of his parish. Everyone seated themselves again on the carpet except Tanya. Tanya stood near the radiator and stared through the large window at drifting, luminous snowflakes. Arthur was surveying his predicament. I presumed he thought it appropriate to talk to Tanya in another room and was trying to gracefully shift the circumstances. As he started to raise his tall frame from the floor, Sebastien softly motioned with his hand for him to remain seated. Without warning, and as if excluding the interruption, Sebastien spoke in a casual manner to those of us seated.

"I visited friends on the beautiful island of Eleuthera a few months ago. Raoul is eighty years or so old with the prideful respect of many children and grandchildren. He lives in a spacious and unpretentious home on a small bluff overlooking the white water mile of his beach property. Though he has never left the island, he has met with kings, queens, and presidents on their visitations."

The room became silent. Sebastien softened his voice.

"His wife, Elese, encouraged me to accompany them to a neighbor's party down the road. She promised me conch fritters, a delicacy from her menu of a regional restaurant she has owned for over thirty years. With dignity and grace, island people have a way of making choice seem superfluous. Obviously, I accepted." Sebastien patted his belly and paused.

"Ahead of schedule, I seated myself in a cushioned bentwood chair on the front porch. The stairs descended to sand dunes gently pitched toward the surf. A silhouetted sunset was symmetrically balanced against a pale blue sky."

"Raoul opened the screen door and walked onto the porch in island attire of fashionable distinction. From the bottom to top he was in his formal dress of leather sandals without socks, white cotton pants, a brocade white shirt, and a black felt top hat with a single gray and crimson feather stretching from the band. Wiping his brow, he scanned the skyline. Knowing he was a person of few words, I spoke ahead. 'You've made a fine life for yourself here my friend. No man could want anymore.' Raoul grinned so that the wrinkles on his face bared the last shadows of remaining sunlight."

Tanya now stood facing the group seated on the floor, warming her back to the heat rising from the radiator. Sebastien paused, sipped his tea, and continued.

"So, we went to this wonderful party. It was a grand gathering of neighbors from the surrounding area. There were tables of fresh fruit and an iron cauldron of fish stew with potatoes, onions, currents, and garlic. Among the delicious dishes, however, none surpassed Elese's conch fritters. Dipped in a spicy hot sauce, I finished a score, and surely approached two, less aware at evenings edge."

Sebastien patted his belly again and poured some more tea into his adopted cup. It was plain clay without a handle and an enameled blue ring at the sipping edge.

"It was past midnight. I looked around for Raoul. I found him sitting on a hewn wooden bench in the shade of a grove of banana palms. He looked tired. His hands were folded in his lap as he gazed toward the crowd with partially closed eyelids. I noticed that Raoul had never moved from the bench for the entire five hours of the party."

"I walked over and touched him on his right shoulder. I said, 'You have never moved from this spot all evening.' He looked at me, smiled, and said, 'No place to go!' I laughed. You see, Raoul was not saying that he did not have a place to go. He was not talking about being homeless, friendless, or resigned to old age. He was beautifully expressing the simple and complete contentment of being fully present without having to move around. He did not need to participate like other people often do to believe they are enjoying themselves and having a good time."

Sebastien paused, looked at Tanya and spoke to her. "I experience you as calmer now and present with us. Am I correct?"

"Yes, I am. Thank you," Tanya said. Tears softly rolled down her cheeks as she seated herself within our small circle on the floor. Sebastien continued.

"Like people who go to parties with an agenda to have a good time, you came here with a purpose. Seeking some imaginary resolution, you came here to find answers. What can we do so you might discover answers for yourself?"

"I don't know," Tanya said.

"Then, how about we listen to your complaint for two minutes," Sebastien said. Perhaps, then we can jiggle something loose."

"Two minutes?" Tanya said. "I don't even know where to start."

Sebastien countered in a firm voice. "Start at your end's wit, where you are now. Crunch what you think is your problem into a capsule, the way you have already swallowed it."

Arthur and I smiled, amused at Sebastien's gentle humor and focus. Tanya gathered a breath.

"Okay. I'm thirty-five. I've never been married and I am tired of being alone. I met this man last year. Until recently, I was terribly attracted to him. He is a wonderful and responsible man. We have spent a couple of nights together every week for the last six months. We hiked into the woods last weekend and he wanted to make love in the snow. I wanted affection and not sex that day. I refused and he walked ahead without me. He complains that I am not sexually adventurous or spontaneous enough for him. However, I do want more of his emotional self. I want more of his time. He doesn't even return my phone calls right away."

Tanya noticed Sebastien look up at the ceiling.

"I know, I'm running beyond my two minutes. I am almost finished. The capsule is that I don't know whether he is being too distant or whether I am being too demanding. I don't know whether something is wrong with him or something is wrong with me."

"Good!" Sebastien responded. "What makes you think that something must be wrong with someone?"

"Our relationship isn't working."

"What makes you think it should be different from the way it is. Maybe its working perfectly well and you don't know it."

"Well, when my pipes in the house freeze in the winter, they need to be thawed."

"That's strange. I always thought it quite natural for water to freeze in the winter, no matter where it is."

"Yeah, but the plumbing doesn't work that way."

"For whom?"

"For me. I mean I don't like it that way."

"That's a different matter, the issue that you don't like it. Right now we are talking about your belief that something is wrong with someone. You think someone has to do something about it. Thus far, your evidence is that the relationship is not working according to your needs, expectations, or desires. Suppose for a moment that your needs and desires are being perfectly fulfilled by a cosmic design to which you have contributed. Suppose this relationship is working perfectly according to cosmic principles. Suppose nothing is wrong with anyone. Suppose this is the way it is. Suppose the pain and conflict you are experiencing is merely present to teach you something."

"That sounds great, but it doesn't make any practical sense."

"To the contrary, it makes impeccable sense by human experience and the laws of nature. Just for a moment, recall a time in your life when you were in absolute bliss, in the pure enjoyment of an experience. Maybe it was an orgasm. Maybe you were running in an autumn breeze with liquid amber drifting all around. Maybe you were watching the flight of an eagle or watching the ice thaw in a spring stream."

Sebastien paused. The room was silent as the rest of us participated in his invitation to Tanya and allowed our minds to drift to memories of ecstatic experiences.

"Now, do you have an experience in mind?"

Tanya nodded.

"Good! Now, is it not true that when you had this experience, there was no difference between you and the experience? There was no observer watching the observed. It was happening without boundaries between you and your object of focus."

Tanya smiled for the first time.

"Yes, that's exactly the way I remember it."

"Was there anything wrong?"

"No, not at all," Tanya enthusiastically replied.

"So, when you don't separate yourself from that which you experience, life is exactly what you would like it to be. You see, when you separate yourself, you make interpretations, judgements, and evaluations of whether the experience is good or bad, enjoyable or aggravating. When you start referencing yourself as the one who is having the experience, you rate the experience by your fictitious expectations. They are fiction in that you created them from the artificial reference of being separate, of being a self that merely observes and records."

"When most of these experiences do not then meet your imagined fantasies, you believe that something has to be wrong with someone. You are then in conflict and pain because you believe that someone needs to change. Something has to be fixed. Someone needs to be something different than they are. Someone or both people are at fault. This circle of the mind continues to reinforce its own reality until you become further isolated from both the world and your experiences. Eventually, you become removed from your experiencing unit of being, your essence that is an integral part of the universe. Do you understand?"

"Yes, I think so. If nothing is wrong with anybody, then I can get on with learning how to deal with the relationship the way it is rather than trying to change it. I can accept the relationship the way it is and focus my attention on what I can learn about myself as my participation in the relationship serves to teach me."

"Excellent! So, now what is the problem?"

"I guess there is none."

"You sound unsure. How do you know?"

Tanya smiled and replied, "There's no place to go."

"Excellent! Now I think it time that we discuss our plans for tomorrow."

Tanya thanked Sebastien, Arthur, and all of us for our time. After another cup of tea, she excused herself and left. I never saw her again. Sebastien insisted that we collectively spend time on the land the next day to determine its "designated currents" in relationship to our desired purposes. We agreed and all went to bed.

The following morning, we awoke to the smells of Arthur frying bacon and baking buttermilk biscuits. Margo energetically depleted the refrigerator and packed a basket for our trip. Following breakfast, we eagerly boarded the wagon and drove to the farm. Snow plowed banks lined the highways from the blizzards the week before. An hour later we turned into the entrance road.

In a blanket of ivory against an ashen sky, the only colors were the chestnut barn, silvery black slate roofs, and veins of emerald from beneath the snow laden pines. Securing our necks in wool scarfs, we paraded behind Sebastien on a tour around the parameter of the lake and north to the barn.

Sebastien remarked that the top of the barn looked like God once sat upon it. He stated this was a good omen, for God never sits twice upon the same throne. I took his meaning to reflect the idiom that lightning never strikes twice in the same place. Inside the barn, Sebastien marveled at the hand hewn beams the entire length of a tree and the two by twenty oak planks of the second story. That glory stated, the remainder of it was a wreck.

A couple of hours later, we returned to the spring house as the focus of our architectural survey. Actually the word, "house" is misleading though accurate. One attic, one room, and one basement does make a house, just a very small one. This house was almost two hundred fifty square feet. Sebastien suggested that since we were planning to live in the spring house, we needed to live in it now for a few hours to feel its soul.

Spontaneously, the five of us divided chores. Karen hauled the supplies from the wagon. Arthur and I shuffled down an embankment and gathered rotten and broken limbs. Margo ripped newspapers she had brought into shreds. Sebastien proudly removed a box of matches that he kept in his breast pocket for his occasional smoke of a pipe. The five of us gathered at the hearth in collective anticipation. Ritualistically, Margo lit the match. The fireplace that entirely encompassed one wall of the spring house choked and billowed smoke into the room.

Sebastien ran outside and looked at the chimney. He came running back inside.

"This old draw hasn't been used in years. It's capped!" he exclaimed.

Not easily swayed by rifts within directed plans, he urgently ran back outside again.

"Arthur, come here!"

Arthur and I bolted outside to find Sebastien dragging a ten foot ladder, the entire length of which was embanked beneath the snowdrifts except the first rung. As we helped Sebastien lean the ladder against the east wall, he quickly climbed onto the roof.

"A hammer. I need a hammer!" Sebastien yelled out.

Arthur ran toward the car and brought back a crowbar. Climbing the ladder I handed it to Sebastien who repeatedly clubbed a steel plate atop the chimney. Several minutes later a cylinder of smoke surged from the smoldering fire below gasping for air.

Inside the latched door we thawed quickly and shed our hooded parkas and soaked boots. Margo spread a wool blanket on the floor and emptied the basket with enough food for all the creatures in the forest. Arthur stabbed a combat knife into a block of cheese, uncorked a magnum of Italian red wine, and poured five crystal glasses to the brim. Sebastien fashioned a toast, he said from a surly, bearded, Irish helmsman he met in younger years on a barge traveling down the Rhine. "May your soul rest in heaven before the Devil knows you're dead."

After our picnic the fire was waning. As a signal for departure, we gathered our gear and returned to Arthur's home. Sebastien started working on rough architectural drafts. He told us after he left that we needed to consult George Nakashima. George Nakashima was a renown Japanese woodworker of samurai lineage[1] who lived in New Hope, Pennsylvania. A previous architect in Japan, he was now a master woodworker teaching ten apprentices the craft of making furniture.

Sebastien left a day later. He promised to forward architectural renderings within a month. Arthur and I made an appointment with George Nakashima for the following week. Arriving, we knocked at a wooded gate entrance to Nakashima's property.

A sign read, "Public Welcome Sundays 12:00–3:00 PM." His business hours were appealing.

After a few moments, a stout, almost bald, Japanese person strolled toward the gate and welcomed us forward. He introduced himself as George Nakashima. The three of us walked to his main studio, an architectural marvel with a cone shaped ceiling of concrete. The ceiling jetted wide and tall toward an entire circular wall of expansive glass that viewed a snow covered valley. Polished planked floors displayed a variety of Nakashima's designed chairs, stools, tables, and cabinets within a home atmosphere.

I asked George why he had surrendered architecture for woodworking.

"After I left Japan, I burned all of my architectural books. They conformed to pedestrian beliefs of architecture that are arbitrary and invasive to nature. They represented conventional consciousness that failed to meet spiritual needs as they tried to control nature. Though, I still occasionally offer my architecture services to churches and temples of worship on special occasions."

George withdrew an album within a sliding door from one of his polished hard wood credenzas. He opened it on a lengthy planked table. It was full of photographs of churches and temples of worship. I casually asked about his recent assignments. George told us the following story.

"Philip Kapleau[2] called me and ask me to design a Zen sanctuary or temple on land he had either recently acquired or was thinking of purchasing in New Mexico. I agreed to experience the land and then decide."

"I flew to New Mexico and spent a few days living on this beautiful mountain. After considerable meditation, I became aware of the design and the exact location of the temple, where it wanted to be placed. When I told Philip of my visions, he said he wanted the temple on the other side of the mountain. I told him that it belonged with the other exposure. He became adamant about it being on the other side of the mountain. I refused the contract. Philip is not Zen.[3] Had he been Zen, he would have known where a temple should be built on this land."

"Other than those instances, I like working with trees. I like taking the discards from all over the world and helping them achieve their proper destiny. Trees don't lie. Their souls are pure."

George was interrupted by one of his family members. He excused himself and took a phone call. As Arthur and I continued to stroll about the room, the interior reflected a distinct austere and modern Japanese style. The only art on the walls were several original Ben Shahn lithographs. They were signed and dedicated to George. George had framed them in walnut, rose, birch, and koa woods. The few books above George's personal desk in a small enclave to the east were all by Sri Aurobindo. George returned. I inquired as to his interest in Sri Aurobindo who, I knew as a Hindu spiritual leader for world union and peace.

George casually replied, "Most books hold little interest for me anymore. These writings are an exception. During 1937 to 1939 I went on an architectural assignment to the ashram of Sri Aurobindo in Pondicherry, Tamil Nadu, India. I was to design and supervise construction of a major building, Golconda, a dormitory. I became a disciple and was honored by being given the Sanskrit name *Sundarananda* ("One who delights in beauty") by Sri Aurobindo."

George excused himself again. He was a person of few initiating words, though most cordial, disclosing, and even intimate on inquiry. He was decidedly more interested in discovering our essence and meeting our inmost interests by sharing his works of nature.

After an hour, George asked if we would like to see a few of the other structures on his property. We toured his warehouse and workshop where ten people were industriously working with both hand and power tools. Next, he asked us into his home completely made of a multitude of hard woods from floor to ceiling. We felt this invitation to be an unusual honor. As a result, I felt comfortable in asking him whether he would consult with Sebastien on the architectural rendering of our property. Somewhat surprising to us, because of his previous declarations of reluctance for architectural consignment, George readily agreed. He invited us to call when Sebastien submitted his plans and said that he would like to experience the property. We were delighted. Thinking that perhaps we were exhausting our welcome, Arthur and I subtly motioned to each other that exit was in order.

At that very moment, George turned to us and asked, "Would you like to see my tea room?" Delighted at the invitation, we graciously accepted. On entry I noticed an entire wall of two mammoth sliding *soji* screens. Inlaid tatami mats covered the floor. In front of the wall opposite the *soji* screens was a small altar. George walked over and proudly slid open the *soji* screens. Though massive and framed in solid hard wood, they softly glided in near silence with the push of a finger. A panoramic view of a serene snow laden valley extended beyond. The air was still and comfortable with a high cloud covering.

We sat on the tatami mats and on our inquiry, George humbly discussed the variety of hard woods used in the tea room and home. Also, he discussed his view of cooperating with nature.

"You know, I often order trees and wood from all over the world that no one else wants. Sometimes they are considered too large for sawing or shipment. At other times these mighty designs of nature have fallen and the land owners merely wish to have them removed. Still other times I have intervened and saved trees from vain destruction in the hopes of restoring their virtue. Most all of the wood I use is unwanted. I do what I can to make it beautiful again, to renew its life into our continued wonder and appreciation of its own."

George paused. In the complete stillness of several minutes we gazed through the opened wall at the tranquil snowflakes beginning to fall.

George summarized, "It is a simple matter of respect. It is a matter of alignment with and not against the nature that we sometimes mistakenly view as outside ourselves. George touched a large supporting beam. These trees, this wood, I like to resurrect their life, their very soul."

The door resounded with a subtle knock. George excused himself. After several minutes, he re-entered and closed the *soji* screens.

"I must go now. There are some matters that need my attention. Perhaps you will come again and visit. And, of course, please call so we can set a time so I can visit with you on your property."

George walked us to the gate. He shook our hands and bid farewell. It was the last time I ever saw him. Several months later, with impending divorces of Arthur and myself again, the project of the farm faded into a disappointing memory.

Zen is Diverse, Intuitive and Synergistic

Similar to currents in a stream, Sebastien Hagenau and George Nakashima exemplified different experiences of the quintessence of Zen. Sebastien was neither pretentious nor presumptive. He was a pensive jester of irrepressible wit. With uncanny provocation, he blended his mirth with a recognition of natural laws and spiritual respect. George lived Zen as traditionally austere. His orientation toward Zen was practical in appreciation and application. With a solemn manner, he reflected a reverence for what he believed to be conspicuous designs of nature.

George lived the first part of his life as an architect designing structures that complimented nature and the land. Feeling that the field of architecture was becoming increasingly commercial and based on profit rather than spiritual harmony with nature, he became a master woodworker. Similar to the sword smiths and calligraphers of ancient Japan, he practiced his craft such that Zen currents became embodied in the physical manifestation of his work. Scrupulously, he selected more than ten apprentices and taught them the craftsmanship of nature in a workshop on his property. He taught them every facet from the selection of a fallen tree to polished furniture. He believed that intelligent awareness was programmed in every cell of life, though he specialized in the souls of trees.[4]

Eido Tai Shimano, Abbot of the Zen Studies Society in New York, wrote of George Nakashima after his death, "He absorbed and introduced three aspects of Japanese craftsmanship; the beauty of simplicity known as *wabi*, a natural uniformity through the achievement of oneness known as *sabi*, and Zen. George's sophisticated skill in cooperating with the nature of nature was appreciated in this country....His greatness as a human being arose from his interest in spirituality, Hinduism, Catholicism, and Zen Buddhism...He was perhaps one of the most spiritual individuals I have ever known...He knew intuitively and sensitively what is for and what is against. He went for the nature, never against. He understood the cooperative nature of nature and his philosophy arose from this universal conformity."[5]

Neither Sebastien nor George pursued their professions solely for monetary gain, notoriety, nor as a result of prestigious and personal requests from their celebrated clientele. Inspirations for their architectural designs, furniture, and craftsmanship were dictated by a confluent awareness of the relationship between people and the living earth. Intuitive sensitivity permitted them to synchronize with natural resources and allow this awareness to influence their designs. After spending intimate time with potential clients in their homes and on the proposed sites of projects, they meditated at length to discover a design that matched a respect for the earth with the needs of their clients. Designs and construction emerged from an intuitive understanding of the mystical harmony and alignment of purpose, person, land, and project.

Sebastien's and George's everyday experiences did not usually originate from conventionally thoughtful deliberation. For Sebastien, every moment was often urgent. For Nakashima, every moment was filled with an automatic acceptance, as if already known. For these artists of nature, living the currents of Zen was an intuitive awareness of the interplay of cosmic forces. Life was to be first intuitively experienced and only then shaped when all components were agreeable and synergistic.

Zen Buddhism is Not Zen

As an organized religion and philosophy, Buddhism migrated from India in the fifth century to China, then to Japan, Korea, and the Western world. As with all major institutional religions, mystically oriented adherents develop methods extracted from nature and oriented toward self-transcendence. In Zen Buddhism, the mystical orientation developed from Indian Buddhism of the Visuddhimagga tradition. This tradition focused on a transcendence of self and a union with the universal beyond worldly identity.

A maverick from orthodox authority and scriptural practice, Zen Buddhism developed through many different lineages, schools, and prominent teachers who initially practiced in China through the *Ch'an* school of meditation. The equivalent Korean translation is called *Son*. With historical development, the practices of meditation for pure awareness and self-transcendence remained as consistent as the orthodox scriptural doctrine of the religion. Zen Buddhism became a religion, philosophy, and meditative method.

Zen Buddhism is now practiced in most countries. However, traditional meditative practice has declined over the last decade. This occurrence is not because of the message, but because of the arduous time required by members of orthodox sects. Meditative practice has also declined in favor of religious doctrine and scriptural knowledge.

Today, there are two prevailing schools of traditional Zen Buddhism in Japan. They are the Rinzai and Soto schools. Each school offers a different emphasis and complementary method of practice. These two schools globally represent divergent views and methods by which people awaken to enlightenment. Both schools agree that while people are already spiritually whole and enlightened, they need focused attention to realize this awareness of completeness.

The Rinzai sect emphasizes that people need to concentrate with the intention of making a dynamic breakthrough of insight, known as a *satori* or enlightenment experience. The Rinzai sect emphasizes the use of the *koan* study, a method employed by Alan Watts and D.T. Suzuki.[6] A *koan* is a puzzling question that cannot be answered by the rational mind. Of course, this is exactly the reason for its use. Well known examples include, "What is the sound of one hand clapping," and "Does a dog have Buddha nature?"

These questions are given to students in meditation to break their normal way of rational thinking. By focusing attention on the *koan*, it serves as a point of concentration. Similar to a *mantra*, spiritual dance, drumming, or song within other mystical traditions, a *koan* re-channels the usual flow of thoughts. Eventually, the rationally unanswerable question begins to make sense with intuitive understanding. Within Rinzai, the use of *koans* is supervised by a *roshi* or teacher who closely checks progress.

The Soto sect believes that people are already completely enlightened. To think that people must "break through" and achieve yet another insight is only one more obstacle people put in their way to free their minds from self-absorption. Even the belief in enlightenment is one more illusive barrier against the simple presence of being. It is another fantasy of desired achievement that people think they want in the future. The imaginary constraints of this illusive goal needlessly require years of struggle and self-deprivation of preferred addictions.

The Soto sect emphasizes *zazen*. *Zazen* is merely sitting in practice. People who practice *shikan-taza* or "just sitting" do not sit with the idea of attaining a breakthrough. They sit with the confidence and faith they are already enlightened. Sitting is merely manifesting this enlightenment. Soto Zen focuses on ceasing to do all those usual activities that people do resulting in believing they are not already enlightened.

The Soto school's focus is on what George Gurdjieff called "objective consciousness" through self-remembering. Similarly, it is what J. Krishnamurti called "choiceless awareness" through self-knowledge. "Just sitting" is a non-activity to allow the stream of consciousness to continue flowing without becoming attached to any invitation. "Just sitting" is practicing "just being" without giving attention to being all those images people think they have to be to live in the present moment.

The practice of "just sitting" includes no conceptions or specified objects of meditation. "Just sitting" is a simple exercise designed to shut down the programmed radio of conventional dialogue inside people's minds. "Just sitting" is "not doing" which helps "no mind." Statues of the Buddha sitting in meditation are not idols. They are representational reminders of a non-attached and empty mind. Buddha icons serenely symbolize the state of total enlightenment without dreaming and without the dramatic interpretations of everyday life.

The Rinzai and Soto schools focus on integrating Zen awareness into the changes and habits of everyday life. The daily integration of increased awareness fortifies new insights. Zen, by any following, requires application rather than naive faith and casual belief. It requires acting on former insights. Each succeeding experience increases an awareness of the similarity and differences between the observer and observed.

Zen itself, however, is not a religion, philosophy, method of meditation, nor intellectual abstraction. Zen does not embody secret wisdom. Zen is not even spiritual in the conventional sense of other-worldly. Neither is it philosophical within conventional academic logic or reason. Conversely, as a method of meditation, it focuses on the miracle of the ordinary in this world and is an anti-religion and anti-philosophy. Zen aims toward an awareness of present events without conventional interpretation that has attached meaning and purpose.

Experiencing or living Zen does not require that people sit in traditional *zazen* or attend a monastery for twelve[7] to thirty years.[8] All tasks can be conducted with an attitude of awareness. The practice of *just sitting* is intentionally the same as Gia-fu's Taoist walking. For that matter, it could be similar to using chop sticks, peeling potatoes, washing dishes, sweeping the floor, cleaning a latrine, or motorcycle maintenance.[9] However, Zen is not similar to activities that encourage a lack of present awareness or preoccupy thoughts. Neither is Zen similar to applying paranormal abilities or mindful intentions.[10]

Zen exaggerates the non-attached mindfulness of being and is illusive to people who prefer laziness or the complication of meaning over the simplicity of being. Understanding Zen is as ineffable as intellectually envisioning the changing currents of a stream. For Zen is to be intuitively lived and not philosophically understood. Through intuitive living people identify with the essence of Zen and not through the linear processes of the rational mind. Specifically, Zen cannot be understood through the bicameral left hemisphere of the brain.

Even the word *Zen* conjures a multitude of varying perceptions, prejudicial associations, and categories. Zen has a reputation that simultaneously misrepresents and confirms itself. Indeed, this is the symbolic message of its essential theme. The vital message of Zen is that people's ideas of reality merely represent an illusion of personal confirmation. Personal identity is attained optimistically at puberty, in adolescence, or at least by mid-life. However, continual affirmation and glorification of identity is not just swimming upstream; it is the monkey of the mind.

Zen is Ecology of Mind

Meher Baba [1894-1969] was an Indian Sufi mystic. He taught his lessons through silence for the last forty-three years of his life. When Meher Baba was in the United States, he was visited by a person who had passed thousands of examinations on his astute telepathic abilities. He was always correct in his readings. This telepathic performed his abilities by writing the thoughts he received on paper rather than verbally communicating them. When he sat before Meher Baba, no thoughts of the mystic registered in his mind. Meher Baba's mind was blank. There was nothing to read. Meher Baba's mind was so vacant that the telepathic wondered whether he was still there when he closed his eyes. He had to open his eyes again to confirm that Meher Baba was still sitting in front of him.

This is similar to what Ram Dass reported with his experiences of Neemkaroli Baba in India. Maharaji, as Ram Dass called him, ingested a large dose of LSD, and to everyone's surprise, nothing happened. When the mind is empty, even psychedelics cannot have an effect on the content of consciousness because there is no attached content.

The conditioned mind acts as a reactive slate upon which sensations and perceptions impress themselves. It is a register. The intentional mind shapes and channels sensations in particular patterns. It is a director. The empty mind allows sensations to pass through without attachment or instruction. It is an empty mirror.[11]

Zen is sometimes translated most simply as "no mind." The basic principle of Zen is there is nothing we have to do. There is no place to return. As Raoul said, "no place to go." Zen awareness begins when people recognize their belief in being a separate observer of an objective reality is ridiculous. This belief is a disguised fantasy they come to believe from an initial and convenient, developmental necessity. However, people do not need to remain the scribes of what they assume to be an external reality. Zen awareness begins with an ability to separate attached, personal concerns from what is conventionally considered as all of "external reality." Most people consider "external reality" as that which is outside their skins. Zen awareness continues with an expansive consciousness of knowing there is no difference between the observer and the observed.

The belief that people need to get rid of an ego to have a mystical experience is non-sense. This mistaken belief raises a couple of important distinctions about mystical experiences that are helpful to clarify. The first distinction is about the idea of possession. No one *has* or owns a mystical experience. People have a personal reference of self. This is often called a well defined ego or self with boundaries. People have a sense of identity, a sense of differentiation from each other and the environment. People have a personally structured consciousness. For better or worse, this individual sense of self is all ours, to have and to behold. However, people do not have a universal self. Human beings are quite naturally part of the universal self.

While people can have a personal experience of the mystical or universal self, it is not personal. They do not own it just because they experience it. People don't have mystical experiences. In a mystical experience, there is no experience of a separate self. When there is not a personal experience of self, people are either crazy[12] or they are the mystical experience.

The second distinction is about the idea of negation. There is no material entity, often called *ego*, to discard. There is usually a disintegrated personality. From bits and pieces there is a disguised personal reference and experience of the most frequently displayed self. This results from a personally structured and conditioned consciousness. However, people cannot get rid of it either directly or entirely.

In trying to directly dismiss it, the effort of will is activated by the personal domain itself. All processes of reflective thought reinforce themselves. All personal belief systems reinforce their own exclusiveness. When the personal self-reference tries to get rid of the personal concern, it empowers itself rather than abandons itself.

Also, to get rid of an ego entirely misses the point. A personally structured consciousness is the only reference and experience that differentiates people from each other. The ego is not an enemy. It is the only reference and experience that makes people unique and personable. The sense of individuality, collectively, is merely the way in which the universe expresses itself.

The simple point of Zen is actually no point at all. In living Zen, people notice that the finite is an inseparable expression of the infinite. Zen students discover their essential nature in the presence of their living. While Zen offers a variety of structural methods to re-awaken people's awareness, they are an extraneous and sometimes cumbersome part of the entirety.

Zen Allows the Stream of Consciousness to Flow

It is a misconception that the point of Zen or the practice of *zazen* is to get rid of thoughts and feelings. Zen allows people to abandon the power they attach to thoughts and feelings. Thoughts and feelings are as enlightened as everything else. The point of "being present" is to allow thoughts to continue so they do not empower conditioned abstractions and negative interpretations of experience. Zen allows the stream of consciousness to flow.

Common sense indicates that each person is an accumulation of conscious and unconscious experiences. Identification is a process by which people attach to favorite stories to describe and substantiate the storyteller. While this is initially essential for human development, insidiously, the process becomes a burden. To establish illusive security or self-importance, people cloud their abilities to experience the present. The methods of Zen simply provide a structure to permit the student to initially dis-attach and inevitably live a life of non-attachment.

Attachment to thoughts and feelings blocks the stream of consciousness. Such attachment blocks accurate perception because people become distracted from the fleeting new moments of the present experience as it continues to change. As the Zen current moves swiftly, people cannot put their feet in the same stream twice.

Separating experiences of the moment from ideologies and even tested opinions is emotionally cleansing and spiritually freeing. Pains and emotions that people harbor in their minds become entities. Anger, sadness, guilt, and feelings of betrayal become barriers because of people's incomplete experience of their fleeting emotions. Prejudices and frozen interpretations do not a fresh experience provide. People miss the show that way. They then wonder why events are not as they expected them to be. Or, they wonder why they are unhappy. Even when people experience unpleasant emotions to their fullest, the energy and power of the displeasure drains. Zen allows people to be more of themselves and increase the wakefulness of ordinary life.

Those paths that focus on the spiritual domain at the exclusion of experiencing emotions miss experiencing the ordinary through the sensual. Pleasure and pain are signals for learning. Soon enough, we all leave this physical body. For a time, we can experience this world through physical sensuality. This is, indeed, cause for celebration and not for cries of desperate relief. As the personal is not in conflict with the universal, neither is the body in conflict with the spirit.

Zen is not a puritanical or aesthetic program. Neither is it a principle of organismic or mental health. Its techniques merely provide a helpful foundation and structure for people to harmonize with the universe and live with satisfaction.

Difficulties arise when the indulgence of personal thoughts and feelings exclude unitive consciousness. Desires, by definition, are particular and not universal. The way in which people determine the personal is by preference. Too many people are as one small leaf, so caught up in their own show they miss the dance of the rest of the tree. They forget their existence is inter-dependent on everyone and everything else. They not only throw the baby out with the bath water, they negate the tub.

CHAPTER SIX
MINDFUL INTENTIONS

With an intention to heal from a second divorce I returned to San Diego and purchased a thirty-two foot Kettenburg sloop. This was a Scandinavian designed racing sloop with which I had less familiarity than the cutter-rig cruiser I grew up building and sailing with my father. I rented a slip in Mission Bay, twenty miles north of the Mexican border, and moved aboard.

I awoke each morning at dawn to the squawking racket of sea gulls scanning in observation of food. Floating winged hunger, they scavenge for breakfast beneath the glass surface of the glistening bay. Diving into the water with concentrated force, they scoop their fresh meals. Then, acrobatically they frolic in the air as if to express joys of satisfaction.

Fishing trawlers silhouetted the sunrise. I began my days in the galley with a breakfast of herb tea, cantaloupe, and grain biscuits from a local bakery that I warmed in the toaster oven. Afterward, I regularly attended early morning sessions of aikido at a *dojo* a block from the beach. Sessions began with the intention of centering existence through concentrated meditation.[1] Students then exchanged turns of defensively throwing attackers on a padded mat. As in *t'ai chi chuan*, the focus of bodily movements was to cancel the opponents force and redirect unbalanced energy with the least amount of opposition. Following this abrupt awakening to body and a quieting of my mind, I returned to the docks.

On overcast days, I fished, read, or visited a kaleidoscopic mélange of boat-people. People who live aboard are exceptionally hospitable, spinning tales of catching trophy-fish or candidly discussing the joys and woes of personal affairs. With a passionate appreciation for the transiency of mortal existence, they follow appetites more often than others in the middle of the day and week. On the docks, invitations for sailing or motoring to sea are usual. Generosity, however, is with an expected code for crew labor, food, or a six pack. Even on the docks, there is no free lunch.

I met a former motorcycle-gang member with a tired belly and tatoos on his arms who frequented his Catalina sloop. Once a week he took overnight voyages. Anchoring at sea, he fancied companionship with two or three of the lesbian strip dancers from local clubs. There was a seasoned Portuguese hermit who lived on an old tug boat and only spoke English to children. Whenever I passed his slip in the evening, he offered me fresh calico bass, yellow tail, or halibut with a wide grin that showed his few remaining front teeth. There was a former millionaire, real estate broker. After an imprudent affair, he lost his fortune in a divorce. Attempting to pull his life back together, he sunk all of his remaining assets into a forty-two foot Grand Banks, a classic motor-sailing vessel. There was a gypsy poetess who cultivated herbs on the starboard railings of her house boat. On occasion, she offered sassafras tea with readings from the Tarot. There was a former minister of the Christian Science Church who had studied in a Himalayan monastery for nearly a year with Tibetan monks. Confused with the ethical principles of religious counseling and Tantric carnal pleasures, he thrived on rescuing sensuous damsels in emotional distress.

On sun-basked days, when not emersed in indulgent laziness, I undertook solo voyages to sea. This experience was entirely different from when I was an adolescent. With solo voyages, alone I was responsible for rig and course. As in life, a sailing craft is never exactly on course. There are winds, calms, currents, tides, and the need to tack to compensate and take advantage of the changes in weather. However, from sailing, I learned that maintaining a course toward a distant target was the only way to reach a destination.

Sunsets viewed from the aft cockpit draped the encroaching evenings with a palate of color. Ravenous pelicans deftly dived beneath refracted mirrors of the sun for their supper. Floating in the bay, a lonely seal claimed a defunct and anchored wooden raft as its territorial home. Mesquite and hickory smoke scented the salty air. Grills ablaze smoked the seascape as hibachis scattered along the docks grilled either catches *de jour* or generic hot-dog and hamburger picnics.

Natural environments create a surreal edge. Their absorbing presence draws attention away from the encroachments of everyday life. Environments of either grandeur or mystery sabotage self-absorption, requiring us to connect with the natural environment. Emotionally purging and then emptying a clouded mind allows time to refocus on emerging central images and themes with mindful intent. The mystical challenge is to clarify and then target precise dreams and visions. Following procedures demand that people accommodate focuses of attention into ordinary life with directed action.

After two months of living aboard, paying detailed attention to the shifts of weather, wildlife friends, and pursuing aikido, a close friend of mine offered a thought. Since he was a psychotherapist, it was conspicuously more than a thought. It was uninvited advise. He suggested I become more socially involved with other people and the mundane activities outside the dock. His concern surfaced that I was withdrawing from the ordinary world and becoming recluse. Outside my casual acquaintances at the *dojo* and on the dock, I had quite comfortably become a hermit. My fixed schedule of rehabilitation did not include social activities by desire. I assured him my waterfront life was well intact and that he need not be concerned. I told him that the ocean, seabreeze, winged and aquatic creatures were the only support I needed. Furthermore, my refuge was a preferred selection of experience.

Stubbornly judgmental and righteously opinionated, he did not accept my rationale. Instead, quite cleverly he suggested that if I wanted to continue being morbid, that he knew of a hospice that was sponsoring a death and dying seminar. It was scheduled the following week at a local mortuary. How enlivening I thought. He continued the thrust of his manipulative and paradoxical invitation by telling me that he had met an attractive, surgical nurse with coal black hair at the last seminar he attended. She was a free spirit and single. Handing me his business card with the time and place of the seminar written on the back, he told me her name was Nichole.

It was strange to me that a hospice seminar on death and dying was meeting at a mortuary. Paradoxically, modern mortuaries are denying theaters of mortal death. Symbolic of embodied immortality, decaying and decomposing corpses are preserved in chemicals. Disfigurements of the ravages of age and destruction are cosmetically restored and then dressed in grandeur gowns of majesty and splendor to look as youthful as possible. After a few years, the only surviving elements are the skeletal remains of bones, teeth, and bits of clothes.

Nonetheless, with pensive reluctance on the scheduled date, I adventured from my encapsulated world. On arrival at the mortuary, the grounds landscaped a pine wooded grave yard. Immediately, after entering through a black, iron gate, I questioned my decision. I viewed the beauty of the grounds as a waste of real estate and would rather see this gardened earth used as a meditative sanctuary or even a park with children flying kites and lovers laughing and kissing on picnic blankets.

Entering the administrative building of the mortuary, I followed directions to a barren room. It was packed with people standing against the perimeters of four walls. There were no windows and no art. I experienced this as an ominous sign of events to come. An empty polished rosewood coffin commanded attention high in the center of the room on a scarlet draped alter. Whispers telegraphed along the rows of mobile bodies leaning against the bare walls. I missed my sea gulls and the cool ocean breeze.

Scanning the nearly thirty participants, it was easy to ferret out Nichole. Shown by her indifferent gestures of grace, she was all that my friend advertised and mysteriously more. Her shoulder length, black hair shinned with a crimson sheen. She dressed in an oversized silk blouse, forest green walking shorts, and heeled sandals. She was charming and the only person talking audibly in the cramped room. She had the full attention of both men aside her. As if two were not enough, she looked at me across the room and smiled. Awkwardly, I returned the same gesture.

An elderly person in a sable suit entered the room and introduced himself as our tour guide. It then dawned on me this event was not a meeting about death and dying. It was not a seminar preparing people for death, postmortem survival, nor compassionate counsel for grieving survivors. No, it was a behind-the-scenes direct sales sojourn through a mortuary. We were now viewing Act One. The opening presentation was a lecture on selecting coffins. This, of course, included much more than I ever wanted to know about various materials, scents, and costs. One coffin even included a music box, the charged batteries of which would probably outlast the remains of the corpse.

Act Two was a stroll through the chapel with an explanation of memorial services that ranged from the frugal plan to the costly grandiose. All during the lecture, a solitary canary chirped in an imprisoned white cage that hung from a rafter. I could only assume this was some designer's concrete metaphor to console the emotionally bereaved and symbolize a duplicate, embodied existence in the kingdom or queendom of heaven.

Act Three was a field trip to the mausoleum in single file. What did they think? That we were going to get lost? Also, I wondered why the remains of any cremated body, the ashes of which are only from bones, should be placed in a tiny box in a marble tomb above the earth. I remembered my father placed the remains of my mother under their favorite rose bush in a garden by their home. And, a Hungarian friend of mind threw the ashes of her deceased husband from a ship near a seaside retreat that he visited often because it impassioned his soul. These ceremonies made sense to me.

The entire performance took more than an hour and seemed like an eternity, perhaps a message the guide was attempting to entrust. For the duration, there was no talking among the audience and therefore no honorable opportunity to introduce myself to Nichole. While somewhat intrigued with her, I had no desire to pursue any companionship at this point in my life anyway.

The production complete, the audience adjourned and walked toward their cars in the parking lot. I thought this to be an excellent idea. As if by destiny, Nichole and I were suddenly walking across the lawn toward the parking lot among rows of tombstones together. I rather nonchalantly introduced myself and mentioned our mutual friend as an excusable reason for introduction.

She smiled and provocatively inquired.

"So, do you believe in reincarnation?"

"Sure, I'm kind of Buddhist."

She laughed and asked, "How are you kind of Buddhist?"

"Well, I don't recite orthodox cannons or habitually sit in *zazen*, but I know about the other side."

"How," she asked candidly.

I suddenly felt cautious, secretive, and embarrassed. From experience I knew not to share mystical beliefs and experiences in casual conversations. Beyond my usual doubt however, I selected Nichole as an exception. She was as curiously empathetic as anyone might imagine.

"What do you want to know?" I inquired.

With a clear track of memory, she responded, "How do you know about the other side."

Not wanting to offer details I said, "I left my body and floated with the wind once."

"Only once?" she said in a playful tone.

I laughed and said, "Well, it's not an experience I have everyday."

"Why not?" she countered.

"Well, it's difficult to get anything else done when you're cruising around all the time."

As we reached her car, we both looked at each other at the same time and laughed. I asked for her phone number in case I became interested in calling her later. She fumbled through her leather, shoulder purse for a pen and scribbled her number on the back of an old grocery list that included a host of fruit and vegetables. I thanked her and left by saying that perhaps we would get together for lunch sometime.

Safely back on my waterfront, I was more fascinated with the strangeness of the afternoon than dazzled by fantasies of Nichole. All memories of the afternoon tranquilly faded as I gazed across the bay watching a lost dove making its way inland.

Two weeks passed. I awoke one morning to a news report on my miniature clock radio. I heard the announcer report that a recent analysis discovered that Chinese food, in particular one portion of either my favorite *kung pao chicken* or *moo shi pork*, contained the same amount of fat as four Big Macs and the same amount of cholesterol as two Egg McMuffins. Also, each of these dishes contained roughly the same amount of salt as two large bags of potato chips or enough sodium for an entire family for a week. The report continued that the reason Chinese people often escape this nutritional travesty, aside from the unmentioned detail that legions awake every morning to exercise with t'ai chi, was they ate twice the amount of steamed rice. This was not the fried rice with the bits of egg in it that I liked. Inevitably, the winner of the most conservative fat and sodium dish was steamed vegetables and rice. That, I could cook in a tin can on the dash of my car in a hot afternoon sun. This was, indeed, depressing news. Now, I knew that nothing was safe.

This same afternoon I was mailing letters and washing laundry. I remember becoming particularly despondent. I concluded that if there was a reason beyond the dismal news of Chinese food, it was that I was becoming lonely. Never intending to call Nichole, her phone number, nonetheless, remained in my wallet. Big hint! If I was planning not to use it, why keep it? Maybe my psychotherapeutic friend was correct.

Impulsively, I stopped at a phone booth and telephoned Nichole. I was pleased to hear her voice. I asked whether she would join me for this evening at an outdoor patio of a restaurant overlooking the bay. Enthusiastically, she eagerly accepted my invitation.

I arrived on the patio early. I ordered a draft beer and looked across the bobbing docks. A late afternoon breeze tossed the rigging lines that clattered against an array of aluminum masts. Nichole arrived late. Again, she was wearing an oversized blouse. Not that I minded, but it was surprising to me I had not noticed that she was either fat or pregnant before. After a proper exchange of introductory remarks, I inquired to satisfy my curiosity.

In a flash of brilliant tact I said, "I don't know how to ask this, but I am wondering whether you are overweight or pregnant."

She laughed and said, "I'm pregnant. Why, does that make a difference?"

I stumbled ahead, "No, no, not at all. Except, who is the father?"

"I don't know," she said. She tossed the right side of her hair back over her shoulder.

"What do you mean, you don't know?"

"I mean, I just found out I'm pregnant."

"Well, how far along are you?"

"About three months."

"Didn't you use any birth control?"

"I was on the pill for several years. I didn't like the side effects. So, I stopped. I didn't expect to involve myself with anyone and didn't give it much thought. Anyway, I favor nature. So, when I did get involved, I used the rhythm method. I felt that if it was meant to happen, then it would happen."

Her explanation was getting weaker by the moment.

I laughed and said, "Well how can you be a nurse and just now discover that you are pregnant. My experience is that most people who are not even nurses dawn a few clues within the first month or two."

In complete candor and still smiling she answered, "I just thought I was getting fat."

By now, both of us were laughing enough to attract attention from the fashionably dressed people sitting at the table nearest us.

"You're kidding," I said.

"No, I'm serious. I just found out a couple of weeks ago."

"Well, how is it that you do not know the father?"

"For six months during the winter I was on ski patrol as a nurse in Aspen, Colorado. I dated three fellows during that time. So, one of them must be the father, but I don't know which one."

I was becoming more curious.

"Are you interested in finding out?"

"No!" she said firmly. "I don't know how I would do that and it doesn't make any difference. Anyway, I don't care."

"Are you going to keep it?" I asked.

"He's not an it," she said.

"How do you know it..., I mean how do you know the fetus is male?"

"I just know."

"Well then, are you going to keep him?"

"I don't know. I only know that the forces of nature have combined for this child to be born. Abortion is out of the question. It's not a religious, ethical, or pro-life issue. Intuitively, I have a simple understanding this particular child needs to be born. I don't know why and I don't know what I'm going to do about the baby."

"What do you mean, you don't know what to do?"

"I don't know whether I want to be a mother beyond the birth. I need to meditate on this."

Nichole shifted the conversation and inquired about me. I was later to learn that she was an exotic blend of Rumanian gypsy heritage and Cuban blood. She was raised in Bermuda and educated on the island as a surgical nurse. Thirty-two years prudent, aggressive, and flirtatious, her only early marriage of two years ended in annulment. Indeed, Nichole devoted herself to passionate adventures with a nourishing riptide of spiritual optimism.

We continued our conversation on the boat that evening and in the bunk below. It is my esteemed male opinion that pregnant women are extremely sensual. Nichole was exceptional in supporting my sentiments. The evening was a delight. Nichole was grateful and surprised. She respected my sensitivity and physical pleasure of her body with child. I was captivated by her mystery and passion, and emotionally comforted by her cheerful and metaphysical nature.

We continued our relationship several times a week and well into the autumn months. My life was inspired. Her baby was stretching "his" limbs. I had fathered two children in my first marriage. As an outside participant, I was familiar with pregnancy and the natural birth process. This time, however, was different. I wasn't the natural father. I did not feel responsible.

Also, Nichole was an unusual free spirit with her own sense of destiny and spiritual responsibility. I never heard her complain nor give the baby the obsessively focused attention of many mothers who notably alter their patterns of everyday activity. With eternal laughter and joy, she was simply living an elated life. Continuing emergency nursing as usual, she was ecstatic about the pregnant experience. She was excited about offering new life without knowing what she was going to do with the child. This was an emerging conflict that I sometimes reminded her she needed to address.

Winter approached. The deciduous trees bordering the dockside shed their leaves. Nichole and I now spent several nights a week together. Arriving home from her hatha yoga class one evening, she arranged fresh flowers and Japanese incense she had just bought. She informed me she had wonderful news. Nichole had practiced yoga for a few years and was now studying with an acclaimed master. People would drive twice a week from three hundred miles away in Santa Barbara and Arizona to study with this master.

"What is it? What is it?" I said enthusiastically.

"Not yet! Light the candles and incense and put on a tape. This is special. It is a gift from the universe."

I followed directions, all the while wondering while watching her silhouetted shape dance about the room. The atmosphere was now suitable according to Nichole. We sat at a small oak table with accents of harpsichord and sandalwood. Nichole was radiant in the flickering candle light across the table. She reached across the linen cloth and gently caressed my hands.

"When I finished class tonight, I walked outside. I just stood there with my arms up in the air, breathing life before I walked to the car. I want the baby to breathe. I want to feel free and unencumbered myself. I want the baby to feel free and unencumbered by any limitations that I might impose on him because of the way I want to live. I've been meditating all week. I am not in the right stage to be a mother. Maybe I will never be. I know I could handle the responsibility and do a good job. It's not that! It's that I feel this baby deserves more than I can give to him now in my life. It's true that I'm afraid, but somehow it feels much more profound."

Nichole sighed and rose to change the tape. She returned excitedly and continued her story.

"Anyway, as I was standing there, this older, quiet lady that's in the class, touched me on the shoulder. She asked me about the baby, my health, and his due date. I told her the baby and I were fine. I told her I had about two and a half months to go and didn't know whether I wanted to keep him. Both of us remained silent for a few minutes. Then, like I'm holding your hands now, she held my hands in hers at my side. She looked into my eyes. 'Nichole, I want your baby,' she said."

The lady continued, "You are not meant to keep this child. I am the family member of a Cherokee Chief. I am married and I am studying to be a medicine woman. The entire Cherokee Nation knows of this male child's birth. You are a chosen person. You are merely meant to be the vessel. You were especially chosen because of who you are for the birth of this boy. You are absolved of guilt by giving him to us. I have been driving this distance from Los Angeles to study yoga and watch you. I know this may sound strange to you, but you were specifically chosen for your understanding of this wisdom. As it's now late, I need to drive back to Los Angeles. However, I would very much like you to call me and let me know your decision. Then, she gave me her phone number on a piece of paper."

"So, how do you feel about this?" I asked.

"I believe in these events, but I never thought this would happen to me directly. I believe her because of her presence, but the plain weirdness of it makes me skeptical. Not only that, but I want to believe in it. If I give the child to her for adoption, it will relieve me of responsibility. Knowing this makes me even more cautious."

I looked in Nichole's pensive eyes.

"How can I help you?" I asked.

"I want you to go to Los Angeles with me and check this lady out."

"You've got it," I promised. "Call her and set a date within the next week and let's complete this decision."

Nichole looked at me and clasped my hands tightly.

"Thank you," she said and added, "I love you too."

The following week we arrived at a typical ranch, three bedroom house in West Los Angeles near Clover Field. After knocking, Carmen opened the door and warmly greeted us. She invited us in and introduced us to her husband who held a doctorate degree and was a physicist teaching at the University of California,

Los Angeles. Also, she introduced us to her three-year old daughter who was well mannered and dressed. The husband gave us a tour of the small back yard. Aside from the freshly mowed lawn, most of the yard consumed a giant cage. It sheltered two handsome Aikita dogs to whom, he proudly introduced us. Carmen continued the tour inside their home. It was immaculate, orderly, and tastefully furnished.

Suddenly, I felt strange, as if I had stepped into a black and white episode of the Twilight Zone. The home was perfectly arranged. The family was perfectly well mannered and socially appropriate. Time only increased the bizarre nature of my experience. If I was watching this experience on television, either I would not believe it or would be waiting for something out of the ordinary to happen. I was aware the family was performing, but then so would I under the same circumstances. After all, they were attempting to show an ideal home and parental environment within which to raise a child.

I felt like a detective or social worker rating the merits of whether the "Smith family" is worthy of adoption. Rationally, I knew I was here to impartially investigate the integrity of the people. I was here to check the environment and support Nichole. However, after an hour, I realized I had no criteria by which to fulfill my assumed role. I knew how to support Nichole. I did not know how to accurately evaluate potential parents, one of whom was claiming mystical identification and destiny. There are few classes for learning this skill.

Detectives look for clues, breaks in patterns, and for objects out of place that don't make sense. Social workers follow a predetermined and Victorian check-list that reads like the qualifications for the Miss America pageant. Here, everything was so perfectly sensible that I felt estranged and absurd.

Carmen abruptly interrupted my thoughts by offering tea and cookies. Her husband served a plate of crisp vegetables, spicy dips, and delicatessen meats. Over lunch, Carmen told us that she and her husband could not birth any more children themselves and wanted to adopt. They had looked for a child for two years. Infants were in such demand they had not been successful.

It was then Carmen had decided to approach the situation through intuitive channels. She stated her "mindful intentions" were consistent with her native American heritage and apprenticeship as a medicine woman. By my curious inquiry, she told us that by authority of her relatives in Oklahoma, she was conducting a three-year apprenticeship, at seasonal intervals, in New Mexico. Obviously, she did not wish to go into more detail. I understood and easily respected her wish.

As Nichole and I had a long drive home, we were ready to leave. Carmen said that she wanted to know Nichole's decision as soon as possible. She would need to prepare. Time was already short. Carmen said that she and her husband would take care of all medical expenses and legal fees for adoption. She added they had the financial assets to provide well for this child. Also, she had two requests. She wanted herself and her husband to be present at the natural birth. And, she wanted the boy to be separated from Nichole and given to her immediately after the birth. Surprising to me, Nichole responded that the conditions and arrangements were satisfactory, should she permit adoption.

Again, Carmen reassured Nichole.

"Remember, you were chosen as the vessel for this child to enter the world because of the timing of this event and your intuitive, spiritual nature. Once you have delivered the child, your task will be complete. You do not need to feel any guilt. This event is a matter of destiny. As such, the child has already been given a name that is known to our tribal elders and holy people."

In a daze, Nichole looked at me with a naked smile as if she felt relieved.

Carmen explained further. "This is why it has been unimportant for you to know the specific father. In fact, it has been in both your and the child's best interests for you not to know. Think about the circumstances. You don't know the father. You are a nurse and didn't even know you were pregnant until nearly three months. You never questioned completing pregnancy and bearing the child. However, for the past three months you have seriously questioned whether you want to keep and raise the child yourself. Nevertheless, if you wanted to offer the child for adoption, you had no idea of how to go about securing or having a voice in the right parents."

Carmine continued, "On this side I have wanted a second child and cannot physically bear one. I have had difficulty in adopting one through ordinary channels. These circumstances are both occurring within the same temporal time. Additionally, it is no accident. Separated by several hundred miles in an area that has nearly twenty-five million people, you and I connect in a yoga class. This occurs only two months before the child is to be born."

Carmen and her husband cleared the table and walked into the kitchen for a few minutes.

I whispered in Nichole's ear. "Did you tell her you didn't know the father?"

"No," she whispered back.

"Did you tell her you didn't know about the pregnancy until three months?"

"No."

"Did you tell her that bearing the child was never a question for you?

"No!"

"Are you sure you didn't mention these events to her?" I pressed.

"Yes, absolutely! Anyway, what difference does it make. They're coming back in. Be quiet now," she whispered and then kissed me on the cheek.

I had listened carefully to Carmen. I took her statements not as a persuasive argument, which they were, but as an orderly account of events beyond ordinary coincidence. Nichole thanked Carmen and her husband for their hospitality. She said she would decide by the next morning and invited Carmen to call at her convenience.

We were about ready to leave when Carmen asked me whether I was still interested in pursuing studies with a medicine man. I had casually mentioned some interest in our earlier conversation, but was ambivalent about her direct query. I said that perhaps I might be interested, but would need to think about it. I said I would get back to her if interested later. She nodded showing approval and said that she would call us in the morning.

The phone rang at seven the following morning. I knew that Nichole had decided to follow through with the adoption. Nichole finished the phone conversation with a smile on her face. She had relinquished the burden of indecision. I asked her what Carmen said on the phone. The conversation was a confirmation of more of the same as the day before. I felt relieved as well. Nichole made some coffee.

"Oh yeah, I'm so excited I almost forgot," she said.

Nichole's conversational manner was always to leave me dangling in thoughtful suspense. She always invited me to tease out informative details.

"Forgot what?" I asked impatiently.

"Carmen said to tell you that right after we left, Archie Fire Lame Deer called from Santa Barbara or somewhere. He said that if you wanted to study medicine with him, it would be okay."

"What?" I asked.

I knew that Archie Fire Lame Deer was the son of John Fire Lame Deer, a Lakota Sioux medicine man.

"You mean she didn't call him. Spontaneously, he just called and offered that invitation?"

"That's what she said," Nichole responded, preoccupied with frying bacon, boiling eggs, and burning toast.

"Oh yeah, and she said a couple of other things."

"What else?" I asked.

"She said that she was preparing her breasts for nursing immediately at the birth."

"Can she do that?"

Nichole laughed.

"Of course, she can do that!"

"How?"

"I don't know; she's a medicine woman."

Fantastic, I thought, and we emotionally settled for breakfast. In the middle of my meditative meal, Nichole popped up again."

"Oh yeah, and another thing."

This time she didn't give me an opportunity to ask.

"I want you to be present with me at the birth. Carmen agreed. What do you think?"

"I like that. I like that very much," I said.

Ahead of time, we appraised the staffs of several major hospitals in the area. Nichole chose one and informed them of our unusual circumstances and special requests. One month later Nichole delivered a healthy son by natural child birth. I was there to support her as was Carmen and her husband. The staff was sensitive and courteous to a caring birth process and respectable celebration. Less than five minutes after birth, Nichole was removed from the room and Carmen took the child as agreed upon. In the same room Carmen started nursing the infant. Nichole, as might be expected, initially had misgivings as she was removed from observation or emotional bonding. However, within a few weeks she accepted her decision as wise for the child and herself.

Reluctantly, I did not accept Archie Fire's invitation for what I now view as mundane priorities in my life at the time. Instead, I sold the boat and reinvested the money. I moved to the suburbs in a cookie-cutter, single family house. Its saving grace was that it was at the end of a development on a canyon. Nonetheless, it was in a neighborhood complete with tricycles on the sidewalks, campers in the driveways, and oil slicks in the street. I took a position as the psychological director of a pain rehabilitation center sponsored by a local hospital. For the next year, I practiced avant-garde psychotherapy in a hundred thousand dollar furnished office in a wealthy suburb and wondered whether I had sold my soul.

Nichole moved in with me. After a year, the relationship ended in disaster. Equally responsible for generating a break in compatibility, Nichole and I simply chose to create conflict to separate. We realized we had well served personal and universal purposes for our time together. Emotional healing and spiritual support were our conscious needs for briefly touching in this world. Little did we know in the beginning that the collective mindful intentions of Carmen, her husband, and the medicine and holy people of the Cherokee nation were also fostering a known child that needed to be born. These events fulfilled the immediate needs of all and spiritually shaped our lives forever.

Mindful Intentions Govern Destiny

Mindful intentions are deliberate beliefs practiced with congruent thought and action that are oriented toward programming future events. They are integrated techniques in which the mind observes itself focusing on fixed mental objects or events.[2] Mindful intentions are not to be confused with casual ideas, attempts, or efforts. They are focused thought forms shown by congruent behavior. Also, mindful intentions are a product of directed attention to a specifically desired way of being. As such, they provide an enhanced experience and quality of life by focusing on a mission and purpose for the living of life itself.

Intentions make the world work. All circumstances and experiences result from either mindful or oblivious intentions. Oblivious intentions occur by default from a lack of awareness and inattentiveness to the field of experience. They are the result of vague awareness, distracted attention, and scattered thoughts. When people are oblivious to intention, they allow others who are attentive and mindful to influence their thoughts, beliefs, and actions. People who are unaware of their intentions often attribute circumstances to luck or fate. Luck and fate are assumed external forces outside personal control or deliberate influence.

Luck is accidental. People who believe in luck think that fortunate or unfortunate circumstances occur by chance. With this belief, good or bad luck is an accidental force that results in fortunate or adverse events by the interpretations of the beholder.

Fate is similar to luck except that it is predetermined rather than accidental. From a mystical paradigm, fate is an excuse for people who do not empower themselves. It is an excuse for people to confirm their victimization by perceiving life as subject to predetermination without any personal intervention.

People who believe in luck and unalterable fate think that some people are especially selected by external forces to experience punishment, misfortune, and suffering, while others receive reward, fortune, and happiness. This superstitious belief serves as a mythical justification for events that appear accidental and occur outside a conventional explanation. Within conventional experience, luck and fate justify belief in hope and existential despair.

There are no accidents within traditional magic. Different from luck, mindful intentions govern destiny by purposeful rather than accidental conditions. Different from fate, they influence destiny by choice rather than by any predetermined pattern. Mindful intentions create the empowering events in our lives by which people spiritually evolve. They require awareness and attentiveness to a limited stimulus field. Mindful intentions provide optimal experiences when people direct courses of action that unite humanity and environment in an interactive system.[3]

Mindful intentions are directed by an active energy that provides a nourishing environment, leading to a *kairos*. *Kairos* originates from Greek and means "ripe moment." The *kairos* is essential for fortunate discovery and creation to arise spontaneously. However, fortunate discoveries and creations only arise spontaneously following a period where concentration or focused attention temporarily exhausts.

After complete effort and a period of relaxation, desired events often occur spontaneously when people do not think about them. They occur when categorical and logical thinking become clear and committed, then confused, and finally relaxed without conscious focus. Direction is initially given by deliberate effort. Integration, though it has structure, seemingly occurs by happenstance. This is the reason people often attribute some circumstances to luck or fate rather than use them as evidence of mindful or oblivious intentions that shape the course of their destiny.

Many people wait to dream until after midnight when all the lights are out and the rates are cheaper. The difficulty with such negligence is that people forfeit opportunities for directing their life. Mindful intentions demand that people expand beliefs, direct actions, and take increasing responsibility for their destiny.

Mindful Intentions Require Commitment

Mindful intentions are different from filling the available time people find themselves having during their leisure life. No matter how pleasant or entertaining, filling leisure time with projects or entertainment is pursuing temporary satisfaction. The only requirement for activities of transient satisfaction are that they adequately satisfy us in the moment by: (1) the impulsive meaning we grant them, (2) the fleeting emotional enjoyment they provide, or (3) through the cognitive distraction these activities provide from unwanted feelings and preoccupied thoughts of dissatisfaction.

Many people learn pessimistic patterns of failure. Eventually, they believe these failures represent all of reality. However, these patterns represent not failings of performance as much as a neglect of setting standards of satisfaction and commitment ahead of time.

A mystical life journey starts the same way as charting a course on the open sea. Charting a direction in life needs to be carefully considered and committed to ahead of opportunity. Various distractions, interferences, and unforeseen events are to be expected. Indeed, this is the reason to predetermine a course rather than allowing varying emotions and unforeseen circumstances to determine life by beliefs in luck or fate.

Varying emotions are *state-dependent*. State-dependency means that as emotional reactions to different circumstances occur, people alter their actions and beliefs accordingly. With state-dependency, people remain puppets to both the events of life and their transitory emotions. Mindful intentions are *trait-dependent*. Trait-dependency means that people follow predetermined values of priority they initially set by a plan of focused attention. Mindful intentions begin by a non-addictive, yet meaningful passion.

Similar to satisfying needs and addictions, mindful intentions demand specific object fulfillment. However, different from failing to satisfy needs and addictions, mindful intentions are a commitment to a specific passion for the long term. Mindful intentions start from contemplated choice and not from habitual hunger. As such, no other passion will satisfy. Mindful intentions are the result of considered commitment and living the charted course as if it were already well traveled territory.

Mindful Intentions are Teleological

In the conventional world, deliberate focuses of attention occur everyday with most everyone. People make breakfast, attend appointments, and follow daily routines. Focusing on goals offers the challenge of continual achievement, always with a focus toward the future.

Motivational psychotherapists suggest affirmations for achieving desired goals. Positive thinking is a valuable process as far as it goes. It is hypnotically suggestive, reinforcing, and self-supportive. However, goals and affirmations are oriented toward the future. They require talking oneself into believing that a desired result will occur in the future. The assumption is that when the goal is fulfilled, it will grant satisfaction or fulfillment. The basic problem with this conventional orientation is that it places the goal of happiness in the future and the object of satisfaction outside one's self. The additional failure of goal-focused behavior occurs when people lower personal goals so, they have a more reasonable chance of achieving them to avoid dissatisfaction. This method fails because focus is on attempts to compromise negative experience rather than experience satisfaction.

First, when people want to win and do the best they can, they cannot compromise their goals to less than socially expected achievement. People cannot settle for the bronze medal and then be satisfied with achievement when they believe the bronze medal socially represents less than the best. Second, if people were successful in convincing themselves that the bronze medal meant limited success, which they cannot do because of the first reason, then they would likely not work hard enough to achieve the bronze medal. This is an expected result when people settle for "less than" and then expect to achieve what they believe represents complete success. While it reflects conventional experience, it does not work by the process of the unconscious mind. Its workability is doomed by dissonant intentions.

Mindful intentions are dissimilar to goal setting. Also, they are not to be confused with Pollyannish inspiration. Pollyannish inspiration is irrepressible optimism. It is the belief that regardless of circumstances, everything will work out for the best. This belief is simplistic and naive. This is like a coach telling an amateur team they will get to the finals by just trying harder. Pollyannish inspiration is a locker-room approach of bolstering wishful courage for the competitive edge. Pep talks have limited effectiveness because people base the suggestions on conscious desires that are in disagreement with developmentally unconscious beliefs.

Mindful intentions are teleological. Teleological means that they are a way of living as if the desired results of expectations already occurred. Being mindfully intent is a way of living as if the selected and passionate purpose in the future determines the reality of the present. All personal reality becomes a once lived mindful intention.

Within conventional experience, pretending is trying to talk yourself into feeling and thinking that you could have what you want if you just tried hard enough. Within mystical experience, pretending is acting by the belief that you already have what you most passionately desire.

Initially, living this mystical way is a new pretend-game. However, people are always pretending, and then pretending they are not pretending anyway. Initially, the conventional disadvantage of focused pretension is that people feel fake. The generic pretense most people play is believing they are a separate and encapsulated ego, only interfacing in limited ways with the universe outside their skin. On a more observable level, millions of people pretend in their professional roles every day. These include mechanics, construction personnel, surgeons, financial officers, politicians, attorneys, and astronauts. Professional actors and actresses merely acknowledge the obvious and make a career of pretending various acts in life.

Mindful intent begins by *acting as if* and is accomplished by imitation, copying, simulation, mimicry, and modeling desired roles. Initially, there is no other way to learn than by pretense. Learning begins by following the successful results of others. The only choices are to: (1) pretend that we are not pretending with the result of developmental and spiritual regression, (2) pretend that we can learn without pretending and stagnate, (3) pretend to achieve the hopeful fulfillment of goals in the future and be continually dissatisfied with the progress, or (4) pretend to live as if goals were already achieved with the result of developmental and spiritual evolution.

Most people already well know, believe, and live the first and second choices. The third choice is the standard for people who believe that are doing something significant about choice one. Mostly, these are people who attempt to succeed and "be real." People who choose this alternative are on the trying treadmill. Living the transient joy of their achievements, they neglect to reach a state of complete satisfaction and accomplishment. The fourth choice requires mindful intention and provides the only satisfactory method for realizing the result of the future in the present.

Mindful intentions expand the opportunity for fulfillment, mastery, and empowerment. However, they are separate from cultural or social standards of success. For, their development is from the ego to the soul to the spirit. As such, mindful intentions provide the framework for transcendence, a shift from the everyday consciousness of gratification to a focus of "making the world work."

Mindful intentions are an expanded belief beyond the conventional experience that the world is either there to serve us or ends up being a disappointment. Living with mindful intentions brings forth a living awareness of satisfaction in being present and not in the wishful fantasies of the future.

Universal Forces Support Mindful Intentions

Thoughts are forms of energy molecules in continuous motion. While people typically expect objects and events to remain the same, change is the constant. Oblivious intentions create haphazard events and chaos. Mindful intentions create ordered motion within programmed fields of encompassing reality. Not only is the universe in order, it maintains a structure through which all forms of energy pervade.

This is particularly observable in the human organism when people determine their path. People who appear lucky actually direct results through mindful intent, commitment, and compatible acts and not through what appears as random or hopeful occurrence. Magicians of the soul create opportunities that mysteriously appear. What appears as coincidence is a collectively orchestrated cosmic dance of designed vibrations making the world work and conducting the spiritual evolution of humanity.

CHAPTER SEVEN
DISCARNATE SPIRITS

Several years ago, two professional colleagues told me about a person they visited often who was especially adept in mediumship. She was a minister and healer of a Spiritualist oriented Christian church. I knew Spiritualists believe that discarnate spirits actively reside in "other worlds." Spiritualists are mediums who claim to contact these spirits and channel their messages and information.

Reverend Anna Franz lived two hours away by car in Colton, California, east of Los Angeles in an agricultural farming community. I drove to an address posted outside a small, wood house directly next to railroad tracks. I knocked on the door. A younger person than I expected opened the door and asked my name and purpose. I introduced myself and said that I had an appointment.

Politely, she invited me inside and said that she was Anna's daughter. I recognized her voice as the person on the phone with whom, I made the appointment. She asked me to wait in the living room. The room was a disheveled conglomeration of books, figurine statues, and worn antique furniture. On waiting, an unkempt, miniature, white poodle hobbled around the house on three legs, occasionally sniffing at my pant leg. I couldn't tell whether it was injured or arthritic.

A door opened down a narrow hallway. An aged woman with a cane left the room. Before she left the house, she pulled money from a tapestry purse and handed it to Anna's daughter. Another elderly woman emerged from the same room. Dressed in a rainbow of layered clothing, she was stout, mildly frumpy, and puffing a cigarette. She introduced herself as "Anna" and ask me to follow her into the same small room down the hallway. She held the door open and called for the dog. As soon as the poodle passed the door entrance, all of its crippling movements suddenly stopped. The poodle became immediately normal in posture and more alive. It walked perfectly well, came over to sniff me again, and casually laid down. Astounded, I made no comment.

Anna motioned for me to take a seat. I sat on a lumpy fabric couch. A wool blanket covered stuffing that appeared through the worn fabric. I looked around the room. There were more than twenty owl images of various sizes, shapes, and materials. The first time I met someone with an inclination for displaying owl icons was with a licensed masseuse I visited as a client in Milwaukee. She had more than a hundred of them. On inquiry, the masseuse told me they were a symbol of wisdom and kept evil spirits away.

The Venetian blinds were closed. The room was dimly lit with a small Victorian lamp with crystal beads dangling from the shade. Nearly a dozen framed portraits hung on the wall. On inquiry, Anna told me they were drawings, paintings, and pictures of her spiritual guides and other psychics. She smothered her cigarette in a battered and filled tin ashtray and immediately lit another one.

Anna looked past me and said, "So, I see that you are in a helping profession also." I had said nothing to her about any personal information. It was likely, however, that this was a good guess, considering my referral sources. She continued telling me about other pieces of information in my past and current situation. All of her information was detailed and accurate. Half of it, no one else could have possibly known, not even my mother. This "reading" took her about ten minutes. I was not aware she was in trance. She talked casually, as if in cordial conversation. I took advantage of a pause in her introduction.

"Okay, I understand that you know what your doing. Let's not take time for credibility issues. I trust you."

She immediately looked at me. "In that case," she said, "let me tell you how we are going to proceed. I am going to tell you some other things about yourself for a while. Then you can ask me questions at the end, if you want." I nodded in acknowledgement.

Anna gazed to a corner of the room and called out a name, "Jason, Jason!," she said, "I need your help." She paused. "Yes, yes, there you are." I did not see or hear Jason. Anna's eyes were fully open. She inquired about me, my past, and my current affairs through Jason, who I later learned was her principal spirit guide. Jason could contact other spirit guides about particular issues or needs. Through Jason, Anna related information about several accurate issues of my immediate past and current conflicts. The primary reason I wanted to meet with her was to gain a better understanding of my previous divorce.

Regardless of other valued relationships, I didn't feel as if I was progressing with my life. Anna completed her reading with a statement about the name of my spirit guide. She then asked if I had any questions. Foolish question, I thought. I began by asking all about my Native American spirit guide, his abilities, tribe, and his etheric being. Evidently, Jason needed to go through a chain of command in the spirit world for this inquiry. Nonetheless, after a while, Jason and Anna transmitted the requested information.

I became sad. She looked at me and asked, "What is it?" I started to cry. With a crackling voice, I asked why my wife had left me. I continued with a rationale of our devotion, mutual compatibility, and romance for more than four years. Our marriage being her second, my wife told me her reason for leaving was that she never wanted to be in a committed relationship. She had said that while I was a perfect partner, she wanted complete independence.

Anna looked directly at me. Her coarse voice raised and she confronted me, "Well, what did you think you were here for, to sit comfortably back and just enjoy the rest of your life?"

My tears stopped. "What are you saying?" I inquired angrily. "Are you telling me that I or anyone else emotionally needs to suffer?"

"No!" she emphatically stated. "I am telling you that your marriage ended because you have more spiritually serious work to do. I am telling you that you have too much to give to the world to deserve an early retirement in mere emotional comfort and passionate paradise."

She stopped. I had no response. I looked at my watch. We had extended beyond my hour appointment. She acknowledged that she had another appointment waiting. Nevertheless, she asked whether I had any other questions. I asked her, whether on future appointments, she would mind if I tape recorded our sessions.

She responded, "You're welcome to do that if you wish. However, I need to warn you. Several other people have recorded sessions, only to later discover their tapes were blank. Jason doesn't like tape recorders."[1] Again, I didn't know what to say.

Before leaving, I inquired further about the framed portraits on her wall. She quickly described the people by name and personal association. I stood to leave and asked her how much I owed her for the session.

She responded, "The session is free. I am a minister and I do this in the name of the church. If you want to make a donation to the church, you may give it to my daughter."

I walked out of the room and handed her daughter what I understood was a usual donation, a twenty dollar bill. The daughter thanked me. As I turned around, the little white poodle walked out of the room. As soon as it passed the door sill, it resumed its crippling posture, hobbled into the living room and curled upon the edge of the oriental carpet.

Ten years later I wondered whether Anna was still available. A friend and a patient had recently ask me whether I knew of a good medium. Also, I had some questions about out-of-body travel. After several attempts of trying to reach her by phone, I discovered from the inheritor of the new phone number, that she had moved with no forwarding information. The elderly person on the phone apologized for being little help as he had received many calls the past year from all over the United States, all asking of Anna's whereabouts. Suddenly, I intuitively knew Anna's spirit had passed on to other worlds. I even considered this another influence as to my recent thoughts of her.

In attempting to locate a new medium, I reviewed a couple of "new age" newspapers. I was discouraged by the language and claims within several advertisements by people offering such services. I then called an owner I knew of a "new age" bookstore. I told him of my dilemma and requested the names of reputable mediums. He gave me two names and scanty information about each person. I immediately rejected these people for the same reason I disliked the newspaper advertisements. I then called a local university that specialized in transpersonal studies. I was given the name of a psychotherapist who knew of a medium with whom she was extremely impressed. In attempts to secure respectable occult contacts, I felt as if I was in the underground of the allied resistance in World War II. However, I knew that effort was an inherent function of the mystical process to show sincere intent.

I called the psychotherapist. She gave me the name of Reverend Chris Meredith. I understood he was British with formal training in England. Later, Chris told me, he discovered his clairvoyant gifts at the age of seven. He began developing his mediumship or channeling abilities at the age of thirteen when he joined a Spiritualist-Methodist Church in Dukinfield, Cheshire, England. Later, he became president of that church and studied for several years with the Spiritualist National Union.[2] Now thirty-seven, Chris lived within a rural Spiritualist community. It was the same one within which I knew Anna had offered readings, healing, and training.

I called Chris to make an appointment. I introduced myself and asked him whether he had known Anna. He said that he had worked with her in healing ceremonies at Harmony Grove and that she had passed on to another world. It was a year later before I made an appointment. I called Chris and reminded him of my association with Anna. I also told him that I was writing a book on magicians of the soul and wanted to continue my mediumship experiences with Anna by including experiences with him. He agreed. We decided to meet for two hours. The first available appointment was three weeks away. Chris informed me that his fee would be one hundred dollars. I ask for directions and he suggested that if I brought an audio tape, he was already equipped to record. Both the fee and the recording invitation were a departure from my earlier experiences.

On the appointed day at eight in the morning, I drove north about twenty miles and into an agricultural countryside. The mountains and rolling hills were lush green as southern California had just received twice its annual rainfall in the last three months. The winding road became narrower and narrower. As I turned onto an even narrower road, I noticed a dairy with several hundred cows feeding in line around a large field. A half mile past the dairy was an overhead sign above a road that read, "Harmony Grove -Spiritualist Association."

I drove through the gate into a miniature community with a score of tiny cottages. I later discovered there were seventeen Spiritualist families on the property, four of whom conducted active practices like Chris, with the others retired. Outside one large bungalow was a sign that read, "Healing Center." A white church with a tall steeple looked more like it belonged in Vermont.

The silence of the morning paused only for a few sparrows and a lady watering geraniums up the road. I located the street address of Chris's small home. To the right of the house was a private garden. A waterfall cascaded into a *koi* pond with several Buddha statues. A picket fence lined a small front yard with a curved path the width of my body to the front door. An orange plaster sun hung on the wall to the left of door. Beside it, a sign read, "Casa Lumininara," which I quickly translated as "house of light."

The door opened and Chris warmly shook my hand. Looking robust and healthy, he wore a royal blue and black wide-striped shirt. It was closed at the neck without a collar and tucked into comfortable matching trousers with black dots. He wore black woven huaraches without socks. In a delightful English accent, he invited me inside.

The interior of his home was modestly furnished. I barely noticed the small reading room to the left with a large sofa and a raised, birch, planked floor. Within the entry was an iron Franklin fireplace elevated on slate. He informed me it was the only heat in the house. Ahead was a kitchen with Spanish paver tiles.

Quickly, we entered through sliding doors to the right. The room encircled three large sky-blue sofas with a patterned oriental carpet in the middle of the room. Chris seated himself on the smaller sofa and requested I sit across from him.

We sat quietly for a few moments. Spontaneously, he arose and seated himself beside me. He instructed me to place my palms on top of his to receive my particular vibration. Following a couple of minutes of silence, he returned to a chair across from me. He told me that he did all of his work in an altered state of consciousness. Depending on the depth of the altered state, he said that sometimes he might even assume personalities of spirits in the other worlds and not to be alarmed.[3] He also asked that when he questioned me, only to answer "Yes" or "No" and that later I could ask questions. He then closed his eyes, inhaled and exhaled a deep breath, and began with an introduction to his work.[4]

"Spiritualists believe that our life here upon the earth is a journey of self in search of self. The purpose of this journey is to evolve spiritual awareness and endeavors. Our mission is to notice and fulfill our potentiality while our spirit manifests in the physical body."

"As we journey in this life, we contact a variety of personal challenges. These challenges provide opportunities for increased awareness and changes in our life's course. Yet, through all of the challenges and changes, we will not be any more spirit than we are at this point here and now. This includes that major change that one day will remove us physically from these surroundings and place us in a more spiritual setting. We are born of spirit. Therefore, it is to the world of spirit that we return when this earthly journey is complete."

"Inevitably, the direction we take is irrelevant. Rather like the roads to Rome, all pathways ultimately have the same destination. At the completion of our current life journey, we return to the world of spirit. There is nowhere else for spirits to return. Our spirit, as the greater part of us, survives physical death and continues beyond the boundaries of this physical world."

"Before even coming to this world we consciously choose the physical body in which we have our being today. In this sense, our body is only a vehicle allowing our spirit to express itself upon this level of life. Our body also allows our spirit freedom of movement here upon the earth. How we manifest our being on this level is entirely our responsibility."

"We arrive upon this earth for a specific purpose. While here, each of us has a mission to accomplish. Each of us has a spiritual blueprint to our life. We come into this world physically to fulfill this spiritual blueprint. Therefore, it makes sense to be given the opportunity to choose this body as a vehicle. The body brings us into contact with those events that will ease the necessary awareness to continue our spiritual quest."

"When we were born into this world, we were born with a second body. This second body is a spiritual duplication of our physical body. As our physical body matures into an adult, this second body evolves with us. This second body is a fraction outside the physical body. It is called the etheric body because it is not visible. The etheric body belongs to the spirit world. Its frequency is normally outside the range of the five senses to which we are accustomed. Even so, it is always present with our physical body as it permeates the physical shell. Without this etheric body, we would not physically exist. The etheric body is that which consciousness will move into. It will become your vehicle in the spirit world. Your consciousness is being deployed through this physical manifestation today."

"As such, your physical manifestation is not a true representation of you. The etheric body always remains with our mind. Once the cord is severed between the etheric body and the physical, the physical body will cease to be because the nourishment will cease. This process is rather like the child when connected to the mother by the umbilical cord. As the umbilical cord is severed, the mother ceases to give nourishment. Similarly, the etheric draws in the energies necessary to maintain the physical body. It is the life source for the physical body. You may eat your food. You may supply nourishment on that level, but without the etherial connection, your body would cease to be."

"The etheric body is joined to the physical by what is called a "silver cord." This silver cord is often seen as a silver light emanating from the crown chakra[5], moving across and attaching to the head of the etheric body. We feed our physical body with food and liquids and this sustains the life force here on this level. However, our mind, body, and spirit, as the trinity of life, needs much more than physical nourishment if we are to maintain the synchronization between the mind and the body."

"Around us in our spiritual surroundings there is an energy that Spiritualists call the "vital force." The Hindus call this *prana*, the breath of life.[6] This energy is vital to maintain structure and form on the earth. Without it, everything around us would simply fall apart. Physically, we cannot draw in this vital force. As a spiritual power, it is now beyond our frequency. However, our etheric is already operating on a higher frequency. As it opens, it can draw the vital force into its being. Allowing it to pass through, the etheric distributes the vital force across the silver cord. The vital force comes in through the back of our physical head, and moves down the spinal column, contacting each of the seven *chakras*."

"Clairvoyantly, these *chakras* are seen as orbs of light all working in unison within the body. Contacting these *chakras*, it disburses the energy and vitalizes the organs of the physical body. Just like our breathing, all of this happens on a subconscious level and continues as long as we need our physical form."

"Death is only an incident in the continuous journey of life. That which is born of spirit can never die nor be destroyed. Death is like walking from one room into another and gently closing the door behind us. When we pass from this world, our spirit releases itself from our physical vehicle. Our mind has been gathering and recording all of the important lessons for our spiritual self while we have been here upon the earth. The mind is the consciousness of our spirit. It is not a physical organ. The mind is pure energy."

"The purpose of physical death is to allow the mind to disconnect from the physical body, move back along the silver cord and reconnect with the etheric body. When this process is complete, the mind force is withdrawn from the physical structure. The cord that joined the two bodies together is severed. The physical is then returned to nature."

"Mindful consciousness is now relocated in the etheric body. The etheric body becomes our vehicle of expression for us in the world of spirit, as today our physical body is expressing our consciousness on this side of life. We are as solid and as real in appearance in the etheric as we are in our physical body. Health conditions in the physical body are not transferred into the etheric."

"Upon arrival in the spirit world, we are met by either family members, friends, or spiritual guides. Spiritual guides are companions who work with us in our journey. Not becoming angels, our character and personality remains identical to what it was in the physical body. The only change that death brings is that we cease to interact on the physical level of the human experience."

"In summary, each person is an important individual thread of the great tapestry of life. We chose this time to come into this world, because we knew that the experiences and events of this vehicle, this body, would bring us into contact with particular earthly experiences. These earthly experiences provide the opportunity for increased spiritual awareness. The responsibility for this awareness allows us to reach increased understanding so we can continue through the many worlds that lie beyond the physical."

"As we begin to look at life in a wider perspective, through the eyes of the spirit, we begin to recognize that each experience that we draw into this journey becomes a platform upon which we develop the higher self. There are no mistakes. There are no coincidences. There is a Divine plan that supersedes all the planning and organizing that you and I may do on this level. This is quite often why we get involved in an experience. We assume that experience is going to work in a particular way. Suddenly, we find the direction of our journey changes. Quite often, we see this happening within the lives of individuals here that need to be brought back into contact with their personal blueprint."

"Many people are often desensitized to the Divine part of their nature. They break contact and distrust their higher self. Quite often then, the journey becomes silted with various fears and problems of these material surroundings. Instead of harmony, we find an inner frustration that is often depicted in their journey. When we come into the light of the eternal truths of life after death, we begin to recognize the essence of the soul's immortal quest."

"Now, as we start to come into contact with you this morning, we want to look into your auric field and share several of the colors that are beginning to emanate. The aura is a field of electromagnetic energy that surrounds the human body and displays aspects of the etheric body as well. It usually extends from six to eighteen inches from the periphery of the physical body. It is like having a rainbow draped over the body because the aura is segmented into seven major rays. Each color correlates to one of your psychic centers."

"Now, if you could view yourself going through this world spiritually, you would see these colors constantly mix and change as you are developing from the human experience. So, it is like viewing a story book of living color that surrounds you. And, this is how the spirit people see you when they come into contact with you. This is how I see you when working on this level. We don't see you in your physical form. We see you in your true colors."

"Now, looking into your aura this morning, one of the predominant colors that is beginning to manifest is a deep, almost turquoise blue. This is coming from the crown chakra at the top of your head. It is moving down the head and shoulders toward the waist line about eight inches from the body. The turquoise ray signifies that your inner being, the Divine part of your nature, is now shifting. It is beginning to reform itself on a much deeper level of awareness. Quite simply, this means that the winds of change are beginning to blow across your life."

"Whenever the origin of change is spiritual, it means everything you come into contact with here upon the physical level is going to be influenced. This is not something to be concerned about because it is positive."

"Beyond the turquoise blue, we see the crimson red around your head and shoulders and moving about seven inches from the body. The crimson red comes from the root chakra at the base of the spine. It deals with the emotions and passions of life and quite often the frustrations and challenges. It is a high energy color. It is being depicted in this part of your journey because you are coming into contact with a variety of emotional challenges. Don't take this part of your journey too personally. This is a time where you need your sense of humor. Try to live lightly, particularly as we move through April and forward into the twenty-second of May."

"Also, we see the daffodil yellow around the head and shoulders, moving toward the waist line, and out again about ten inches from the body. This is emanating in the shape of a sphere. Yellow is the color of creativity. Often, we will see this color in relationship to writers, musicians, and artists. Usually, as individuals on this level aspire to higher levels of mental activity, this color becomes more pronounced in these people. However, it is not limited to them. Although the yellow is governed by the solar plexus, or the natal chakra as it is known, it is a mental color. What this means is that you are beginning to experience creative mental stimulation, moving from one level of understanding onto another."

"This means there is a transition to the super-consciousness. It is known also as the Christ consciousness. The timing is correct for this shift to take place within you mentally. It deals with an expansion of mind. That means this year for you is going to be a year where you can develop your creative flow in a much more pronounced manner. So, there is an awakening that is occurring on an inner level that is mobilizing the mental aspect of your nature. It is your receiving station, if you like, between this world and the next."

"Beyond the yellow, we see the light powder blue ray that is enveloping your whole physical body. It moves out about fifteen inches. This is more in the shape of a cylinder. This color is often depicted as the healing ray. This is how we see it in correlation with you this morning. This means that you have a propensity to come upon the earth here, bringing this healing field with you, to allow you to be in a position of service to others."

"You will find that in many of the lifetimes that you have had here upon the earth, you have been in service to others. You have brought through understanding. You have brought through wisdom. So, there has always been this part of you that has brought enlightenment into this darkened world. So, you have become a light house for those who have become shipwrecked on the ocean of life. And, you see, you are a teacher by your natural self."

"The spirit-people who work with you, work not just on a mental level to bring through knowledge and education. Also, they work through the vibratory tuning of the voice. Communication is an important tool for you on this level of life. We see the throat chakra becoming active for you. The spirit people often will work through the vibratory toning of the voice to bring about physiological and psychological changes of healing with those that you come into contact. Now, it doesn't matter whether they be here or in New York, or in another part of the world. Time and distance do not matter in the spirit world. They will use the vocal tones of the body to bring about changes."

"You can transfer energy through the hands, as well. We noticed that when we held your hands for a moment in the beginning of the session. The energy was building in the palms of the hands. This is a more common way of transferring the energy. However, we feel, for you, that it will come more through your spoken word for now."

"Now, the coloration around you tells us you are an old soul that has had many faces, many places, many times, wearing many hats. And so, in this lifetime here today, you come upon the earth again, not to complete a cycle, but also to bring understanding into a time as our world is changing from one frequency to another. Although there are many stresses and problems, there is new enlightenment coming into this world. Through this, we see an eternal light burning."

"Now, last, but not least, we see the emerald green ray being brought into the aura. This is coming from your waist line, encapsulates the top part of your body, and moves out about ten inches. The emerald green is governed by the heart chakra. It deals with harmony and balance. Quite often, you will notice in this world individuals in the inner cities who seek recreation by the ocean or the countryside. The ocean's blue represents healing. The green countryside of nature represents harmonizing balance. When we come away, we feel refreshed because we have absorbed the energy's frequencies that are necessary for our well being. This is why there are so many problems in the inner cities today, because there is a considerable void of these blue and green colors. You will note that in cities of the world where people have taken care of their immediate environment, parks, and waterways, that personal difficulties decrease."

"Putting these colors together, what does it tell us about you? Well, it tells us that you are coming into a state of balance. It means there is shift beginning to occur mentally and emotionally, causing a spiritual change. There is an alignment where the mind is becoming much more open and receptive to the minds you are attracting from the spirit world."

"Now, this is a mission of partnership for you. There is a partnership occurring where you are connecting with the Divine part of your nature, a shift from one level onto another. You are ready to receive information and understandings that are prevalent to you. Remember, everything in this world and in worlds that surround it are governed by laws. We cannot always force the time. There will be a union with the higher self. It will give you the opportunity to recognize more of who you are and what you are about. With this knowledge, you can recognize the Divine nature that is now becoming active within your being. We could say, now, that you are contacting your personal blueprint that is rising from the ashes."

"You see, a part of your life in which you have been living is now coming to a close. A death is being experienced, but this death is only symbolic. The way of life for you that you have lived is becoming invalid. This is because of the growth that has occurred within you. So, you are releasing and letting go."

"This is a time, where the spirit world is saying to you that you need to recognize your Divine nature by discarding emotional baggage of the past. It is rather like putting a seed into the correct environment so, that it can gain from its environment that which it needs for its nurturing and well-being. There is a joy coming from within, an illumination of the soul. Now, just because we tell you events are going to happen, it doesn't mean they are written in stone. You must play an active role. This life is not passive for you. It has to be active."

"There are opportunities in May that will give you new insight. Be prepared to be flexible. We try to quell many of the anxieties that loom around here, but we do feel, there has been a breakthrough from the spirit world, where you are concerned. You will find, that the dream state is actually becoming active for you. There are particular symbols being brought in and the spirits are experimenting with you in the out-of-body-state. So, sometimes you may get up in the morning and wonder where the night has gone. Sometimes, you may feel as if you have not slept the whole of the evening. Quite often, when the etheric is making shifts like this, it will affect, momentarily, one's connection to the earth vibration. However, they are taking you out of the body.[7] While you are traveling here, you may not have conscious awareness of this experience. More information will be revealed as people here in the spirit world are aware of your work and what you are doing."

"You have had to put to rights much of your personal life before this work could be undertaken. Now is when we have to learn to trust the process, you see. You are coming into a period of wholeness. This will bring to you a heightened sensitivity that is going to allow you to see beyond the physical aspect of what is going on. I said to you earlier that you are an old soul. There is no doubt about this. There are strong karmic influences operating in this part of your journey."

"Now, we feel also at this time that you are drawing from the spirit world a gentleman who is interested in what you are doing. His origin is German. When he was here upon the earth, he would work mainly within hospitals. His work was that of a surgeon. He has continued his work in the spirit world using the forces that are available to him. He is interested in your work. He comes to bring new information and be part of your group. You may well find that your work is going to lean a little more toward the healing side. You may well find there are opportunities for you to understand more about the transference of energy and the impact it has here in the physical world. This gentleman is going to continue to be with you now until the end of the year. Momentarily, a name is not being given to me. He may offer it a little further along in our session."

"We feel this gentleman would have passed with a heart condition into the spirit world. He reached into his later eighties before he came to the spirit world. He came from the Cologne area and it seems that he had traveled several times into the United States where he had a favorable response. He prefers working with you silently because there is a mental compatibility between you and him. I feel too that, he has been working with your physical body. It seems he has been working with the lower part of the neck down the spinal column and the lower part of your back. He is talking about doing some extra work there, bringing the body back into alignment. Have there been any past conditions or problems, especially with the middle part of your back?"

"Yes."

"Is this the result of an accident some years ago?"

"Yes."[8]

"He is aware of this and says we should start to see improvement within the next few months. He says that the stress factor is much better handled now with you than it was some time ago. We think, perhaps in the last two years, that events have started coming together here in your life. There was a time here that events fell apart in your life. Your stress became of great concern to those here in the spirit world. We feel now you are on track with where you need to be and we are working diligently in trying to remove the obstacles that have been placed in your path here in the past. So, recognize there are not one or two personalities working with you. There is a group that is operating in your behalf now."

"There is a lady that also comes to you from your mother's side of the family.[9] She is probably about five foot nine in height. She doesn't carry much weight on the physical frame. Her hair had turned almost white before she passed over to the other side. It appears to be wavy or curly. Her complexion is rather light and

I feel that at the age in which she showed herself to me today, she would probably be in her early eighties when she took her transition. I feel there were complications that were similar to a cancer condition because I feel there was a wasting in the body. This lady would have not suddenly gone over to the spirit world. She suffered a little here before she went over."

"She is gentle within her nature. It seems to me that this lady is associated to your mother. I feel that she would have been here physically when you would have been here around the ages of six to seven years of age. It wouldn't have been much more than that when she took her transition. It seems this lady would have been in and out of your life as if she had seen you born and seen you grow up into your early years, but then she took her transition. She was good with her hands. She would do sewing. She would crochet. She had a wonderful way of making things with fabrics, working with colors you see. She was a spiritual person. She had belonged to one of the orthodox religions here. Has there been connections to the Catholic Church with your family?"

"No."

"Okay. If it is not Catholic, it is high church then, because I feel she had a religion that she tried to live up to. Also, she had a natural sensitivity. Do you know if there is any Scotch in your family?"

"Yes, there is."

"I am seeing some sprigs of heather that is symbolic of connections to that part of the world. This lady draws close to you. She seems to be wanting you to enjoy the journey a little bit more. Have things been rather intense for you over the past five months?"

"Yes."

"She wants you to find the little boy within yourself, you see. She is talking about you being too serious. She sends the message that sometimes you get lost in situations here and forget the joy of the journey."

"Now, to shift, you are going to get an opportunity to see some physical phenomena which is not common in this world today. It will give you the opportunity of seeing the manifestation of psychic energy building here on this level where objects can be moved. This will give you the opportunity to see the powers of the spirits."

"Hum, because of the way the energy is, I would like you to ask some questions about the revealed information and our experience here, if you would. Then, we can probably build up the contact with you again. What would you like to know?"

"What do you mean when you say I will have the opportunity to experience additional psychic phenomena, such as of a psychokinetic nature?"

"We feel again, that we saw this type of mediumship which was prevalent at the turn of the century. It was needed then to gain interest of those within the scientific field. It was also necessary then, to show proof of survival, something that was apart from the medium and could be seen by others regardless of belief system. We feel, again, that this is now necessary in your world as it has become more materialistic. People now need to see and experience from personal vibrations. So, we feel that where you are concerned, there will be opportunity under the protection of the spirit world, to bring you that information and experience the phenomena in a psychokinetic way."

"Also, I can begin to see the ectoplasm beginning to form. This type of mediumship has many dangers for the medium. It is why most of this practice has gone underground. However, it is still prevalent in this country in certain locations. We feel again, that you are ready to have a first hand contact from this experience so you can include this within your work. Do you have other questions?"

"Anna told me the name of my spiritual guide. Can you tell me the same name and even contact this spiritual guide?"

"This is not always possible. You must remember that each medium works on a particular level. He or she will attract those people to them from the spirit world at the same frequency. Now, they are not with us twenty-four hours a day. I can only relate information to you that is brought to me. I cannot demand or determine that unless the information is there available. However, you will find, that if the individual is here and conditions are correct, then they too will give me that particular name. At this point, I do not have that for you."

"Every particular medium, every particular psychic works on different levels. Sometimes, where communication with the spirit world is concerned, we can work on a spiritual level. We can receive that communication or we can work on a psychic level where we pick up more information from the earth and from the character of the individual. So, quite often, depending on the conditions available, there will be a fluctuation of the two levels."

"Also, could you tell me your experience of the similarities or differences between you and Anna?"

"I knew Anna not as well as I would like. I knew her briefly and was familiar with her work. Perhaps in our teaching skills, we differ a little. Perhaps in her personal experiences, in that she came here on the earth, and my own, there was a difference. So, we would interpret events with a little different terminology. However, I would say there is a closeness within Anna's work and my own. I feel that she too, was a medium with psychic abilities because she had spiritual depth, compassion, the light."

"You see, there are psychics and there are mediums. They are different in their work. When we come into this world, we are all psychic because we have the gifts of the spirit. For some people it is latent. Sometimes it does not come into being until there is an experience, lets say like an out-of-body experience or an experience of something traumatic that can awaken that psychic ability."

"There are those who are born into this world, like myself, who experience the opening of the psychic faculties at a young age. Now, I believe from what has been given to me, that both Anna and I are mediums because it is a pathway that was chosen before coming into this world. This is rather like being a cleric, singer, or actor. I believe that mediumship is a chosen profession before coming into this world because there is a spiritual purpose behind it. Now, as I said, a psychic is not always mediumistic which means that the psychic is moving onto an extrasensory level, but is still connecting with the earth. Now, the medium can go beyond the physical level and connect with the spirit world. So, where a medium is psychic and uses psychic abilities, a psychic is not always a medium."

"You see, one of the problems and frustrations with our work is that because we are governed by mental and emotional conditions around us, even aspects of the weather can affect mediumship. So, it is rather like your electricity that exists. We know little about the compound of it. With mediumship, few of us here know exactly how it works. It's like someone saying to you, 'Well, how do you walk?' 'It's something I do, something that is natural within my being.' And, you find that sometimes that the spiritual links are clear and defined. At other times, we might as well go to the beach. There are times, when by circumstances, the information is not prevalent. I have found sometimes that people ask me questions for which I cannot give answers. We find later they needed to find the answer for themselves through the experience of their journey."

"Is the association with our spiritual guides based on karmic lessons that people need to learn or on different reasons for the relationship?"

"Usually, the relationship with the spiritual guide is undertaken long before we come into this world. It is a continued process of evolving here, you see. So, the guides or the spiritual companions, as I like to call them, are those with whom you have made an agreement. They know that when you came into this world physically, they would spiritually help you through the evolving process that you are trying to attain."

"Now, there are some people who come here purely upon the earth, to develop the soul part of their nature. There are those that come upon the earth to bring about specific changes upon the earth and the earth history. For example, if we go back to people in your world, Winston Churchill said before the Battle of Britain that his entire life had been in preparation for that moment. He was quite correct in saying that. He came back, solely upon the earth to help create those necessary changes."

"You said that upon arrival in the spirit world, we are met by either family members, friends, or spiritual guides. Why are these spirits serving our personal needs rather than advancing their spiritual evolution?"

"Oh, now, this is twofold. Through them helping, not with just your needs, but others with whom you come into contact here upon the earth, it is also fulfilling their plan. We see this as like a tier system. There are those from the higher levels helping those in the lower levels, helping those in still lower levels. So, the best possible way in which we can serve the Great Spirit is by serving those around us. Those who have become your spiritual helpers desire to serve. Being of service to you, they help the progression of their own soul nature."

"Remember, reincarnation is not obligatory.[10] It is a law in operation that allows the spirit world to bring persons into this world that are going to help evolve civilization. In other instances, there are those who can continue their evolvement through the many levels of the spirit world. We must remember, again, that one of the primary reasons for coming into this world physically is to individuate the soul. It is to notice the union between yourself and the Divine that we will call God. So, in this world, we can begin to recognize that we are a co-creator. We are part of the Divine force. The more we make the Divine force active in this world, the more defined becomes our path. So, development can take place on both levels."

"How does the mind[11], within the vehicle of the etheric body, know the lessons that need to be learned?"

"When we pass into the spirit world, we notice the many lives that we have lived as they are brought back into consciousness. You see, if you were to come into this world with all the awareness of what you had experienced here in the past, you could not live in this world. You could not complete the cycle with the interference of this information. So, for a time that information is suppressed."

"Now, when you return to the world of spirit, you no longer have the mental or emotional limitations that you do in this physical world. There is greater clarity. A veil lifts. You can review your life and the lessons learned from this journey. It is rather like going to the movies in some respect. From your life experience, you will apply it to your soul nature and what you now need to do. One life does not always need to follow another one. You could remain in the spirit world for hundreds of years before you incarnate again upon the earth.[12] So, we find that within personal awareness and understanding, that you *know* instinctively what you need for the evolution of the soul. Do you have any other questions?"

"Not now."

"Last, we want you to know that in your diversity of pursuing mystical paths, it allows you to be more objective. So, we become a part of all and remain a part from all. It is with diversity that you will find truth. We take from each of these particular areas and put together an understanding of people's expression through the many faiths and beliefs that are available here today. This allows us to understand the God within that we are here to personify. And, because there is such a diversity in the human race, we will see this done in many different ways, each being correct for that person then."

"Interpretation is a problem in this world. Language has barriers and many misinterpretations that historically have created many problems with the organized religions. Psychic phenomena have had to be understood through personal experience. So, we have unfortunately had colorings of these influences throughout history. Unfortunately, we have given religious significance to them. It has been the downfall of mankind. In spite of one's religion, you are going to survive death, you see. Unfortunately, this world controls people. As you well know, religion has been used for political control. So, if everyone today came into a realization that life after death is a fact, and that this world is only a temporal state, then we no longer would need churches. We no longer would need the help of the priests. We no longer would need religion as a way in which to connect with the Divine force."

"I am sure you understand there is wealth and politics in religion today. So, it is not in the churches' best interests to reveal these truths. If you go to the Vatican today, you will find locked within secret chambers, libraries of books that have not been adulterated. There is truth within them that the church does not want people to know. It is an unfortunate state of affairs that man has not learned of his folly. So, your journey will bring to you many areas of the mystical field that will reveal to you the same earring spirit that is manifesting in different manners. For inevitably, God speaks in one tongue, but is understood by all."

I thanked Chris for our morning together and walked onto the small front porch. Without prompting, he added, "Let me in closing just say that your work is going to take some rather interesting turns this year that you have not considered, but life is that way, isn't it. I do feel that your connection to mystical factors is going to become more pronounced. You will find that various cultural aspects will have a great effect upon you throughout your life time here because you have at one time walked through that life experience. In connecting this time around, I see it as completing a cycle. It is almost a sense of coming home. I want you to watch what transpires here. Something special is going to be given to you of a spiritual nature that will carry you through your journey."

As I left Harmony Grove, the reverse of the entry sign read, "No Accidents Today." I took the double entendre to be both a carefully stated suggestion for vigilant living as well as a reminder that no accidents occur in the universe.

Mediums, Channels, and Spiritualists

Anna and Chris demonstrated unquestionable clairvoyant and precognitive abilities. This was also reported by nearly a dozen professional colleagues, most of whom were scientifically oriented and initially skeptical. Whether Anna's and Chris' *psi* abilities were the result of mediumship or the direct channeling of information from discarnate spirits, I cannot confirm or deny their personal experiences.[13]

Anna and Chris were professional in their manner and integrity of presentation. Each had a sincere motivation to lessen human suffering and give to the evolving planetary consciousness. Each devoted her and his entire professional life to this chosen career. Chris believed they chose this service specifically for reincarnating upon this earth again. With a conservative estimation, Anna and Chris have performed more than 125,000 mediumship readings and psychic healings.

The University of Chicago's National Opinion Research Council found that 42 percent of American adults believe they have been in contact with a discarnate spirit. Of this forty-two percent, seventy-eight percent reported they saw spirits. Fifty percent reported they heard the voices of spirits or noises of their interference in the material world. Eighteen percent reported they talked with a spirit directly. Curiously, thirty percent of Americans who report they do not believe in after life, still claim personal contact with a discarnate spirit.[14] This statistic is important in that prior beliefs usually influence later experiences by a "self-fulfilling prophecy" or determining interpretation.

A *psychic* is a person who demonstrates telepathy, clairvoyance, clairaudience, precognition, or other paranormal phenomena and altered states of consciousness with unusual frequency. Identification of being psychic is usually made by people who claim intentional control. However, the term is also applied to those who have frequent uninitiated spontaneous occurrences. The problem with using the word *psychic*, particularly as applied to mediumship, channeling, or Spiritualism, is that it is too general to differentiate variant paranormal phenomena. Also, it is unspecific whether there is consciously directed intention rather than spontaneous occurrence. Further, the term "psychic" does not specify whether the method of receiving information should be credited to discarnate spirits.

A *medium* or *channel* explains acquisition of information by stating they receive and send their information from discarnate spirits of people who have passed on to other worlds. This definition assumes that information comes from the spirit world and not from personally generated paranormal abilities or internal states of consciousness.[15]

In North America, South America, and Europe, many mediums work within Spiritualist associations or churches. These mediums call themselves *Spiritualists* in North America and *Spiritists* in South America and Europe. Since 1939, when England recognized Spiritualism as a religion, it has split into two primary factions. The Greater World Christian Spiritualists acknowledge Jesus Christ as its leader. The Spiritualist National Union does not recognize a particular God-head. These two primary orientations also encompass more than two hundred separate sects or associations. Spiritualism has about a quarter of a million active and regular attending members in Britain. Recent estimations include about 200,000 members in France, 10 million in Brazil, and 150,000 in the United States, with five hundred practicing mediums in New York.[16]

Some Spiritualists also practice psychic healing, psychic surgery, spiritual detachment [ghost busting],[17] out-of-body experiences, and conduct seances. Seances are conducted with a medium and one person or more. Attention focuses on the transmission of energy from the spirit world to prove the "reality" of discarnate spirits. This "reality" reveals "itself" as tapping noises, verbally speaking through mediums in a change of voice, levitating material objects, or in rare instances, the body of the medium.

Anna and Chris were mediums, channels, and Spiritualists, who demonstrated psychic abilities and performed psychic healings. Anna also taught out-of-body experiences (OBEs) and Chris conducted seances. Simply, I refer to both of them, by their preferred choices, as mediums.

Mediums Experience Time and Space as Illusions

Mediums collectively agree that the conventional experience of time and space are perceptual illusions created by attached mental constructs. Within the world of the medium, time and space do not exist. Units of conventionally measured time of the past, present, and future are simultaneously experienced in the present moment. This is the primary reason mediums have difficulty determining the exact conventional time within precognitive experience.

I remembered Chris saying that "we are as solid and real in the etheric body as we are in our physical body." I asked him to clarity the word, *solid*.

"Everything around you today in this physical world appears solid because the molecules and atoms are all vibrating at a particular rate. Everything vibrating at a particular rate makes it appear solid to you. Now, in the spirit world, there are many different frequencies. So, when you move out of the physical body, all that is happening at the change of death is that the spirit becomes quickened. The vibration increases. These vibrations take us out of the ordinary solid world and obstructed universe. We arrive in an unobstructed universe to where again, we deal with a vibratory level that is compatible to us because of our energy. So, again everything will appear as solid because it is vibrating on the same frequency."

"The spiritual world is like an onion, with many layers and skins. Each vibrates on a particular level. Your developmental experience in the world determines the particular vibratory rate and frequency of your spiritual being. When you leave the earth migration, you will move onto that level that is spiritually applicable for you. Each will go according to his or her understanding. If that was not so, it would be like taking a small child in kindergarten and putting him or her in a university. You couldn't comprehend the immensity of your environment. So, as on earth, the spirit world has various levels of consciousness."

"Now, when one moves from the physical into the astral domain here upon this earth, then usually we progress on that level and go into the spiritual halls of learning. We study more of our purpose here upon the earth and receive information that will help us. For some people this comes consciously, depending on their spiritual evolution. For many, it is on a subconscious level.

Mediums Work in Various Levels of Trance

There are many levels of trance. Light trance is almost like inspirational speaking. There is a slight change where there becomes a flow of thought without one having to think about what one says. The intermediate trance state with a medium occurs when he or she contacts and connects with the personality of a spirit. A rapport between the medium and the spirit occurs such that certain personalities speak through the medium. The medium, however is still conscious of what is being said. A deep trance state occurs when the personality and the consciousness of the medium is removed to one side. In this altered state, the spirit functions through the physical realm. The medium assumes all the characteristics of the individual as he or she was here upon the earth.

Later, I asked Chris whether spirits enter physical bodies. He replied, "Now, there has been much dejection about medium trance because many people think the spirit enters the bodies. It is not so. When a spirit person works through a medium, they stand directly to the back and work through the medium in neutralizing the voice box and other personality aspects. They never come into the body."[18]

Assuming personalities or personal characteristics of discarnate spirits does not mean such spirits enter, control, or possess a medium. The event may appear so, because the trance is deep enough for the medium to "role play" the discarnate spirit. However, the assumption of "entry" presumes that the medium is without some experiential point of reference. The assumption of "possession" infers that the medium is without command of exit from the altered state of consciousness or experience. Within this context, the issue is the amount of control the medium retains while in the trance state. While it is possible, these distinctions simply reveal a difference between an amateur and an expert. My experience indicates that most mediums temporarily delegate control to the altered state of consciousness and may exit whenever they choose.

Uninvited Spirits and Demonic Possession

Many people and healers believe that during physical and emotional states of vulnerability, people unknowingly allow earth bound spirits to enter their energy bodies. These spirits are called *alien spirits* [19], or more commonly *lost souls* or *disoriented spirits*. Reportedly, these discarnate spirits are often not aware they have physically died. Others are confused, bewildered, and fearful. As Charles Tart has stated, "dying does not necessarily raise your IQ."[20]

Reportedly, these energy bodies enter, inhabit, or attach to physical beings. Without realizing it, the possessed people are depleted mentally, physically, and emotionally. This event is sometimes called *spirit possession*. I ask Chris whether his experience and knowledge supported this belief.

"I do believe this exists, although, it is not as prevalent as we would have thought it to be. It is true, first, when one uses substances like alcohol or drugs to extreme levels, this affects the spiritual balance of the body. And, as it was once enlightened to me, that is like going to bed at night and leaving your back door open. You see, anything can enter. Quite often, particularly with souls that have gone over with no understanding of life after death, or have gone over in traumatic circumstances, often they will be attracted by the light of those still here in the physical body."

"There were individuals in Great Britain, like Dr. Carl Wickland[21] and his wife, who studied people in mental institutes. Bertha Harris, who was also a well known medium in Great Britain and passed some years ago, also took this line of study. They found there were many people in mental institutes who actually were under the influence of these discarnate spirits and didn't know the effect that they were having upon the incarnate individual. So, I do feel there are many souls who unwittingly get caught and entangled in the life energy of those still in the physical body."

"I assume that you differentiate between spirit possession and demonic possession," I stated.

"Absolutely, most spiritual possessions are not malice."

"You mean, also, they are not intended."

"Correct! Demonic possession is an area that is difficult to define, because the mind has so many undiscovered areas that can create apparent though not actual demonic possession. Rather than an event of possession, these events more accurately depict a psychological obsession of these individuals. Let's remember, just because people pass into the spirit world, they don't suddenly become a saint or a sinner. The only event that changes is one's physical state. The personality and the character remain the same. However, those souls that have been materialistic in their nature, or angry towards themselves and their world, will remain on the lower frequencies of the spirit world."

"It would make a mockery of divine justice if we would think there are spirits waiting here to jump in and grab our bodies from us.[22] The laws of the universe do not allow that! Unfortunately, there are times when there can be these shadowings. Often, possessions that do take place are from those who are a little weak-minded or have a lack of control or esteem. It is for this reason, that we need to attend to matters of the soul."

CHAPTER EIGHT

REINCARNATED LAMAS

For the past five years, my morning routine is to walk five to ten kilometers everyday. Crunching a green apple in route, I combine exercise with a meditative focus of nature. Racoons, skunks, rabbits, and morning doves are frequent at dawn. Occasionally, I am fortunate to see deer, pairs of red fox, or a solitary eagle soaring the landscape in search of prey. Beyond superstition and sometimes even peculiar to me, I watch for ravens and hawks to traverse my right shoulder as optimistic signs favoring my immediate thoughts. Many of these sojourns stretch into the rugged hills, valleys, and dry river beds of Mission Trails Regional Park. More often I journey within the local suburban neighborhood.

A few weeks ago I met a wolf at dawn. I met the animal with mutual realization like respectfully nodding to a familiar stranger. The tradition of shamanism experiences the wolf as a protector. In a moment, I experienced a cordial and respectful contact of understanding beyond words and linear language.

Parked cars flanked a paved roadway. Unusually, I walk along the left curb facing oncoming traffic that is usually oblivious to joggers. I turned a corner and found myself on the right side. In the distance, what I thought to be a large German Shepherd casually trotted toward me on the opposite side of the street. I moved to the left side. The animal crossed at the same moment to the right. Casually passing me, I recognized it to be a wolf. It sauntered without fear as if owning the passage way. After it passed, it looked over its shoulder three times acknowledging to me a courtesy of cautious respect. I felt humbled within its presence of sovereignty and boldness in what mistakenly I had considered was humanized territory.

Within my busy schedule, early hikes in the nearby canyons guarantee the opportunity for communication with guests who join me. In this respect, my daughter and I started walking together the first morning of her visit. She was returning for the holidays after living in Geneva, Switzerland and three months of travel in Western Europe. The last time I saw her was six months before she returned from living two years in Japan and traveling Southeast Asia.

Two days before her leave and during our walk, she asked me about reincarnation. I knew that Karen believed in reincarnation. So, it was not only an unexpected question, but abrupt within the context of our chat that morning.

"Why do you want to know?" I inquired.

"Well, when I try to explain it to other people, they ask me questions that I cannot answer well enough in my mind. This makes me doubt my beliefs and then myself. I mean, is there any proof for it?"

I was quiet for a few moments.

"Proof is a relative issue. The consensus you may be looking for does not exist separate from your personal experiences and beliefs. I only know I have had experiences that confirm life after death and believe there to be a choice in rebirth, the higher one is evolved in consciousness. As a result I don't question it anymore. I even experience reincarnation as superficial as long as I am attentively evolving my life here. On the other hand, it may be an essential belief. Similar to near death and out-of-body experiences, a confirmed belief in reincarnation strengthens mystical realization."

Karen was now quiet. While I wanted to offer her some profound wisdom that would resolve the doubts in her mind, I felt my answer was weak. Our walk ended shortly and I continued my usual activities of the day.

I went to sleep that night feeling compelled to offer Karen something more substantial. I drifted into sleep before any thoughts emerged. I awoke in darkness before dawn and was clearer about my thoughts from a dream. I mentioned the subject of reincarnation again during our walk.

"I want to add a few thoughts to what I said yesterday about reincarnation. If you had absolute proof that your essence would continue, how would you live your life differently now? Or, suppose you had absolute proof that reincarnation did not exist. Suppose your energy will disperse in an unrecognizable form back into a nebulous cosmos. Suppose that beliefs in eternal life or reincarnation merely sooth emotional discomfort. How would you live your life differently now?"

"The answers to these questions are more important than determining consensual or objective reality. I have told you before that my focus is on being and evolving my spirit in this life with gratefulness. I cannot explain how I know my soul will continue after physical death, and how that knowledge makes little difference once you know it. It is simply the way the universe works."

Karen did not respond. We were near the end of our walk, on the same street and at exactly the same time and place she had asked about reincarnation the day before. I continued.

"You asked for proof yesterday. I told you that the proof you may be looking for does not exist. I remembered a story last night, however, that is difficult to discount. As you probably know, His Holiness the Dalai Lama is the spiritual ruler of Tibet. The reigning Dalai Lama was discovered in a village when he was nearly three years old. The Tibetan Buddhist tradition has special ways in which the Dalai Lama and other ranking lamas are to be rediscovered once the current one passes from the physical body. The Dalai Lama knows ahead of time when he will die. So, do other ranking lamas."

"At the time of death, they call forth the senior *geshes* of the order and tell them the next village and time at which they will be reborn. After physical death and at the predesignated time and location, a group of priests visit the village. There, they ask the villagers to bring all the small children who are of the pre-designated age stated by the lama at the time of his death. Some reborn child-lamas can recite scriptures though they have not been taught them."

"While age varies, usually children are before the age of five. Sometimes, the senior monks draw a large circle on the ground. The monks place a multitude of toys and objects within the circle. With the Dalai Lama, they placed several of his former prized possessions randomly within the circle as well. One by one, the monks place each child of the expected age in the village within the circle and watch his or her behavior."

"It's kind of like an ultimate cosmic game. The goal is for the reincarnated lama to touch all of his previous possessions and none of the other objects. The monks determine that the child who accomplishes this task is the reincarnated Dalai Lama, or in other instances, ranking lamas. This process has occurred successfully thirteen times in the succession of the Dalai Lama. It has occurred countless times with other ranking lamas. Now, I would say the odds of that occurring by chance even one time, let alone repeatedly, are several billion to one."

It had been several years since I had told this story. Karen appreciated my story and comments. Our walk ended. We did not discuss reincarnation further. Rather, we gardened and talked about family matters. She left for Switzerland the following morning. I thought nothing more of reincarnation the following week.

The next Sunday, I returned from my walk alone. As usual, I slid quarters in the local machine and grabbed a paper. The feature article on the front page of the *San Diego Union-Tribune* was entitled "Victorville's Little Holy Man—Boy, 5, To Become Buddhist Monk."[1] The article discussed a five-year old boy named

Simon Heh of Tibetan and Chinese ancestry. Geshe Lobsang Tsephel was merely visiting Victorville, California when he met five-year old Simon and later discovered him to be his former reincarnated tutor.

The article reported that Geshe was surprised by their initial conversation. "'I know you,'" the boy told Geshe. At first, the religious leader on a cultural mission authorized by His Holiness the Dalai Lama, dismissed the boy's comments. However, Simon persevered telling him, "'You have been my best friend.'"

Geshe returned to San Diego where he directs a Tibetan meditation center in his home. That night he had a dream about a teacher he studied under as a boy. It was a ranking lama named Lobsang Phakpa. Lama Phakpa died in China in the early 1950's. In quest of the truth, Geshe Tsephel first talked to Simon's mother and grandparents. The boy's natural father did not live with them. Geshe discovered from the grandmother, Dolma Lhakyi that Simon showed precognitive abilities that reliably came true.

The article reported that Geshe wrote to the holy leaders of his earlier monastery in India. Guarding against influencing the outcome, he merely informed the holy leaders that he thought the boy might be the reincarnation of one of five former monks. After consultation, the leaders wrote him back. They ruled that the boy was a monk once named Lobsang Phakpa. With this confirmation, Geshe gave Simon the names Sanggyal (which means Buddha in Tibetan) and Dorjee (which means strong) and gave him a crimson robe made especially for him in India.

On January 3, 1993, one hundred Buddhists in addition to eleven monks visiting from India crowded into Geshe's home for the ancient blessing ceremony of Sanggyal's debut. This was the first step of his journey toward becoming a lama. Following a year, Lama Sanggyal Dorjee would go to India with Geshe to further his training.

After reading the article, I reached for my calendar. The blessing ceremony performed for five-year old Sanggyal Dorjee was on the same day I discussed with my daughter the Tibetan methods for confirming reincarnated lamas.

While the event was an obvious lack of coincidence, I did not understand the meaning of my involvement. Three days later I awoke from a dream that clearly indicated I must write about the subject of reincarnation and include it as the last chapter of this book. There were five pieces of evidence that supported this interpretation. First, the idea to pursue this experience arose within a dream and was not the result of deliberate thought. Second, I was not interested in researching nor writing about reincarnation. Third, there was the obvious synchronicity[2] of the conversation with my daughter, specifically about Tibetan reincarnation. Fourth, we discussed reincarnation at exactly the same time and on the same day as was the official blessing of the reincarnated lama. Fifth, our discussions occurred within the same small suburban location as was the blessing celebration of a reincarnated lama.

The following week I called Sandi Dolbee, the staff writer who wrote the article for the *San Diego Union-Tribune*. A receptionist told me she was on vacation and gave me the phone number for inquiries about the article. Another week passed before I called the referral source. Reaching a recording of the Center for Healing and Growth, I left a message. I then called Sandi Dolbee again. She answered the phone and told me that the phone number given was that of Dr. Walt Rutherford, the appointed contact for the article. Although we had never met, I had known of his name for the last ten years in San Diego as a clinical psychologist. A sixth synchronicity fell into place. We both intermittently taught at the same university. After mentioning this to Sandy, she offered the phone number of Geshe.

I called Geshe immediately and received a message stating only the confirmation of the phone number by an elderly female. A couple of hours later Walt returned my call. Walt was cordial. He said he had meditated within the Buddhist tradition for more than twenty years and specifically with Geshe Lobsang Tsephel for the last three. Several years ago, Geshe had led a team of three Tibetan monastics, representing the Council for Religious and Cultural Affairs of His Holiness The Dalai Lama to the United States. He visited thirteen American Benedictine and Cestercian Christian monasteries and shared inter-religious experience and dialogue for a duration of six months. Walt mentioned that Geshe had recently achieved the distinctive honor of Master of Tantra, an achievement level of which only two monks every year attain in the world. Tantra embraces the highest mystical teachings of Tibetan Buddhism that deal with the transmutation of energy. Geshe had recently flown to India for a fifteen day oral examination and passed. This achievement authorized him to perform and teach any of the Tantric doctrines or practices.

Geshe called back an hour later and said, "Hello! This is Geshe. How are you?"

He responded as if we were already friends. I told him that I just spoke to Walt on the phone. I was writing about reincarnation and wanted to meet with him. After a pause, he said, "You come two o'clock Saturday."

I asked him for his address and we ended our conversation. It was then that I discovered a seventh synchonicity. Geshe lived only one block from my home. The location of his home was not only in the same suburban neighborhood. It was exactly the same house that Karen and I had passed on the two consecutive days when we discussed reincarnation within our five mile walks. It was also at the exact time when the Tibetans prepared for the ceremony and conducted the blessing.

The following Saturday, I arrived at a small suburban house late in the afternoon. The curbside appeal was nondescript. It was so ordinary that in over a thousand times of passing it on my walks, I had never noticed it. I walked into an enclave and knocked on a wooden door. No one answered. I pressed the door bell. A small child opened the door and smiled at me. Across the entryway a group of six people sat on cushions. Beyond the group was a sliding glass door that opened to a small patio with a panoramic view of a canyon to the east. A person with a solid build turned around. He called my name and motioned for me to join them in the living room. I removed my shoes and placed them in line among the others in the entryway. The person stood and introduced himself as Walt Rutherford. Walt gave me his cushion and grabbed another one. He then introduced me around the circle of people seated on the floor. Sequentially, each of the persons rose and warmly extended a hand shake.

To my left was Tenzin Dhonden, a twenty-six year old lama. He began living in the Dalai Lama's palace when he was three years old. At six he entered a monastery where he had studied for the past twenty years. He arrived here a year and half ago. He was bald and dressed in the traditional crimson robe except for a bright red, fuzzy cotton jacket that he wore unzipped. Tenzin was to be a helpful translator since Geshe spoke broken English.

I was next introduced to Geshe who warmly welcomed me. Next Walt introduced me to Ron Wong Jue, a clinical psychologist and past-president of the Association of Transpersonal Psychology. I discovered later that the Dalai Lama commissioned Dr. Jue to conduct workshops in India for instilling spirituality into business. I then met Woody Fulmor, who for the past twenty years had worked in structural integration, a somatopsychic orientation of psychotherapy.[3] Also present was Ann Wen Chang, the Assistant City Editor for the *Chinese Daily News* from Monterey Park, California.

I looked around the room. Five children were running and playing in the hallways, kitchen, and dinning room to my right. I noticed one of them to be the boy lama, Sanggyal Dorjee, who the group casually called Simon the rest of our time. Including Tenzin's mother, several other adults wandered in and out of kitchen, dining room, and the living room during my visit. They took a multitude of pictures and filmed the activities. To my left was a lengthy altar with lit candles and fragrant incense softly scenting the room. Above the altar and extending to the ceiling were several large pictures of Tibetan Buddhist lamas.

Walt interrupted my brief sensual survey of the surroundings. "It's good you came now. Ann was just asking Geshe about the method the leaders in his old monastery in India used to determine than Simon is the reincarnation of his old teacher Lobsang Phakpa. Actually, it was the Abbot of Gaden Jangtse Monastery that finally decided."

I grabbed my tape recorder and turned it on. Geshe looked at my tape recorder, nodded and smiled. Knowing that Native American medicine people and many shamans prohibit tape recorders, I appreciated the approval.

Walt continued, "Tenzin, could you ask Geshe again how the lama in India determined Simon's reincarnation?"

Tenzin turned to Geshe and spoke in Tibetan and responded, "Geshe says he does not know."

Ann, the reporter, interrupted, "In other cases they go to the lake[4] and find it out, but in this case Geshe does not tell."

Tenzin looked at Ann and said, "Yes, Geshe either does not know or will not tell. However, usually, high lamas will tell servants or people who are working for them. They will say, 'I'm going to be born in this or that certain family and when I come out from mother's womb, there should be some letter on my tongue.'"

Tenzin opened his mouth, pointed to his tongue and continued, "So, they make some kind of prediction like this and it will happen exactly as he said. Some lamas don't wish to return. They don't wish people to recognize them. This is the kind of power high lamas have."

Geshe spoke in broken English, "Yes, high lamas say, 'Don't worry. I am guide. I am very tired of this body. I change the body and after this, I come back. So, don't worry. Maybe come, maybe no come. If I don't come, somebody come for you in another time, another place. Someone will always come back to guide you."

Ann asked, "So, Simon is the first lama found in the United States?"

Geshe said, "I think this is maybe second. Another one was found in New Jersey."

Ann continued, "Did the one found in New Jersey already go back to India to study?

Tenzin answered, "It depends on the monastery and the lama of the monastery in the past life. You know, he has to study for twenty to forty years on the philosophy and psychology of Buddhism as represented by that monastery."

Dr. Jue asked, "Was it a boy that was found in New Jersey?"

Geshe said, "I don't know."

Ann responded, "Well, it's impossible to be a woman lama, right?"

Tenzin replied, "No, there can be women, sometimes few. Walt quietly motioned toward an elderly lady in her fifties across the room. She was busy talking to people and performing chores. She dressed in a grey robe and stocking cap. I found out later she was a Vietnamese Buddhist nun, the equivalent of a Lama nun.

Dr. Jue entered the conversation and spoke to Ann, "I don't know if it would help you, but there are tests for reincarnation. However, I think what is more convincing is the clarity of mutual recognition. Simon somehow knows that he is to follow this destiny. The same experience occurred with his Holiness the Dalai Lama. At four years old, he recognized that he was going to go to the *Potala Palace*[5] and that this was his destiny. Now, this is very unusual. It would be like having someone recognize, 'Oh yeah, of course I've been in New York and I need to go back to New York.' Similarly, this occurred with his Holiness when he recognized his personal objects from his past life. I am one of the sponsors for Ling Rinpoche[6] who was his Holiness's senior tutor, and again this small boy is not only very wise in his demeanor. He has an enormous faculty for language. I mean he picks up information as if he has done this a hundred times over."

A lull occurred in the conversation as an elderly Tibetan lady served hot leaf tea in a decorative variety of porcelain mugs.

Ann asked, "So, when he goes to India, does he have to start studying at the first level as the other children? Or, because he is a gifted person, does he get to skip some grades and jump to a higher level to start?"

Geshe responded, "He starts at first level and I think it will be easy because of past lives and stored karma."

"So, right now, do you teach him something, like how to read the Bible or how do you call that...?"

"No."

Ann was surprised, "You don't? You don't teach him? Why?"

Tenzin and Geshe talked in Tibetan. After a few moments Tenzin interpreted to the group, "Geshe doesn't have the time." We all broke out in laughter and Geshe joined in our amusement.

Ann, less entertained that the rest of us, continued her questioning, "Can you tell me the special characteristics of Simon?"

Geshe responded and Tenzin interpreted, "He understands things that his grandmother and grandfather do not understand about past time. He has many predictions that events will happen. Also, when Geshe first met Simon, Simon was telling Geshe that he knows him. Geshe did not know that he knows him."

Woody added, "But then the dream came."

"Yes, then the dream came," said Geshe.

Ann asked, "So, when you meet with Simon, is he always very friendly with you? Is he always happy to be with you?"

Geshe spoke with dramatic aliveness, "Yeah. I am very enjoy. He look at me and say all the time, 'I like YOU.'"

Dai Van Nguyen, a Vietnamese person who I later discovered had studied Buddhism for twenty years and was a student of Geshe, entered the group. He passed around a Vietnamese news journal showing pictures of reincarnated lama children. After enthusiastic discussion, Woody handed me the journal. The facing page included three pictures of small children seated cross-legged in repose positions. He then looked at me and said, "With these little boys you can see there is a kind of wisdom."

I looked carefully at the pictures. In a formal state of meditation, it was true they did not look like most little people I have experienced from all over the world. However, I thought that the "kind of wisdom" that was being seen was as much a projection of the observers' desires. I then looked at Simon playing, laughing, and running around with the other children. I couldn't help wondering whether monastic life, at what would be six years old, was such a good idea. I then remembered that the children in these pictures and Simon were different from other children. They were reincarnated lamas.

While some of my questions had been answered, I had not yet had a polite opportunity to ask about reincarnation as a process not exclusive to the Tibetan lama tradition.

Suddenly, Ann shifted the topic. "Do you know of other religions that emphasize reincarnation?"

Tenzin answered, "Hindu and yes, the Christianity of Jesus, though that is not widely known."

Ann continued, "Knowing that other religions believe in reincarnation, do other religions find someone?"

Spontaneously, I replied, "Not like the Tibetans." Geshe roared in laughter and was pleased with my answer.

With my opening I shaped the conversation toward my agenda. "I thought you were asking perhaps a different question. That is, does reincarnation occur outside the Tibetan Buddhist religion? Were you asking that as well?" I addressed Ann.

"Yes," she said.

Geshe quickly responded, "Ah, of course! Yes! This is freedom. This is highest level."

Tenzin added, "Yes, but a critical point is that many of the discoveries have had to occur with the Tibetans since their exile to India in 1959. This is why rediscoveries are occurring in other countries, to continuing the teachings. There is a special and separate vibration for these countries. And, these past lamas choose to be born in these countries to continue what they have already learned."

"Aside from lamas, does everyone have a choice of rebirth?" I asked.

"Of course!" Geshe said emphatically.

Walt had been in conversation with someone else and turned around to help interpret my question again to Geshe. "The word *choice* is important here. Everybody reincarnates, but when I die, can I say I want to be reborn here or reborn there and determine when? Can I make a choice?"

Geshe responded, "If you study *Dharma*!"

I understood *Dharma* to have a variety of meanings, the most important and frequent being the teachings of Buddha. Of course, Buddhism has many different sects. Interpretations of different sects were not now my interest.

Walt helped clarify, "Say, I don't study *Dharma*. Say, no good study Dharma, now what? Can I still make a choice?"

Geshe responded, "No! No choice. No choice for reincarnation."

"What if this person is a good medicine person as in the Native, South American, or African traditions?"

Tenzin quickly understood my meaning and asked, "Shaman? You mean good shaman?"[7]

"Yes," I said.

Tenzin and Geshe consulted in Tibetan.

Tenzin then answered, "It would still be difficult for them to make a choice of where and when, of location and timing. You see, again, it depends on who makes choice. They have certain types of realization, a certain type of understanding you know, of confidence. The shaman's mind is strong."

I continued to clarify, "So, your understanding is that while a shaman would have an easier time, it would still be very difficult for them to make such a choice."

Tenzin confirmed, "Yes that is my understanding."

"So, the more evolved the soul, the easier it is to make choices whether to return or not, and to choose place and time."

Walt corrected me within the Tibetan tradition, "I would prefer to say the more developed the *mind stream*, the easier it is to make choices."

"What do you mean by *mind stream*?"

Walt responded, "It is that aspect of consciousness that goes through time and takes on different vehicles or bodies.

"This is what I mean by soul." I responded.

Tenzin added, "People who are highly developed in meditative ways, after their body dies, they sometimes continue to sit in a meditative pose for days. Their body does not decay or smell."[8]

Geshe interrupted Tenzin in Tibetan and then turned to me. "Yes, sometimes even three weeks, sometimes one hour."

To clarify, I asked Geshe, "The bodies of the lamas that don't rot for three weeks, those lamas have the greatest choice to return."

Geshe smiled and loudly said, "Ohhhhkay. Oh yeah!"

I added, "Or not!"

Geshe laughed loudly for a few seconds and rocked from side to side and spoke through his laugher, "Or not!" He was amused with my understanding that highly developed spiritual beings may well choose not to return. This concept is consistent within both Buddhist and Hindu tradition.

I continued. "So after physical death, is it the spirit that survives or the human personality?"

Tenzin answered, "It is the spirit. When the mind is severed from the body, it continues as spirit."

"So, then the spirit has an organized memory and recognizable life energy to itself and others within the same realm on the same plane, like Simon."

"Yes," said Tenzin. "And, the mind stream is always changing, both here on earth and in other realms. So, when the physical body dies, there is the same continuity of mind stream."

Walt conferred with Tenzin, "When you finish with your body and come into a new life, it is not the same mind."

"It is not same mind because the mind is always changing. It is the same *continuity* of mind. This is like the words of similar and same. There is a difference. So, here when we say the same continuity of the mind stream, we mean not the same mind stream."

Walt offered a helpful metaphor. "I think of it sometimes like a ray of light that goes for a long distance. While it is different at various points of distance, it is the same ray of light."

"So, there is not going to be another Walt?" I asked.

"Never. Not even tomorrow will there be the same Walt."

"Though the destiny of the mind stream of this Walt will continue."

"Yes."

Dai sat beside me and spoke.

"In Buddhism, there are three parts in your body. There is the physical body. There is the soul. The third part is called spirit. When the spirit resides in the body, they call it mind. When it gets out of your body, they call it spirit. In Buddhism, they believe the soul in your body, after you die, will die with it within three days. What is the spirit? In Buddhism, they call it the foundation of consciousness. It includes whatever you think and whatever you do. All this is included in its memory bank. Storage doesn't mean this consciousness goes anywhere. It resides in there and follows the consequences of good or bad actions. The seed is in there. It travels with you with this life to the other life. So, you bring it up in the next life. Your mind is still there, but it's changed because you go to the *bardo*.[9] It doesn't change directly, but it changes because you go from one state to the other state and usually to the other body. That's the spirit. Now, for example, you are reborn. You lived in your old house and it burned down. Now, your spirit moves to a new house, a new body."

I interrupted, "What happened to the soul?"

"The soul dies too."

"Why does it die?"

"It dies because it doesn't have the body. You get a new soul with a new body. The soul is like a connection between your spirit and your body."

Dai looked at Tenzin and asked for agreement. Tenzin nodded with approval. I realized there was agreement between the Buddhist teachings and my original understanding except a translation of concepts and words.

First, the typical Western concept of soul is that it is bodily immanent. It is dependent on the organismic life of the physical body. The Western concept of soul becomes transcendent spirit after bodily death and either reincarnates or resides in heaven or other worldly realms. In Tibetan Buddhism, the soul was the connective force between the physical body and the mind.

Second, the Western concept of mind usually equates to the intellectual brain and does not continue after physical death.

Western thinking views mind as bodily immanent and defined by physical life. In Tibetan Buddhism, the mind equates to the heart force with organized memory. The mind progresses or regresses with the continuity of the mind stream after physical death.

I looked over my notes for any unanswered questions and found one remaining.

"There is an interpretation by Westerners that if people do not attend to their spirit or mind stream, reincarnation may involve spirits being reborn into animals, plants or even insects.[10]" Tenzin smiled when I said *insects* and discussed this matter with Geshe.

Geshe responded, "It is not necessary."[11]

Tenzin interpreted further, "We have many past lives and much stored karma."

"Yes, but can it happen?"

"Yes, sometimes it does happen, but only after many past lives of spiritual deterioration. You still have the opportunity many times to purify what you have done in the past. But, if someone asks you where you come from, you should say 'yesterday.'"

"As you may know, some psychologists and psychics within the United States do past-life, regression hypnosis so people can remember their past lives. What is your opinion on this matter? Is it a good idea?"

"It's a good idea. It doesn't matter you know, but it is a good idea because it gives a belief to the people. It is inferential reasoning. By depending on logical reasoning, you can improve your past life. This is similar to what happened with Simon and many others. They remember their past life. They say, 'I was in that other family in past life. I want to go and see them, visit them you know.' Sometimes the current parents think they are crazy. Sometimes the family gets very angry because the child keeps saying, 'I want to go to my other family because they are my parents.' Eventually, everyone is happy because the boy gets two fathers and two mothers. With Simon, there is much evidence of past life."

Tenzin changed subjects and spoke about the Sanskrit language. "You know in Sanskrit, one small character takes so many English words to explain. For example, we have one tiny symbol that translates to *samsara*. In English, it means cyclic existence. So, *samsara* is the continuing mind stream, the interminable cycle of birth."

I asked, "Is it not also true that Buddhism refers to *samsara* as the *wheel of life* and that the Buddha's *dharma* offers a means of escape?"

"Yes!"

"I have only one more question."

Tenzin nodded as Geshe stood to adjourn guests who were leaving.

"The religion or belief of Spiritualism accepts that the discarnate spirits of family, friends, teachers, and even animals are frequently around us now in this life time. Sometimes, people call these discarnate spirits 'spiritual guides.' There are other people who believe that these discarnate spirits are stuck within the *bardo* as a result of emotional attachments."

Tenzin said he didn't understand.

Walt explained further, "The people who are Spiritualists believe that around us right now, around Tenzin, there are many spirits. These may be old family members, maybe old teachers, people who are here to help you."

I interrupted and added, "or maybe your old dog."

Walt continued, "Yes, and maybe your old dog. Do you believe that?"

Tenzin answered, "Yeah, we believe that."

Walt asked, "Who are they?"

Tenzin laughed, and said "I don't know. I can't see them. Can you?"

After more laughter and Tenzin and I joking around and saying hello into empty space, Tenzin answered more directly.

"We believe these spirits are in the *bardo* for a maximum of forty-nine days[12] when your mind and certain energies are completely separated from your body. Sometimes less, never more. The *bardo* state is an intermediate state in which the mind wanders. The entities that reside in the *bardo* state can see and hear us, but we cannot see and hear them because they are formless beings."

I asked, "Is it automatic that these formless beings leave the *bardo* after forty-nine days?"

Tenzin answered, "Yes, the *bardo* is only a passage way. By exactly one second till midnight on the forty-ninth day they must make their journey."

"What do you say of those Spiritualists that say they can see or hear your grandmother who died more than twenty years ago?"

Tenzin did not understand. Walt explained further.

"Say, I have psychic powers. Could I say that I see next to you your grandmother who died twenty years ago?"

"To give you the right answer, I would need to know and have certain types of psychic powers to know whether you had the psychic power or not."

"Let's say a person does. Is that possible?" I asked.

"Yes, it is."

"Well then, if someone could see or hear someone's grandmother who died twenty years ago with certain psychic powers, how is this possible if she left the *bardo* by forty-nine days?"

"Oh, well that is easy because they could see her beyond the *bardo* state."

"This would mean that she had not reincarnated."

"Yes, she would not have reincarnated."

"Then, where is 'beyond the *bardo* state' in which she is not reincarnated?" I asked.

"It is in other worlds, in other realms. Remember that reincarnation is a change, a transitional phase. The end return is in the other worlds, in other realms."

The conversation shifted to casual dialogue. I stayed for a while longer and arose to leave. Geshe and Tenzin grasped my hand warmly, thanked me for coming, and welcomed my presence again. Geshe handed me a four by six color photograph of himself and Simon that I appreciated as a token of gratification and acceptance. I left as the sun was setting in the West with a sense of heart felt warmth and appreciation for our brief time together, now, in this life time, in this *bardo*.

Reincarnation and States of Consciousness

The broad definition of reincarnation[13] is the belief that the essence, soul, spirit, or mind steam transfers and continues from one person to another born after the death of the first. Dependent on cultural tradition, this continuous entity is called soul, spirit, or mind stream. It is an organized and recognizable life energy both to itself as well as to other entities. It has an organized memory. The experience within and of this spirit or entity is not as the self-focused personality people conventionally experience themselves through their physical bodies on earth.

The human personality includes many different roles and states of consciousness. It represents change more than a fixed state of consciousness. Those roles and states of consciousness that people most frequently adopt become a personal reference. They become a home base for personal identity. It is this ego-defined personality that people often and mistakenly assume survives physical death or reincarnates.

Reincarnation is not a string of beads, each representing an embodied life and strung together by a silk cord representing a soul that travels through successive lives. An accurate metaphor is that reincarnation is like a pillar of dice. Each die represents a separate life and supports the one above it. As there is no functional connection between the die, there is no ego-identity between successive lives. However, each die depends on the one below it for its foundation in the pillar. Similarly, each embodied life depends on the former for it's continuity of mind.[14] Walt's metaphor of a ray of light is another example. While each ray of light is the same continuous source, it is different at random cross sections of it.

It is reasonable to assume that postmortem consciousness between embodied lives reflects the evolution of consciousness before physical death. Enlightened people reach mystical realization. Their state of consciousness before physical death is one that easily continues to change without attachment to role, personality, or identity. It is this ability, to move from moment to moment without attachment that reflects a flexibility of consciousness. This consciousness also represents less pain in this life and after because identity shifts to a universal reference beyond itself.

Reincarnation is an elected and sacrificial choice by those who are spiritually advanced. It is less an option by those less spiritually advanced who require re-embodiment for continuing spiritual evolution. Reincarnation is compatible with spiritual immortality or eternal life of the spirit with the qualification that rebirth is frequently the rule and not the exception.

A confirmed belief in either spiritual immortality or reincarnation is necessary for a belief in mysticism. However, a belief in either spiritual immortality or reincarnation does not presuppose mystical experience nor identification. To the contrary, belief in spiritual immortality is usually a result of optimistic faith unless intentionally confirmed by self-initiated paranormal events. Even then, the predisposing interpretation is theistic in that the experience is defined as the revelation of a separate and transcendent power or Divinity. An unquestionable belief in reincarnation is an obvious revelation from either paranormal experiences or mystical experiences in which the union with the Divine and the self are experienced as one.

Belief in Reincarnation is Separate from Belief in Eastern Religions

Reincarnation is often equated with Buddhist or Hindu religion, particularly in the Western world. As for its foundation in Buddhism, Siddhartha Gautama, the Buddha, recollected his former births by having visions of human beings vanishing from one state of existence and appearing in another according to their deeds. This experience led to his conviction of rebirth and the karmic law of cause and effect.

Repeated polls have found that twenty-five percent of Americans believe in reincarnation.[15] Less than one half of one percent are practicing Buddhists as defined by membership in a Buddhist Temple or church. In North America the combined number of both Buddhist and Hindu members represents less than two thirds of one percent. The world membership of Buddhist and Hindu believers is less than nineteen percent of the world population.[16]

These statistics offer evidence that more United States citizens believe in reincarnation than the combined number of Buddhists and Hindus in the entire world. Additionally, there are over twenty-five times the number of people in the United States that believe in reincarnation compared to those who are card carrying members of the Buddhist and Hindu religions in all North America. By these statistics, belief in reincarnation does not depend on belief in an Eastern religion.

Belief in Reincarnation Embraces Ancient Mythological Roots

Mythologists note that the myth of eternal return is symbolized through the continuing cycles of nature. Joseph Campbell cites the human experience of the sun daily returning, the consistent and repetitive phases of the moon, the seasons of the year, and the perpetuation of organic birth, death, and new birth.[17] Mircea Eliade[18] affirms that these images are found in all cultures throughout the world, particularly displayed in India, Iran, Mayan, and Aztec cultures.

Joseph Henderson[19] reminds us of the modern celebration of Christmas and Easter as representative of the myth of eternal return, where as members of the faith or not, people unwittingly revere the symbolism of rebirth.

The celebration of Christmas echoes the pagan solstice festival before the birth of Christ. It carries the faith that the harshness of winter in the northern hemisphere will return to the colorful rebirth of life and end hibernation. For the celebration of Christmas was appointed by the Catholic Church to coincide with the winter solstice to compete with the pagan rituals. The winter solstice was the time when most of the ancient sun gods were reborn. These mythological sun gods include the Persian Mithra, Egyptian Osiris, Greek Bacchus, the Roman and Greek Apollo, the Phoenician Adonis, and the Phrygian Atys. Mythologically, at the beginning of the cold and dark Winter throughout the world, these spiritual teachers came to illumine the earth as the sun. With the fulfillment of the myth of eternal return nearing Spring, the soft fluffy Easter rabbit, pastel colored eggs and new fashions dawn the symbolic renewal. The completion of rebirth is experienced as millions in the modern world celebrate the Christian resurrection at sunrise. Still untold thousands plant new seeds for food and shelter as rivers rush forth nutrients from the melting snow.

Mythology alone, however, reduces reincarnation to merely a powerful and existential belief, ultimately devoid of the ontological union with either the Divine or cosmic source. Mysticism expands the belief to include a practical dimension of unification with the Divine or cosmic source for individual and planetary evolution and healing.

Belief in Reincarnation Embraces Ancient Mystical Roots

The **Druids**[20] were the original priests of Celtic Great Britain and Gaul in about 2000-1000 B.C. They believed in the immortality of the soul, transmigration, and apparently in reincarnation since what they borrowed in this life, they promised to pay back in the next. They also believed in a purgatorial hell where they would be purged of sins and then progress to a blissful unity with the gods. The Druids believed all people would be redeemed, but some would need to return to earth many times to learn the lessons of earthly life and to master the intrinsic evil of their personal natures.

The **Eleusinian Greeks** were named after the community in Attica and are believed to have been founded in about 1400 B.C. by Eumolpos. This mystical school then spread from Greece to Rome and then to Britain. The Eleusinian mysteries symbolized the human soul by Persephone, however, they believed that the human soul actually resided in the cosmic world free from the bondage of material constrictions, where it was believed to be vibrant and self-expressive. By this belief, human nature was a transitional illusion, a prison of pain and suffering. The essence of Eleusinian belief was that after-life was the same as human life. This, of course, is the same position of Tibetan Buddhism and the reflective nature of the bardos in human life and after life. People not arising above their ignorance during their life upon this earth, transcend into an eternity to wander about forever, making the same mistakes, yet having the same opportunities for correction, which they made in human form. Similar to Hinduism and Buddhism, then, the Eleusinians believed human birth was repeatedly necessary for correction. They believed that union with the Divine required people to transcend from their material attachments.

Pythagoras [600-500 B.C] was born in Sidon, Syria near Bethlehem, Syria, the birth of Christ five hundred years later. The similarities between Pythagoras and Christ also include: (1) Their fathers [Mnesarchus and Joseph] were prophetically informed their wives should bring forth sons who should be benefactors to mankind, (2) Pythagoras and Christ were born away from home on journeys, (3) The multitudes gave each the same title as the "son of God" as both were supposed to be under the influence of Divine inspiration.

Pythagoras referred to reincarnation as *transmigration* and probably derived his views from India or Egypt. Dr. Margaret Murray, a distinguished Egyptologist, believes that Pythagoras should give credit to the Egyptians. The Egyptian Book of the Dead[21] is a volume written in 1500 B.C. It is actually a treatise to the importance of immortality in Egyptian culture rather than about transcending physical death. Dr. Murray reports that in the well preserved Papyrus of Ani (Egyptian Book of the Dead) held in the British Museum and dating to 1500 B.C., there are nearly twelve chapters imparting the precise spells to reincarnate.[22] The important point, here, is that the Egyptians predated views of reincarnation at least a thousand years before Pythagoras.

The Egyptians withstanding, Pythagoras was nonetheless a champion of what was originally called metempsychosis, the belief of the soul's transmigration into successive bodies. Pythagoras' views of reincarnation included the following: (1) human beings were predestined with a Divine pattern or imprint, (2) ultimately, human beings reach a state where they discard their material nature and function in a body of spiritual ether in juxtaposition to the physical body, (3) from this plane of existence, the spiritual ether ascends into the realm of immortals.

Philippus Aureolus Paracelsus [1493-1541] was a Swiss physician and alchemist with a vast knowledge of chemistry and metallurgy. Performing an early experiment of palingenesis, a term that the Stoics and Pythagoreans used as equivalent to metempsychosis or reincarnation, he reconstructed plants from their own ashes. He sought to prove not only that consciousness and intelligence survive bodily death or deterioration of the physical structure, but they keep the individuality they formerly possessed and remain as organized forces.

The **Theosophical Society**, founded in 1875 in New York City by Mme. H.P. Blavatsky,[23] Colonel H.S. Olcott, and William Q. Judge, among others, was the first significant movement in the Western world to synthesize the beliefs of reincarnation among many mystical ideas in Buddhism, Christianity, and Judaism. The purpose of the movement was to integrate and synthesize the mystical teachings of all religions, philosophies, science, and psychology. Mme. Blavatsky believed that the most important goal of the Theosophical Society was to activate the work of Ammonius Saccas, the founder of the Neoplantonic School of in 193 A.D.[24] Her sincere desire was to "reconcile all religions, sects, and nations under a common system of ethics, based on eternal verities."[25]

The common view of reincarnation supported by Hindu and Buddhist religions, as well as ancient Judaism and Christianity believed that the purpose of soul, spirit, or mind evolution was to attain nirvana or eternal heaven. Nirvana is the final liberation from the bonds of existence outside the cycle of rebirth. Theravada Buddhism regards nirvana as an escape from suffering. Mahayana Buddhism views it as an ultimate realization of the Buddha-nature potential in everyone. The Theosophists, however, approach reincarnation differently. They view rebirth as a normal function of evolution and believe there are infinite possibilities for progression and higher consciousness within an infinite universe. With this view, the human soul as the progressive essence of the spiritual evolution of human beings always can incarnate following periods of rest, assimilation, and a reunion with the cosmic source.

Freemasonry, particularly within the higher degrees, shows a serious leaning toward a belief in reincarnation.[26] While Masonic values state members are free to decide their beliefs, the mystical teachings plainly support reincarnation. Many leading masons found the Theosophical Movement attractive. Mme. Blavatsky was even accorded a high Masonic degree because of her book *Isis Unveiled*. Additionally, most of the forefathers of the Constitution of the United States were Masonic members. As a result, the symbols on both the obverse and reverse sides of The Great Seal of the United States, shown on the back side of the one dollar bill, are a direct influence of the Masonic belief in reincarnation.

Some Scientific Evidence Supports the Possibility of Reincarnation

Neither reincarnation, the survival of organized memory or the soul beyond physical death has been substantiated by conventional science.[27] However, there is enough convincing evidence, even by evaluation from this paradigm, that postmortem survival should remain a distinct possibility for further inquiry. Conventional science suggests that reincarnation cannot be dismissed by alternative explanations that propose coincidence, normally acquired information, cultural or religious encouragement, nor developmental childhood fantasies.

Dr. Ian Stevenson, Professor of Psychiatry and Director of the Division of Personality Studies at the University of Virginia at Charlottesville, is the world's foremost scientific investigator of reincarnation cases. For thirty years, he has filed more than two thousand investigated cases. More than 250 of them were investigated extensively with conclusions of merit.[28] The entirety of these investigations suggests that reincarnation is an actual occurrence. The substantial and majority of cases offer repeated instances that cannot be explained nor dismissed by any other scientific or rational evidence.

Scientific Investigations of Children Offer Evidence for Reincarnation

The most accurate way to investigate and confirm reincarnation is with young children who remember multiple aspects of previous lives.[29] The typical characteristics most childhood cases share are: (1) the child is usually between the ages of two and five when first speaking of a previous life, (2) while an incident or observation that is related to a previous life memory may trigger the child speaking about a previous life, the child usually speaks spontaneously, (3) the child frequently uses adult expressions or language skills beyond age expectation, and (4) unless these memories are supported and reinforced, they begin to fade after the age of five and usually disappear by the age of eight. Convincing cases involve children acting in ways that are strange even from the child's perspective, but are consistent and congruent with the previous personality as reported or known by the child or others.

The Original Unadulterated Bible Contained Passages Referring to Reincarnation

The **Kabala** represents the underlying mystical and esoteric wisdom of the Old Testament. An Italian Renaissance Kabalist and Neoplationist, Pico della Mirandola (1463-1494 A.D.) stated the profound teachers such as Moses orally transmitted beliefs through seventy wise men in a continuous tradition until they were written into the Kabala.[30] Those of Judaic faith who initially identified themselves as Kabalists were the Tanaiim living in Jerusalem at the beginning of the third century B.C.[31]

In the modern and altered King James Version of the Old Testament, there are only a few, vague, remaining passages that refer to reincarnation. However, the Old Testament as interpreted by the mystical Kabalists, confirms their belief in reincarnation. G.F. Moore in an Ingersoll Lecture on reincarnation in 1914 at Harvard University, stated metempsychosis [reincarnation] is an essential part of the Jewish Kabala.[32]

The **First and Second Councils of Constantinople** deleted passages referring to reincarnation from the original Biblical texts. The First Council of Constantinople held in 381 A.D., and convened by Theodosius I, confirmed a statement by the Council of Nicaea held in 325 A.D. This doctrine redefined the Holy Spirit as the same Divinity expressed in the trinity of God the Divine, the historical person Jesus Christ, and the Holy Spirit as one will and intentional force. This dictum supported a belief in eternal life, but not in rebirth as was expressed before.

In 553 A.D. Emperor Justinian I further condemned the remaining teachings of pre-existence (reincarnation) and submitted his anathemas (curses) against the Origen for final ratification to an unofficial session of the Second Council of Constantinople, also known as the Fifth Ecumenical Council (of Christendom). As a result of Justinian refusing Pope Vigilius' request for equal representation of bishops from both the East and the West (the Pope's influence representing the West), the Pope boycotted the Council. Justinian convened the council anyway. The voting dominated by the vast majority of bishops in attendance favored Justinian's anathemas against pre-existence. The Council's decrees were well received in the East. However, they were contested by the Pope and Bishops in the Western Church. Finally church differences and politics eroded meaning of the original scriptures supporting reincarnation altogether.

These reinterpretations began and remain well intact through the political development of Catholicism and later in the Protestant Reformation. Biblical passages referring to reincarnation continued to erode by the will of the ecumenical hierarchy. As a result, orthodox Christianity still excludes teaching pre-existence of the soul, and by implication, reincarnation. However, the *Catholic Encyclopedia* explicitly states there has never been nor is there a restraint to a belief in reincarnation for Catholic Christians.[33]

Exploration of Past Lives Should be Used Sparingly and with Mystical Intent

When past lives are either frequently pursued or continuously relied upon for spiritual direction in this life, misguidance is likely to result. By definition, past lives are usually less integrated and spiritually evolved. Assuming the validity of communication with discarnate spirits, the most frequent dead with which mediums communicate or receive messages about past or current lives are not highly evolved themselves. Otherwise, they wouldn't be "hanging around" in the ethereal realm. By definition, these spirits have not completed their homework. While exceptions exist about spirits from other realms outside the *bardo*, who intervene with elevated guidance, these experiences are usually spontaneous and not invited. That is, these experiences occur as supportive guidance when intentional focus is toward *Dharma* consciousness or mystical evolution within this life.

Also, when the exploration of past lives or communication with the dead is with an attitude of amusement, it encourages a diversion from an elevation of mystical consciousness. Gurdjieff[34] believed that knowledge about reincarnation or past lives is a distraction unless people realize that all the repetitions of one's lives can be experienced in this current life. The advantage of this awareness is to escape repetition. Equally important is the dangerous risk that can occur with an indiscriminate exploration of past lives and communication with the dead. These activities have the potential, if not the bidding probability, of evoking a degenerative and regressive evolution for the embodied person as well as the contacted dead spirit. When deceased human entities become habituated in the bardo, their otherwise normal evolution becomes retarded.

W.Y. Evans-Wentz explains from the *Tibetan Book of the Dead*: "According to the most enlightened of the lamas, whenever a spirit is called up, as in such spirit-evocations as are nowadays common throughout the West, that spirit, through contact with this world and the prevailing traditional animistic beliefs concerning the hereafter, being strengthened in the illusion that the *Bardo* is a state wherein spiritual progress is possible, makes no attempt to quit it. The spirit called up ordinarily describes the *Bardo* (which is pre-eminently the realm of illusion), in which it is a dweller, more or less after what it had believed whilst in the fleshly body concerning the hereafter; for just as a dreamer in the human world lives over again in the dream-state the experience of the waking-state, so the inhabitant of the *Bardo* experiences hallucinations in *karmic* accord with the content of his consciousness created by the human world....This is said to explain why none but very exceptional spirits when evoked have any rational philosophy to offer concerning the world in which they exist...as being senseless ghosts, or psychic 'shells' which have been cast off by the consciousness principle, and which when coming into rapport with a human 'medium', are galvanized into automation-like life."[35] Tibetans also acknowledge that some evoked spirits are *bkahdods*, demoniacal and malignant spirits with evil karma, however these spirits are not of people recently deceased. Also, they are not usually within the known sphere of knowledge of the embodied person.

The human personality is a result of an embodied and attached identity and not representative of the soul. Recalling past personalities can interfere or encumber people with misinformation. Liberation from such outworn encumbrances increases people to assume more responsibility for self-development and the quest of their soul.

A disintegrated personality unwilling to separate from the earth plane is a poor substitute of counsel for a majestic identification with the cosmic force, Great Spirit, Christ or Dharma consciousness. While perhaps temporarily consoling, too much cosmic garbage and unreliable information is obtained by spirit guides looming around offering information within the limits of their attached incarnation. Of course, exceptions occur where spirits who have completed their earthly detachment and continued beyond in other realms, specifically return to teach, heal, and protect.

In summary, relying on information received from assumed past lives or discarnate entities is foolish in avoiding the responsibility for personal and spiritual development. Such information should be used sparingly and then reserved for those committed to evolving the soul and emerging with spirit. Indiscriminate exploration of past lives and communication with the dead involves risking: (1) arresting, reinforcing, and increasingly regressing the most frequently available discarnate spirit's evolution, (2) receiving compromised or unenlightened information and guidance, and (3) as a result of believing the information and ignoring more important spiritual matters, retarding personal development and spiritual evolution for the embodied person directing the exploration and communication.

END NOTES

Prologue

1. For the past thirty years, increasing scientific evidence suggests that dolphins are an exception to this statement. Dolphins may have equivalent or higher intelligence than humans. They maintain sophisticated social support systems without species related aggression and have physical healing abilities within their own species and perhaps in relationship to humans. Current research efforts are now being centered on breaking the barriers of communication.

2. For a comprehensive examination of the esoteric symbolism of the *tree of life*, see: Hall, M. *Masonic, Hermetic, Qabbalistic, and Rosicrucian Symbolical Philosophy*. Los Angeles, CA: The Philosophical Research Society, Inc., 1988, ref. index.

3. Examples include clairvoyant readings, the experience of stigmata, and exorcism.

4. Interesting to note is that within the ancient teachings and practices of the Tibetan Buddhist tradition, precognition or fortune telling was not selected for mastery. That is, although it frequently and spontaneously occurred, precognition was not selected as a psycho-experimental skill to be practiced nor mastered. Some of the reasons for this are discussed in Chapter 2 [*Paranormal Stepping Stones*].

5. For a respectable work [one author is a physicist who researched paranormal abilities at Stanford Research Institute; the other is an experimental psychologist known for his study of out-of-body experiences and fourteen years of research at Duke, Maimonides Medical Center, and the American Society for Psychical Research] on the practical aspects of *psi* phenomena including remote viewing, locating lost objects, and pre-cognition see: Targ, R. & Harary, K. *The Mind Race—Understanding and Using Psychic Abilities*. New York: Villard Books, 1984

6. The concept of *meditation* commonly refers to: (1) conventional abstraction and linear cognitive processes similar to ordinary rational thought. That is, to meditate conventionally means to reflect, ponder, or plan. In this respect, to meditate merely means to theoretically "think about." (2) Meditation also means to intentionally

concentrate and focus attention on a specific object of consciousness. The processes involved in this kind of meditation are similar to paranormal experience. (3) A third meaning defines the mind as observing itself without an external object of reference except the process of consciousness itself. The processes involved in this kind of meditation are representative of mystical awareness and realization. In Zen, this is referred to as no-thought, (*wu-nien*), no-mind (*wu-shin*) or empty mind. Various mystical schools focus on either the second, third, or some combination of the second and third definitions of meditation, see Chapter 6 [*Mindful Intentions*]. Various schools of Zen are no exception, see commentary in Chapter 4 [*Zen Currents*]. With this background in mind, any reference I make to *meditation* excludes the first definition. For further reference on no-thought and no-mind, see Suzuki, D. *Zen Buddhism*. (W. Barrett, ed.). Garden City, New York: Doubleday Anchor, 1956, pp. 157-226.

7. The leaders of major world religions were mystics. Interestingly, many of them were killed for their peaceful visions. Zoroaster, the Persian mystic of the sixth century was stabbed to death. Socrates was condemned to death by poisoning. Guatama Siddartha, the Buddha, was stoned by orthodox Hindus. Jeshua of Nazareth was crucified. Mohammed, the founder of Islam, was poisoned in an assassination attempt. Al-Hillaj Mansoor, the Sufi mystic was executed by being slowly cut to pieces.

8. For collaboration, see: Sandweiss, S. *Sai Baba—The Holy Man...and the Psychiatrist*. San Diego, CA: Birth Day Publishing Co., 1975, pp. 182-3.

9. For a perspective of new paradigms as applied to professional psychotherapy, see: Orcutt, T. & Prell, J. *Integrative Paradigms of Psychotherapy*. Needham Heights, MA: Allyn & Bacon, 1994. For a perspective of a new quantum psychology, see: Zohar, D. *The Quantum Self—Human Nature and Consciousness Defined by the New Physics*. NY: William Morrow, 1990.

Chapter One

1. The dialogues representing Alan Watts in this chapter are from my personal experience, conversations, and notes. Within editorial limits, I have taken caution to represent Alan's words, meaning, and robust flavor accurately.

2. Sister Theresa Lentfoehr, S.D.S. (1902-1981) was a poet and teacher through her entire professional life. Many years after my experience with her, I located corroborating testimony of her confidential friendship of twenty-nine years with Father Thomas Merton, from

1939 to his death in 1968. Sister Lentfoehr maintained the largest known collection of Thomas Merton's life and writings. Following her death, and by order of her will, she bequeathed her entire collection to Columbia University in New York. For further reference, see: Daggy, R. (Ed.). *The Road to Joy—The Letters of Thomas Merton to New and Old Friends*. New York: Farrar.Straus.Giroux, 1989, p. 187.

3. Experiences of various forms of levitation are discussed in Chapter 2 [*Paranormal Stepping Stones*] under the subheading *Varieties of Paranormal Experience*.

4. My experiences with Arthur Stirling are also included in Chapters 2 through 4. Arthur Stirling also edited all sections of the narratives in which he is included for collaborative accuracy.

5. While the essence of Alan's mystical message was similar to Jiddu Krishnamurti's teachings, their personalities and expression of life were nearly opposite. Without design, they isolated each others audiences. Those who favored Krishnamurti sanctioned the austere duty of mystical realization. Those who favored Alan valued a flare for the kabuki theater of life.

6. Alan Watts and I use opposite conceptual language to make an important distinction with which we completely agree. Here, Alan uses the concept of belief in the meaning of make-believe, fantasy, or wishful thinking. He then uses the concept of faith to represent a confident and convicted shift in consciousness based on undeniable experience. I use the concept of belief to represent the entire range of any constellation of combined thoughts, from absolute conviction based on scientific evidence or profoundly spiritual experience, to unconsidered opinion and persuaded foolishness. I avoid using the word *faith*, not because it implies there is a certitude, whether the source has objective evidence or not, but because this word implies and conjures other vague associations including hope and religious observance. Also, my experience indicates that beliefs are self-reinforcing and are either quantitatively regressive or evolutionary. A shift of consciousness requires a qualitative shift in beliefs. Reactive qualitative shifts can occur with spontaneous, unintentional, perceived crises. The only proactive shift that can create this qualitative change in a life-enhancing way occurs through mystical realization. And, it does initially occur by a qualitative shift in belief [leap of faith] that is later reinforced by practice of the new belief. Indeed, Alan and I are in agreement that both science and religious faith are based on similar presuppositions and beliefs. That is, science is not subject to the scientific method anymore than religion is subject to evidence for cosmic principles.

7. It is particularly difficult, if not impossible, to recognize and confirm contemporary mystics, unless of course, the observer functions within the same mystical reality. Additionally, mystics are usually disinterested, if not opposed, to proving mystical attainment except to selected apprentices. For further reference on this point, see: Bucke, R. *Cosmic Consciousness*. New York: E.P. Dutton, 1923, p. 131.

8. See: Commentary of Chapter 2 [*Paranormal Stepping Stones*] for clarification.

9. Wilber, K. "Two Humanistic Psychologies?" *Journal of Humanistic Psychology*, Spring 1989, Vol.29, No.2, pp.230-243.

Chapter Two

1. The following text was published ten years after my initial experience. Okada, M. *Johrei—Divine Light of Salvation*. Kyoto, Japan: The Society of Johrei, 1984.

2. The Chinese refer to this process a *nui gung, gigong, chi kung*, or *chi gong*. *Chi gong* is the internal mobilization of vital energy or force. It is practiced in the martial arts, in t'ai chi, acupuncture, acupressure, and calligraphy. This energy is traditionally used to self-heal and revitalize the living organism through everyday practice. When it is used by medical doctors for diagnosis and treatment of malfunctions of accident and mild and chronic diseases, it is referred to as either *nui gung gee liao* or external *chi gong*. Similar to Johrei, energy is extended through the fingers, palm, or hand. For a lay reference on mind-body healing, see: Moyers, B. *Healing and the Mind*. New York: Doubleday, 1993. For an academic reference, see: Rossi, E. *The Psychobiology of Mind-Body Healing*. New York: W.W. Norton, 1986. For a current and thorough examination of mind-body relationships that is well documented and focuses on the possibilities and evolution of the mind-body experience, see: Murphy, M. *The Future of the Body -Explorations Into the Further Evolution of Human Nature*. New York: Putnam Publishing, 1993.

3. The Church of World Messianity also focuses on spiritual detachment for lost souls. Indeed, Reverend Dowd said, during our visit, that she was contacted by the Los Angeles Police Department to survey the extraordinary number of accidents at several freeway off-ramps. Her examination concluded that lost souls were causing the great number of accidents. She reported that after conducting spiritual detachment ceremonies, the accidents ceased at those off-ramps. Further exploration about detached spirits are covered in Chapter 7 [*Discarnate Spirits*] and Chapter 8 [*Reincarnated Lamas*].

4. This book is still in print after more than twenty years. Silva, J. *The Silva Mind Control Method*. New York: Simon & Schuster, 1982.
5. T'ai chi chuan as both a martial art and health exercise is explained in Chapter 3 [*Harvesting the Tao*] and Chapter 4 [*Masters Just Practice*].
6. Targ, R. & Harary, K. *The Mind Race -Understanding and Using Psychic Abilities*. New York: Villard Books, 1984, p. 193.
7. Clairaudience is receiving similar information through the power or faculty of "hearing" something not present to the ear, but regarded as having objective reality.
8. For further clarification on this point, see: Broughton, R. *Parapsychology—The Controversial Science*. Ballentine, 1991, pp. 34-35.
9. The older and more widely used term for psychokinesis is telekinesis.
10. For an enjoyable and witnessed account of this experience, see: D'Antonio, M. *Heaven on Earth*. New York: Crown Publishers, 1992, pp. 244-47.
11. For further reference, see: Gersi, D. *Faces in the Smoke: An Eyewitness Experience of Voodoo, Shamanism, Psychic Healing, and Other Amazing Human Powers*. Los Angeles, CA: Jeremy P. Tarcher, pp. 154-155.
12. For further information, see: Govinda, L. *The Way of The White Clouds*. Berkeley: Shambhala, 1970, pp. 77-78.
13. Even though neither myself nor Jim had been involved in any formal meditation prior to our experiences, we initially believed the events we experienced were quite possible without reservation. This is the same expectation that advanced meditation brings with practice.
14. For collaboration, see: Boyd, D. *Mystics, Magicians, and Medicine People*. New York: Paragon House, 1989, p. 75.
15. Frazer, J. *The Golden Bough—A Study in Magic and Religion*. New York: Macmillan, 1922.
16. *Accommodation* means that mental processes make room for new concepts or ideas by altering the larger concept for the smaller concept to fit it without being perceptually modified. Only through accommodation does a shift or qualitative difference in consciousness occur.
17. *Assimilation* means that the incoming data is perceptually modified to fit into existing structures of beliefs and current concepts of consciousness. This is a quantitative difference which, while functional, inevitably maintains the status quo.

Chapter Three

1. Alan Watts' final book was written from his notes after his death with the collaboration of his friend and colleague, Al Chung-Liang Huang, a *t'ai chi* master of the gentle way. For those interested in Watts' and Huang's practical interpretation of the implication of Taoism in modern times, see: Watts, A. *Tao: The Watercourse Way*. New York: Pantheon, 1975.

2. Gia-fu Feng died in 1985.

3. Feng, G. & Frank, G. *Tai-Chi—A Way of Centering— & I Ching*. New York: Macmillan, 1970.

4. Feng, G. & English, J. (Trans.) *Tao Te Ching*. Lao Tsu. New York: Alfred A. Knopf, 1972.

5. Feng, G. & English, J. (Trans.) *Chang Tzu*. New York: Random House, 1976.

6. For a catalog, write: Esalen Institute, Big Sur, California 93920 or call (408) 667-3000.

7. (A) From a conventional reality perspective, some authoritative styles are extremely threatening to personal identity and social conscience. In more recent times, it may remind people of the mass media coverage of sociopathic religious leaders and cults, wherein the leader "programs" followers. Unsuspicious devotees become "programmed" to follow messages of the leader, tasks that may include exploitative labor, sexuality, or suicide. While this is sometimes the situation with zealous, religiously theologic, and often self-proclaimed leaders, it was not representative of Gia-fu in any way nor is it typical of mystics. (B) From a mystical perspective, (especially exemplified by Christian mystics, Zen masters, Lamas, Sifus, shamans, and medicine people), the relationship between an apprentice and mentor is authoritative by definition and nature of evolutionary development. Indeed, this is necessary to break the chains of rational thought. (C) For further clarification on the difference between psychopathology and mysticism, see: Commentary in Chapter 1 [*Mystical Awakenings*].

8. Following is a reference for the scholarly classic edition of the *I-Ching* which includes a lengthy forward by Carl Jung. See: Wilhelm, R. & Baynes, C. (Trans.). *The I Ching*. Princeton, New Jersey: Princeton University Press, 1967. [Originally published in 1950 by the Bolligen Foundation, New York.]

9. For those persons interested in a practical authoritative edition for casting, see: Hua Ching, N. *The Book of Changes and The Unchanging Truth* (Revised Edition). Los Angeles, CA: Shrine of the Eternal

Breath of Tao and College of Tao and Traditional Chinese Healing, 1990.

10. For instructions regarding casting with either the yarrow stalks or coins, see: Wilhelm, R. & Baynes, C. (Trans.). *The I Ching.* Princeton, New Jersey: Princeton University Press, 1967, pp. 721-24. [Originally published in 1950 by the Bolligen Foundation, New York.]

11. The Merlin Project, appropriately named after the magician's name in the *Once and Future King*, was founded by futurist Paul Guercio and physicist Dr. George Hart. They have programmed a computer with multiple systems of fortune telling. They claim to have created a program that includes all data from the *I-Ching*, Tarot cards, astrology, Nostradamus, Edgar Cayce, and the actuation of major historical world events. The program intends to predict world and personal events. Thus far, they claim to have a seventy-five percent success ratio, including the Gulf War and major earthquakes. Opposite of precognition, they report little difficulty in determining the time a major change will occur in either the world or in a person's life. Their difficulty is in accurately interpreting the exact nature by which the change will occur. They claim it is scientific, in the sense that all of their data is replicable. For further information and their quarterly subscription, write: Merlin Project, P.O. Box C, Cambridge, MA 02140.

12. For an excellent reference on how psychotherapy can incorporate the principles of meditation and Taoism, see: Johanson, G. & Kurtz, R. *Grace Unfolding—Psychotherapy in the Spirit of the Tao Te Ching.* New York: Bell Tower, 1991.

Chapter Four

1. There are four primary theories on the origin of t'ai-chi, dating anywhere from 618 A.D. to 1795 A.D. Each differs by dynasty, province, family or founder, and school. The most rational asserts that the founder is unknown, but that the origin of t'ai-chi dates from Wang Tsung-yueh of Shansi province, who then introduced it in Honan during the reign of Ch'en-lung (1736-95) of the Ch'ing dynasty. This thesis also supports that tai chi originated as a form of hand boxing called *pao ch'ui*. Much later in the 1800's a man named Yang Lu-ch'an became expert enough that he later went to the capital of the Ch'ing dynasty in Peking and taught the emperor's guards. While he met all challenges from a myriad of martial art forms, he was never defeated. For further reference, see: Man-ch'ing, C. & Smith, R. *T'ai-Chi.* Rutland, VT: Charles E. Tuttle, 1966, p. 4.

2. For example, traditional Korean herbalists customarily apprentice for twenty years before opening a practice of their own.

Chapter Five

1. George Nakashima was born in Spokane, Washington, the eldest child of Katsuharu Nakashima, of samurai lineage, and Suzu Thoma Nakashima, who, as a young woman, served under Takeko Horikawa, official court taster for the Emperor Meiji (r.1868-1912). Mr. Nakashima received his M.A. from Massachusetts Institute of Technology, Cambridge in 1930. In 1941 he married Marion Okajima, born in America, of samurai lineage, and a teacher of English at a private school in Tokyo. He received the Craftsmanship Medal from the American Institute of Architects (1952), was named a Fellow of the American Crafts Council, New York (1979), and was the recipient of the Hazlett Award for the Crafts, given by the Commonwealth of Pennsylvania (1981). He died in 1990 at the age of eighty-five. See: Nakashima, G. *The Soul of a Tree.* New York: Kodansha America, 1988, pp. 195-7.

2. Philip Kapleau, American born (b. 1912 -) studied traditional Zen in a Japanese monastery for ten years and in the 1970's became one of the first three *roshis* [ordained Zen Masters] of Occidental descent to receive *dharma* transmission. He then returned to the United States and started the Zen Center in Rochester, New York. *The Three Pillars of Zen* is one of the most popularized books about Zen for Western audiences and is also widely used within college and university courses. For further reference, see: Kapleau, P. *The Three Pillars of Zen.* Garden City, New York: Anchor Press, 1980. Also, see: Kapleau, P. *The Wheel of Life and Death.* New York: Doubleday, 1989.

3. In 1989 Osho Rajneesh resonated George Nakashima's statement that I heard in 1978. "Philip Kapleau does not understand Zen as an experience. His book is beautiful. *The Three Pillars of Zen* is a good intellectual introduction, but only intellectual. Even this statement shows that the person does not understand. Zen is not a 'drive towards enlightenment.' Zen is enlightenment; it is not a drive." Rajneesh, O. *The Zen Manifesto.* [Talks given to the Rajneesh International University of Mysticism in Gautama the Buddha Auditorium, Poona, India during the months of February and April, 1989] Cologne, West Germany: The Rebel Publishing House GmbH, c Neo-Sannyas International, 1989, p. 221.

I have never met Philip Kapleau. Also, while I have carefully listened to many of Rajneesh's tapes and read many of his transcribed discourses, I was never in his presence either. My following opinions are from my own mystical experiences and professionally considered beliefs.

I neither identify myself with being an *intellectual* of mysticism nor Zen, nor purely an experiential wizard devoid of structural reflection. However, if you ask me, I would say that I am mystical and Zen oriented. To be fair within the context of Rajneesh's discourse entitled *The Zen Manifesto*, and in addition to Philip Kapleau, Rajneesh similarly discounts the following persons as intellectualizing Zen and not being Zen: Fritjof Capra, Erich Fromm, Karl Jaspers, U.G. Krishnamurti, J. Krishnamurti, Father Thomas Merton, Paul Reps, Nancy Wilson Ross, D.T. Suzuki, Alan Watts, and Ken Wilber. I find it terribly amusing that the quotes used to discredit the above persons as *being* Zen are obviously biased and in my opinion, the least representative of these persons. Second, I am bored with such self-gratifying exclamations. Rajneesh uses the same dualistic, intellectual rational to discredit persons from being Zen as he claims these persons use to describe Zen. That is, by attempting to justify his verdicts of intellectualization, he intellectualizes, judges, and decides that this is Zen and that is not Zen. Who cares Rajneesh? However, by my indicating this personal fallacy of bias, it in no way discredits Rajneesh's mystical realization or in him being a great Zen Master. Neither does his proclivity for loving women, [mentioned by Hugh Milne in his book *Bhagwan, the God that Failed*], owning roughly seventy Rolls Royces, or being deported from the United States and not being allowed to reside in any other country substantiate evidence to the contrary. For further examination of this last point, see: Orcutt, T. *No Beggars Just Balloons—A Practical Approach to Self-Transformation*. San Diego, CA: Global Village Publishing, 1989, pp. 153-168.

4. For further reference, see: Nakashima, G. *The Soul of a Tree*. New York: Kodansha America, 1988.

5. Letter from Abbot Eido Tai Shimano sent to me by the Nakashima Foundation.

6. For a thorough explanation of *koan* exercise, see: "The Reason of Unreason: the *Koan* Exercise" in Barrett, W. (Ed.) *Zen Buddhism -Selected Writings of D.T. Suzuki*. Garden City, NY: Doubleday, 1956, pp. 134-154.

7. Korean monks who complete the entire standard curriculum spend about twelve years in study. It is also noteworthy, that in Korean monasteries, very few resident monks meditate. Most of the monks support the monastery and involve themselves in seminary study at the exclusion of meditation. For further reference, see: Buswell Jr., R. "Zen Monastic Practice in Korea," *Korean Culture*, Vol. 13, No.3, Fall 1992, p. 37, 43.

8. Osho Rajneesh is acclaimed by traditional Zen Masters in Japan who appreciate his contemporary living of Zen and even use his books in their monasteries. Rajneesh's position is adamant about Zen not needing years of either asceticism or hard training as is usually practiced in traditional Zen in Japan today. His position is that while Gautama Buddha took twelve years to resolve ignorance, evolutionary consciousness is now such that twelve minutes is enough for ordinary people when they learn to relax into themselves. For further reference, hear: Rajneesh, O. [Audiotape No.411-001] "The Awakening of the Buddha." Rahneeshdam, Poona, India, January 4, 1989/7:00 P.M.

9. For a charming read and informative way Zen is applied to everyday life, see: Pirsig, R. *Zen and the Art of Motorcycle Maintenance*. NY: Bantam, 1984. [This book was originally published in 1974 by William Morrow.]

10. For a discussion of mindful intentions where the focus of attention is on an object of desired consciousness, see Chapter 6 [*Mindful Intentions*].

11. Janwillem van de Wetering presents a vivid and humorous record of his experience as a young Dutch student who spent a year and a half in a Japanese Zen Buddhist monastery. See: Van de Watering, J. *The Empty Mirror*. New York: Ballantine Books, 1987.

12. An exploration differentiating psychotic and schizophrenic experiences from mystical experiences can be found in the Commentary in Chapter 1 [*Mystical Awakenings*].

Chapter Six

1. The value of a centered state is that it represents the elements of mindfulness (attention) necessary for mindful intentions (attention of attention toward objects or events). The notion of *being centered* or *centering one's existence* is typically vague and used with a variety of misunderstandings. Western psychology and conventional thinking supports the assumption that we either focus on self or others, that mindfulness or intentions are object specific. With such a quantitative belief, either the self or others are compromised. The essential point of a centered state is that both the integrity of self and an intuitive feeling with others is enhanced. I am grateful to Rod Windle and Michael Samko for differentiating the specific attributes of a centered state. A centered state enhances the "perception of self and others non-judgmentally and simultaneously." Additionally, a centered state includes: slowing or absence of internal dialogue, physical and emotional relaxation, the lack of a startle reflex, in-

creased ability to detect minimal psychophysiological cues from others, and interestingly, "soft eyes" which allows sight to simultaneously focus and use peripheral vision. For further information on a centered state, see: Windle, R. & Samko, M. Hypnosis, Ericksonian Hypnotherapy, and Aikido. *American Journal of Clinical Hypnosis.* Vol. 34, No. 4, April 1992, pp. 263-4.

2. Daniel Goleman classified the mechanics of meditation techniques according to the Visuddhimagga typology. Concentration techniques are those that focus on a fixed mental object. Mindfulness includes those techniques that occur when the mind observes itself. Integrated meditation occurs when both concentration and mindfulness occur in combination. I am using the concept of *mindful intentions* to represent a combination of the mind intermittently observing itself when it is also focused on a fixed mental object of consciousness. This integrated combination is exactly what makes mindful intentions powerful when continuously held in consciousness. Mindful intentions, then, become the marvel of psychic (intentional) coincidence (manifestation). For further clarification, see: Goleman, D. *The Varieties of Meditative Experience.* New York: Irvington Publishers, 1977, pp. 1, 109.

3. Pope, K. & Singer, J. (Eds.). *The Stream of Consciousness -Scientific Investigations into the Flow of Human Experience.* New York: Plenum Press, 1978, p. 344.

Chapter Seven

1. This event is relatively common in the world of spirits. [1] Douchan Gersi, an international documentary filmmaker, known for his television series, *Explore,* shown on both the PBS network and the Discovery Channel, shares numerous incidents of a failure to either film or audiotape extraordinary paranormal phenomena with "peoples of tradition." In attempting to film levitation in Haiti, frequently the batteries supplying the movie camera, portable lighting system, tape recorder, extra batteries, and even the battery of his wrist watch failed more than twenty times. In other instances of still photography, using three Nikons, two with normal and high sensitivity color slide film, and the other with black-and-white film, something equally bizarre interfered with the photographic process. While all of the other frames after processing were perfect with vivid color, only those covering levitation were dark and out of focus. In one instance, this occurred with five rolls of thirty-six-exposures each, on high speed film, all processed by Kodak laboratory in Brussels, where the 138 slides covering levitation were black. The events leading up to levitation and return were perfectly clear. In the multiple

cases, when equipment and film supervisors were consulted for explanation, rational answers that could explain the phenomena were not available. See: Gersi, D. *Faces in the Smoke: An Eyewitness Experience of Voodoo, Shamanism, Psychic Healing, and Other Amazing Human Powers*. Los Angeles, CA: Jeremy P. Tarcher, 1991, pp. 156-158, 182-183.

Also, Doug Boyd tells the tale of photographing an old, Korean, country farmer. The old man had never permitted his picture to be taken, even at family weddings. Although all his other pictures developed fine, Doug Boyd reported that only the farmer's face was out of focus in otherwise clear pictures, however his image, including his clothes, continued to fade on the slides until it disappeared over time entirely. For further reference, see: Boyd, D. *Mystics, Magicians, and Medicine People*. New York: Paragon House, 1989, pp. 14,18.

2. Chris also reported that he was ordained as a minister in the United States through the Universal Church of the Master and then became an ordained minister of the Independent Spiritualist Association. He reported that he has contributed to television and radio interviews. Currently, he does over two thousand readings a year.

3. During this session, Chris did not assume spirit personalities.

4. The following ideas and conversations on mediumship and Spiritualism within the narrative and the quotations within the Commentary are from audiotapes and notes of personal conversations with Chris Meredith, 1993 and quoted here with his permission. I have edited the transcripts for readability and understanding while taking every precaution to maintain original language, meaning, and content.

5. *Chakras* are psychic centers of energy in the physical organism. They are both psychosomatic and somatopsychic. That is, (1) the energy is at once physical and psychic and (2) if we must use the understanding of a dualistic framework where physical is separate from mind, then it could be said that the energy moves from the psychic centers to the body and is transmuted back into psychic forces. These psychic centers of energy are "located" from the root center near the base of the spinal cord to the crown center at the top of the skull. Increasing movement toward a locus of attention, that is centered within higher *chakras*, means that the shift in consciousness moves from self-absorption to universal consciousness. For further reference, see: Chaudhuri, H. "Yoga Psychology" in Tart, C. (Ed.). *Transpersonal Psychologies*. New York: Harper & Row, 1975, p.265.

6. Yogis, with an origin in India, physically practice with *prana*. Hawaiian and other Polynesian shamans refer to "mystical heat" as

mana. The !King Bushman refer to this flowing energy as *n'um*. In China, martial artists practice developing the control of *chi*, and in Japan with *ki*. Each culturally relative psycho-physical discipline focuses on the control of energy and breath as both an organismic and symbolic union with the universal force and a healing energy.

7. I had not mentioned my interest in out-of-body experiences (OBE's) to Chris at this point and only discussed my interest in this area with him in later sessions.

8. When I was twenty-four I led an over night psychotherapy marathon. In the morning and walking in leather sandals to the breakfast room of the lodge, I slipped on a slate stair and landed on it in the middle of my spine. Fortunately, a masseuse from Guam had been in the workshop and immediately worked on the injured area for over an hour. Ever since that time, I have intermittent pain every other year or so in the lower left quadrant of my back and hip. It had recently been in mild intermittent pain for the past month. All pain vanished and normal functioning restored by the stated date and the publishing of this book two years beyond the stated date, considerably beyond usual reoccurrence. I considered this a "direct hit" for Chris, whether or not the restored physical functioning was a result of a discarnate spirit.

9. My father, who is the only physically living relative of my family of origin, distinctly remembers the woman who was my designated guardian for my parent's time away when I was an infant and child. She lived in the same apartment building. She was a close friend of my mother. She was with me weekly from a week after birth to about seven years old when she died. She was in her eighties, about five foot nine, less than one hundred pounds, had curly white hair, was quite religious, and enjoyed sewing and crocheting. However, my father remembers her as Swedish or Danish.

10. This statement is consistent with Geshe Lobsang Tsephel and Tibetan Buddhism. See: Chapter 8 [*Reincarnated Lamas*].

11. I asked this question of Chris after my association with Geshe Lobsang Tsephel. Refer to Chapter 8 [*Reincarnated Lamas*] for a nearly compatible explanation of *mind stream* within the narrative.

12. There is considerable agreement in the paradigms of Spiritualism and Tibetan Buddhism. In other conversations, I mentioned this to Chris Meredith. He said that he almost completely agreed with Tibetan Buddhism, particularly as represented by the *Tibetan Book of the Dead*, and that the views were merely different cultural interpretations. See Chapter 8 [*Reincarnated Lamas*].

13. I find myself agreeing with Ken Wilber when he stated in an interview with Jon Klimo that the extraordinary transformation that can occur with a person in a dissociative state is amazing and that people can generate incredible phenomena in a dissociative state without requiring people to postulate "'something like ghosties running around whispering in their ear.'" Nonetheless, Wilber adds, "'I *do* think there are some ghosties running around whispering in peoples ears.'" Quoted by Jon Klimo in Klimo, J. *Channeling -Investigations on Receiving Information from Paranormal Sources*. Los Angeles: Jeremy P. Tarcher, 1987, p.239.

14. Cornell, G., "Idea of Hell Loses Its Wallop," *San Francisco Chronicle*, May 28, 1986.

15. While I use the terms of *medium* and *channel*, and *mediumship* and *channeling* synonymously and interchangeably, some authorities continue to distinguish between mediumship and channeling, stating the later covers communication with all kinds of intelligences (e.g. extraterrestrial entities) not associated with physical beings or physical reality, while the terms *medium* and *mediumship* are reserved for transmitting communication from discarnate human beings. See: Rogo, D. *Mind Beyond the Body*. New York: Penguin, 1978.

16. Hill, D. & Williams, P. *The Supernatural*. London: Bloomsbury Books, 1989, p. 107.

17. As a matter of accuracy, it should be noted that most esoteric and mystical literature makes a distinction between ghosts and discarnate spirits. Assuming an identifiable energy form of existence, spirits are more highly evolved and free. Ghosts are trapped within an etherial realm seeking freedom from continued attachments within a recently embodied form.

18. Not all mystical traditions agree with this point of view. For example, the Taoist position is that spirits can enter and leave the body as easily as people can enter and leave a house without walls. For further clarification, see: Ni, Hua Ching. *The Book of Changes and the Unchanging Truth*. Los Angeles, CA: Shrine of the Eternal Breath of Tao, 1990, pp. 134-165.

19. Within this context, the concept of *alien spirits* does not refer to extraterrestrial entities.

20. Quoted in Hastings, A. "Investigating the Phenomenon of Channeling," *Noetic Sciences Review*, Winter 1986.

21. For further reference, see: Wickland, C. *Thirty Years Among the Dead*. San Bernardino, CA: Borgo Press, 1974.

22. I agree! However, Edith Fiore, Ph.D. is a psychologist and psychotherapist specializing in the practice of spirit detachment of spiritually possessed persons. Contrary to myself and Chris, she believes that most discarnate spirits are disoriented spirits with malevolent intent. I attribute the reported success of her treatment to a modification of early unconscious belief systems and a reintegration of split parts of the personality, rather than the successful dispelling of "evil" spirit entities from the physical body. For further reference on Edith Fiore's work, see: Fiore, E. *The Unquieted Dead: A Psychologist Treats Possession*. New York: Ballantine Books, 1987.

Chapter Eight

1. Dolbe, S. "Victorville's little holy man." *The San Diego Union-Tribune*. San Diego, CA: January 10, 1993.

2. For a description of synchronicity as discovering "meaning and giving prominence in our lives to the dramatic chance occurrences that take place" see: Arnold Mindel, "Synchronicity: An Investigation of the Unitary Background Patterning Synchronous Phenomena, *Dissertation Abstracts International* 37:2 (1976). Also, see: C.G. Jung, "Synchronicity: An Acausal Connecting Principle," *Collected Works*, Vol.8. Princeton, N.J.: Princeton University Press, 1973.

3. Most psychological theories and methodologies acknowledge *psychosomatic* components to emotional malfunction and physical disease as incorporating some secondary gain. Secondary gain means there is a higher valued benefit that people receive for maintaining an emotional or physical disorder. This benefit is often unconscious and made from former beliefs that were appropriate at the time, but at the current time are life limiting. Structural integration was founded by Ida Rolf and assumes that these beliefs, over time, have been programmed into the skeletal and muscular structure of the body such that awareness is now directly blocked in a *somatopsychic* way. Psychotherapists who employ this theory and methodology use specialized techniques of movement and deep message for relieving muscular armature. These techniques are intended to increase emotional well being and aliveness. For further references on this approach, see: (1) Rolf, I. *Structural Integration: Gravity, an Unexplored Factor in a More Human Use of Human Beings*. Boulder, CO: Guild for Structural Integration, 1962. (2) Lowen, A. *Pleasure: A Creative Approach to Life*. New York: Coward-McCann, 1970. (3) Keleman, S. *Somatic Reality*. Berkeley, CA: Center Press, 1982. (4) Janov, A. *The Primal Scream*. New York: G.P. Putnam's Sons, 1970. (5) Reich, W. *Character Analysis*. New York: Noonday Press, 1967.

4. There are many spiritual lakes in Tibet, but Lhamoi Latso at Chokihorgyal, about ninety miles southeast of Lhasa, is the most celebrated. Tibetans believe that images come forth and that visions of the future can be seen in the waters of these lakes. Sometimes the visions appear in the form of alphabetic letters and at other times as pictures of places and times in future events. The current Dalai Lama was initially discovered in this way and then verified by other tests of remembering objects and people from his former life. For further reference, see: Dalai Lama, H.H. *My Land and My People*. New York: McGraw-Hill, 1962, pp. 21-22.

5. The Potala Palace is one of the largest buildings in the world. Its construction was begun by a king of Tibet 1300 years ago as a pavilion for meditation. It was expanded by the Fifth Dalai Lama in the seventeenth century A.D. It is thirteen stories high, contains about thirty-five chapels, four cells for meditation, and the mausoleums of seven Dalai Lamas, some that are thirty feet high and covered in solid gold and precious stones. In its libraries are housed the records of Tibetan history, culture, and religion, in 7000 volumes. Some of the records are written on palm leaves imported from India a thousand years ago. See: Dalai Lama, H.H. *My Land and My People*. New York: McGraw-Hill, 1962, pp. 52-55.

6. A *rinpoche* is an enlightened high lama who is acknowledged as reincarnated by Tibetan authority.

7. Tenzin made an important distinction here, in that while there are not good or bad shamans per se, shamans use their neutral powers in ways that are either beneficial or detrimental to the life force of others. *Good shaman* refers to a shaman who favors using power for the welfare of their community.

8. As an example of this phenomenon of physical immutability after death, Swami Paramahansa Yogananda [1893-1952], an Indian mystic and founder of the Self Realization Fellowship (SRF) introduced *Kriya Yoga* to the West with international meditative centers located in Los Angeles and Encinitas, California and the Yogoda Satsanga Society (YSS) in India. Following a speech at a banquet in honor of the Ambassador of India in Los Angeles, California, he died. At his physical death on March 7, 1952, Paramahansa Yogananda entered *mahjasamadhi* (a yogi's final conscious exit from the body). The story of his passing was reported in *Time Magazine*, August 4, 1952. The Director of Forest Lawn Mortuary [Mr. Harry T. Rowe] forwarded a notarized letter in which he stated there were no visible signs of decay in the dead body, even after twenty days of death. This observation included no skin mold, odor of decay, or desiccation (drying) of the bodily tissues. Yogananda's physical appearance twenty days

after physical death and just prior to the bronze casket being closed was exactly the same as it had been on the day of his death. For further reference, see: Yogananda, P. *Autobiography of a Yogi*. Los Angeles, CA: Self-Realization Publishers, 1969, p.iv.

9. The Tibetan concept of *bardo* is thoroughly explained in the *Bardo Thotrol*, more commonly known as *The Tibetan Book of the Dead*. The *bardo* is not to be confused with the concept of *limbo*. The *limbo*, as a point of consciousness and state of being, according to Roman Catholic theology, is negatively valued in that it defines a transition of consciousness or being in which (lost) souls are prohibited from entering heaven because of not having received either Christian baptism or the sacraments of Christ, including those good people who died before Christ's birth. To the contrary, the *bardo* is a gap, an interval of suspension, both after physical death until rebirth, and also descriptive of suspensions in life on earth. Suspensions in life on earth include death of ordinary consciousness and gaps of altered states of consciousness. The *bardo* experience is a natural function of our developmental and evolutionary soul. Our entire life and death is a series of mini-*bardo* experiences with life and death being macro-*bardo* experiences. Mini-*bardo* experiences, representative of transitional states of consciousness, occur in everyday life with the possibility of either life-enhancement or life-depreciation. Examples include delusions, fear, insecurity, uncertainty, dream states, and meditation. Psychotherapeutically, a *bardo* experience represents the transition between being stuck in an *impasse* (defined as the position in which environmental support is unavailable and self-support seems insufficient) and conflict resolution. For further reference, see: (1) Fremantle, F. & Trungpa, C. (Trans.) *The Tibetan Book of the Dead* [The Great Liberation Through Hearing in the Bardo]. Boston: Shambhala, 1975; (2) "Secrets of Life, Death, and Rebirth—An Interview with Sogyal Rinpoche." *Body, Mind & Spirit*, Issue 55, Vol.12, March-April 1993, pp.44-45; (3) Rinpoche, S. *The Tibetan Book of Living and Dying*. San Francisco: HarperSanFrancisco, 1992.

10. This process is usually referred to as *transmigration*.

11. The Spiritualist/medium Chris Meredith [See Chapter 7] completely agreed when he stated, "There are certain cultures that do believe in the transmigration of souls. This I have not found to be so. I have not found anyone that has come back as a dog, cat, or bird. I have found that levels tend to progress in the intelligence and consciousness that it is today in the human form."

12. The duration of forty-nine days is confirmed by Carl Jung's 'Psychological Commentary' in: Evans-Wentz, W. (Ed.) *The Tibetan Book*

of the Dead. New York: Oxford University Press, 1960, pp.xxxv, xxxviii.

13. Reincarnation is also referred to as rebirth, re-embodiment, metempsychosis, pre-existence, transmigration, and palingenesis. Transmigration, however, often refers to the regression of souls or mind streams to less evolved forms of life, such as animals and plants. And, palingenesis characterizes the resurrection of the spirit, soul, or mind stream from the material organism.

14. For further clarification, see: H. Schumann. *The Historical Buddha*. London: Arkana, 1989, p. 139.

15. D'Antonio, M. *Heaven on Earth*. New York: Crown Publishers, 1992, p.19.

16. *World Almanac*. New York: World Almanac, 1993, pp. 718, 817.

17. For further reference, see: Campbell, J. *The Masks of God: Oriental Mythology*. New York: Viking, 1962, pp. 3-4.

18. Eliade, M. *The Myth of Eternal Return*. New York: Pantheon, 1954, p. 88.

19. Henderson, J. in Jung, C. (Ed.). *Man and His Symbols*. New York: Doubleday, 1964, p. 108.

20. The modern name *Druid* is derived from the name *Der-Wydd* which is derived from *Gwydd*, the name of priests, instructors, wise people or sorcerers.

21. Budge, W. (Trans.) *The Egyptian Book of the Dead*. New York: Dover, 1967.

22. Murray, M. *The Splendour That Was Egypt*. New York: Philosophical Library, 1949, pp. 210-211.

23. One of Mme. Blavatsky's most influential works is *The Secret Doctrine*, a two volume treatise focusing on the underlying unity among all great religions, esoteric and mystical beliefs. See: Blavatsky, H. *The Secret Doctrine -The Synthesis of Science, Religion, and Philosophy*. (Vol.I & II). Pasadena, CA: Theosophical University Press, 1977, [A Facsimile of the Original Edition of 1888]. Mme. Blavatsky's translation of *The Voice of the Silence*—or "The Book of the Golden Percepts" is accepted by Tibetologists as well as by His Holiness the Dalai Lama. D.T. Suzuki referred to her translation as "the real Mahyayana Buddhism." See: Blavatsky, H. *The Voice of Silence*. Theosophical University Press, 1976.

24. Blavatsky, H. "What are Theosophists," *The Theosophist*, October 1879, p.5.

25. Blatavsky, H. *The Key to Theosophy*. Los Angeles, CA: Theosophy Co., 1930, pp. 3,5.

26. Wilmshurst, W. *The Masonic Initiation*. London: John Watkins, 1927, pp. 123-124.

27. For an excellent examination of the continuation of individual human personality beyond biological death, see: "Human Survival of Biological Death—An Approach to the Problem Based Upon the Orientation of Field Theory in Modern Physics," *Main Currents in Modern Thought*, Vol. No. 2 (November-December 1969), pp. 35-57.

28. Broughton, R. *Parapsychology—The Controversial Science*. New York: Ballentine Books, 1991, p.268. For cases of alleged memories of previous incarnations (past lives) also see Stevenson, I. "Twenty Cases Suggestive of Reincarnation," Proc. Amer. Soc. Psych. Res., 26 (1966), 1-362. Reprinted Charlottesville, Va.: University of Virginia Press, 1974.

29. Broughton, R. *Parapsychology—The Controversial Science*. New York: Ballentine Books, 1991, p. 268-269.

30. Spitz, L. *The Religious Renaissance of the German Humanists*: Cambridge, Harvard University Press, 1963, p. 67.

31. Head, J. & Cranston, S. *Reincarnation in World Thought*. New York: Julian, 1967, p.86.

32. Moore, G. *Metempsychosis*. Cambridge, MA: Harvard University Press, 1914, p. 54.

33. *The Catholic Encyclopedia*. 1913 Edition, IV, 308-309, XI, 311.

34. Ouspensky, P. *In Search of the Miraculous*. New York: Harcourt, Brace & Co., 1949, p.250.

35. Evans-Wentz, W. (Ed.). *The Tibetan Book of the Dead*. New York: Oxford University Press, 1960, p. 187.

About the Author

TED L. ORCUTT, Ph.D. is a clinical psychologist and transpersonal psychotherapist in private and consultation practice and since 1981 has been a consultant to the Psychiatry Department of the U.S. Naval Hospital in San Diego, where he received the Outstanding Teacher of the Year Award in 1989. Commissioned as a Lieutenant in the U.S. Navy, he completed his internship at U.S. Naval Hospital and Saint Elizabeth's Hospital in Washington, D.C. followed by a two year staff appointment at U.S. Naval Hospital in Portsmouth, Virginia. He has served as Director of Psychological Services for Rancho Bernardo Pain Rehabilitation Center, Academic Dean of the Professional School of Psychological Studies, and on the faculties of seven universities and colleges. A Diplomate, American Board of Psychotherapy, Dr. Orcutt is certified in group psychotherapy, clinical hypnosis, and cognitive psychotherapy. His other publications include: *Integrative Paradigms of Psychotherapy* [with Jan R. Prell] and *No Beggars Just Balloons—A Practical Approach to Self-Transformation.*